301

D1180873

LONDON BO

THE ESCAPE ARTISTS

BOOKS BY NEAL BASCOMB

Higher

The Perfect Mile

Red Mutiny

Hunting Eichmann

The New Cool

The Winter Fortress

The Escape Artists

THE
ESCAPE ARTISTS

A Band of Daredevil Pilots
and the Greatest Prison Break
of the Great War

Neal Bascomb

JOHN MURRAY

First published in Great Britain in 2018 by John Murray (Publishers)
An Hachette UK Company

1

© Neal Bascomb 2018
Maps © Maeve Norton, Scholastic Inc.

The right of Neal Bascomb to be identified as the Author of the Work has
been asserted by him in accordance with the Copyright, Designs and
Patents Act 1988.

All rights reserved. Apart from any use permitted under UK copyright law no
part of this publication may be reproduced, stored in a retrieval system, or
transmitted, in any form or by any means without the prior written
permission of the publisher, nor be otherwise circulated in any form of
binding or cover other than that in which it is published and without a similar
condition being imposed on the subsequent purchaser.

A CIP catalogue record for this title is available from the British Library

Hardback ISBN 978-1-473-68677-9
Trade Paperback ISBN 978-1-473-68678-6
Ebook ISBN 978-1-473-68679-3

Typeset in Minion Pro

Printed and bound in Great Britain by CPI Group (UK) Ltd, Croydon CR0 4YY

John Murray policy is to use papers that are natural, renewable and
recyclable products and made from wood grown in sustainable forests. The
logging and manufacturing processes are expected to conform to the
environmental regulations of the country of origin.

John Murray (Publishers)
Carmelite House
50 Victoria Embankment
London EC4Y 0DZ

www.johnmurray.co.uk

To Liz and Susan, my editors par excellence

Stone Walls do not a Prison make. Nor Iron bars a Cage.

— Inscription on Holzminden cell wall,
from Richard Lovelace poem "To Althea, from Prison"

It seems to me that we owed it to our self-respect and to our position as British officers to attempt to escape, and to go on attempting to escape, in spite of all hardships.

— A. J. Evans, inveterate World War I breakout artist

Contents

MAIN GERMAN PRISONER OF WAR
CAMPS IN THE NARRATIVE

A MAP OF HOLZMINDEN

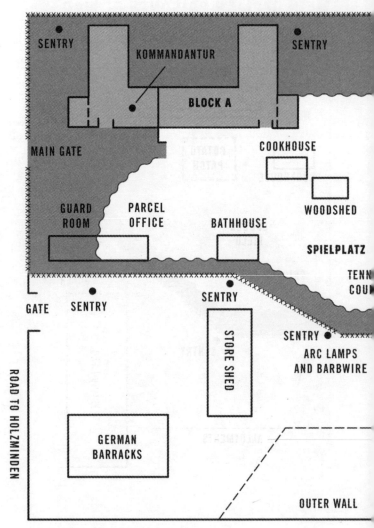

← ROAD TO HOLZMINDEN

SENTRY

KOMMANDANTUR

SENTRY

BLOCK A

MAIN GATE

COOKHOUSE

WOODSHED

GUARD ROOM

PARCEL OFFICE

BATHHOUSE

SPIELPLATZ

TENN COU

GATE

SENTRY

SENTRY

STORE SHED

SENTRY

ARC LAMPS AND BARBWIRE

ROAD TO HOLZMINDEN

GERMAN BARRACKS

OUTER WALL

A = Medlicott and Walter's escape point
B = Block B officers' entrance
C = Block B orderlies' entrance
D = Postern gate
E = Original exit of tunnel

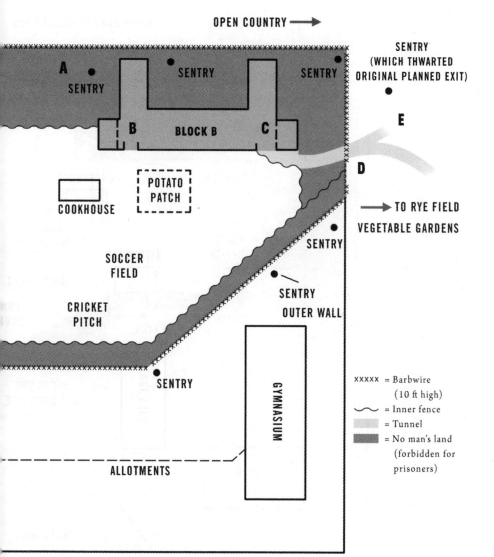

OPEN COUNTRY →

A
SENTRY

SENTRY

SENTRY

SENTRY
(WHICH THWARTED
ORIGINAL PLANNED EXIT)

E

B   BLOCK B   C

D

COOKHOUSE

POTATO
PATCH

→ TO RYE FIELD
VEGETABLE GARDENS

SOCCER
FIELD

SENTRY

CRICKET
PITCH

SENTRY

OUTER WALL

SENTRY

GYMNASIUM

xxxxx = Barbwire
        (10 ft high)
〰 = Inner fence
█ = Tunnel
█ = No man's land
    (forbidden for
    prisoners)

ALLOTMENTS

A CROSS-SECTION OF THE WORKING AREA AND ENTRANCE TO THE TUNNEL

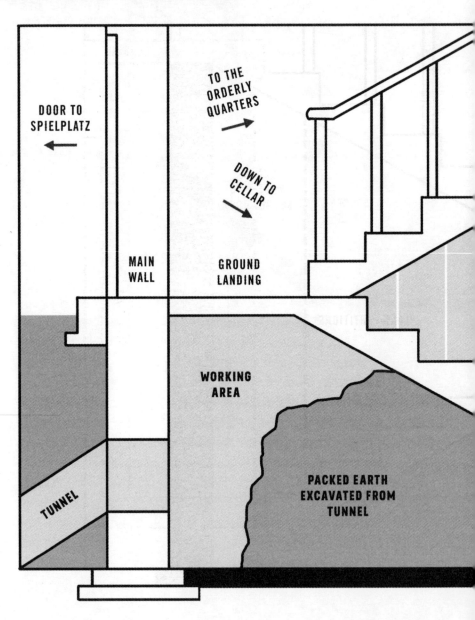

DOOR TO SPIELPLATZ
←

TO THE ORDERLY QUARTERS →

DOWN TO CELLAR ↘

MAIN WALL

GROUND LANDING

WORKING AREA

TUNNEL

PACKED EARTH EXCAVATED FROM TUNNEL

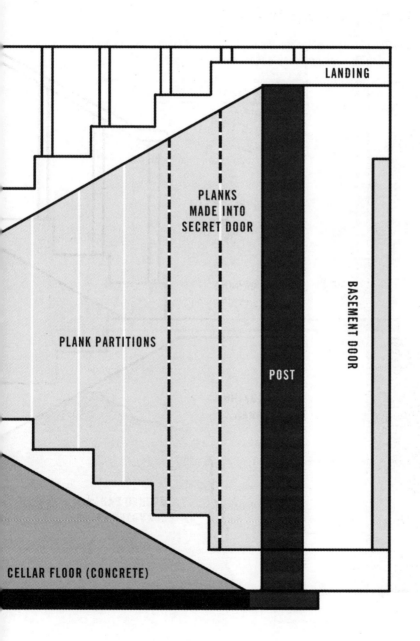

LANDING

PLANKS
MADE INTO
SECRET DOOR

BASEMENT DOOR

PLANK PARTITIONS

POST

CELLAR FLOOR (CONCRETE)

PROGRESSION OF THE TUNNEL

A=ENTRANCE TO TUNNEL **B**=FIRST PLANNED EXIT **C**=TEST EXIT BY BUTLER **D**=FINAL EXIT
E=WINDOW FROM WHICH TEST EXIT WAS OBSERVED **F**=ORDERLIES' ENTRANCE

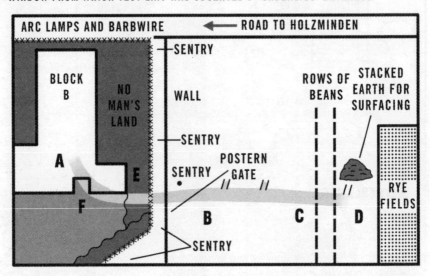

THE FINAL ROUTE OF BLAIN, KENNARD, AND GRAY, AS WELL AS RATHBORNE'S TRAIN JOURNEY

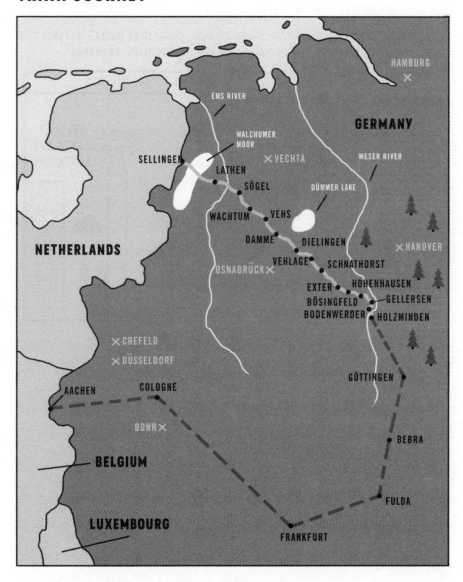

= The final route of Blain, Kennard, and Gray

= Rathborne's train journey

● = Stops

✕ = Cities and POW camps

Dramatis Personae

Key Holzminden Escape Artists

Captain David Gray, "Father of the Tunnel," Royal Flying Corps (RFC) pilot
Second Lieutenant Cecil Blain, RFC pilot
Second Lieutenant Caspar Kennard, RFC pilot
Lieutenant Colonel Charles Rathborne, senior British officer, Royal Naval Air Service (RNAS) wing commander
Sublieutenant Leonard James Bennett, RNAS observer

Other Holzminden Prisoners

Second Lieutenant Frederick William Harvey, "the Poet," Gloucestershire Regiment
Lieutenant William "Shorty" Colquhoun, Princess Patricia's Canadian Light Infantry, originator of the tunnel
Second Lieutenant William Ellis, RFC pilot, originator of the tunnel
Captain Joseph Rogers, member of the Pink Toes, Durham Light Infantry
Captain Frank "Mossy" Moysey, member of the Pink Toes, Suffolk Regiment
Private John "Dick" Cash, camp orderly, Australian Imperial Force
Lieutenant Harold Medlicott, RFC pilot
Captain Hugh Durnford, adjutant to Rathborne, Royal Field Artillery
Second Lieutenant William Leefe Robinson, Zeppelin killer, RFC pilot
Captain Douglas Grant, London Scottish Regiment

German Officers

General Karl von Hänisch, head of the 10th Army Corp Division
Karl "Milwaukee Bill" Niemeyer, Ströhen and Holzminden commandant
Heinrich "Windy Dick" Niemeyer, Clausthal camp officer
Commandant Blankenstein, Osnabrück camp
Commandant Gröben, Gütersloh camp
Commandant Courth, Crefeld camp
Commandant Dietz, Schwarmstedt camp
Commandant Wolfe, Clausthal camp

Prologue

July 14, 1941

For all his wife, Elsie, and two young children knew, Jim Bennett was leaving for an overnight business trip. As he was the eponymous owner of a small import-export business that traded in china, couture clothes, and other fine goods, they expected such absences, even during wartime — perhaps especially during wartime. No effort could be spared in keeping the bottom line from seeping red.

Dressed in a light-gray tailored suit with a white linen handkerchief in his pocket, he bid his family goodbye and walked out the front door of his five-bedroom brick house in Northwood, a bucolic neighborhood threaded with golf courses fifteen miles northwest of London. The son of a farmer, Bennett had come a long way from the rolling fields of Somerset.

Carrying a brown leather suitcase heavier than one might imagine he would need for an overnight, Bennett joined the others heading down Kewferry Road at morning rush hour to the Metropolitan line London Underground station. Few could keep to his normal brisk pace, even with the skies threatening a thunderstorm. At forty-nine and with thinning, salt-and-pepper hair, Bennett remained trim and fit.

On the half-hour ride into the city, there was plenty of time to page through the *Daily Express*. Its headlines read, "Moscow Denies Claims by Berlin" and "Nazis Flee from Syria." Most interesting to Bennett was the story about the British air raid on Bremen, Germany. On the thirty-second-straight night of attacks into Germany, bombers had struck the city's shipbuilding yards and factories. Two British planes had not returned to base, the fate of their crews unknown. With the number of these raids accelerating every month, and more and more airmen shot down, Bennett knew that his particular expertise was in very high demand.

He switched lines at Baker Street and arrived soon after at Paddington railway station, not far from his offices. Three months before, the station had suffered a direct hit by German bombers that demolished the southwest corner and killed eighteen people. In quick order, the rubble was hauled away from the tracks and train service resumed. Still, the piles of bricks and hollowed-out windows bore witness to the destruction that could rain down on London at any moment. Bennett boarded the 10:30 Great Western to Penryn, Cornwall, and settled into the second-class carriage for the five-hour journey.

His firm had no business on the southwestern tip of England. Nor was he traveling there for its sandy beaches, now fortified with pillboxes, minefields, and barbwire enclosures against the threat of a German attack. Instead he was headed to the Royal Air Force base at Predannack to lecture fighter-squadron pilots on what to do if they found themselves captured or on the run in enemy-occupied territory. In his suitcase was an Optiscope projector that looked like a small cannon, a number of slides, purses of foreign currency, silk maps, and compasses hidden in button studs. Earlier that morning, before his family awoke, he had taken these items out of the locked chest of drawers he kept in the house.

While running his import-export business, Bennett also worked for MI9, a top secret organization within British military intelligence. Recruited immediately after its founding, he was sworn to secrecy, forbidden from revealing his involvement even to family or friends. MI9 had been started in 1939 under the leadership of Major Norman Crockatt, a medaled veteran of the Royal Scots and former stockbroker. Its purpose was to codify and teach principles of evasion and escape for the use of Allied soldiers, airmen, and naval personnel caught behind enemy lines.

Crockatt did not draw these principles from *Boy's Own* fiction or moth-balled old tales, although there were stories aplenty of dramatic breakouts in the history of war and strife. Empress Matilda escaped from Oxford Castle in 1142, avoiding her pursuers by hiding in the snow under a white sheet. In 1621 the Dutch jurist Hugo Grotius was smuggled out of Loevestein Castle, where he was being held prisoner, in a book chest. In 1870, during the Franco-Prussian War, the French statesman Léon Gambetta rose up and away from a besieged Paris in a hot-air balloon. Winston Churchill himself escaped from a Boer prisoner of war camp in South Africa, by jumping over a fence and making off. These true stories were sedate compared with the adventures of the literary Count of Monte Cristo, to say nothing of Odysseus's supernatural deliverance out of Calypso's grotto.

For MI9, however, Crockatt called upon the lessons learned from the firsthand experiences of those who had escaped the Germans in World War I. And one of the participants in the greatest, the most successful, breakout of that war was Jim Bennett.

Late in the afternoon, Bennett arrived at Redruth station, where he was met by an RAF driver who whisked him southward to the newly built Predannack Airfield, near Mullion. On the apron of grass stood a line of Hawker Hurricanes and Bristol Beaufighters. They were a sight more advanced than the wood, linen, and wire-strung contraptions in which Bennett used to hunt U-boats as a Royal Naval Air Service sublieutenant.

At 8:45 p.m., his slide projector at the ready, Bennett stood at the head of a crowded hall. In his hand, he held a sheet of paper roughly torn from a notebook, upon which he had scrawled his lecture notes in bullet points. Addressing the assembled airmen, he spoke of the possibility of their being taken prisoner by the enemy, and stressed that if captured, they had a "duty to escape." Britain needed them back in its ranks. An escape attempt would also divert the attention of the Nazis, requiring the allocation of men and resources that might otherwise be used on the front line against Britain and its allies. Bennett added that if captured, the men's best opportunity to flee was the "earliest opportunity," either while in a makeshift detention spot or during transport to a POW camp. Once arrived, their chances of breaking out diminished precipitously. Yet even suffering extreme mental and physical stress, Bennett stated, they were to remember that their war effort was by no means over.

He went on to detail escape routes from Germany and to explain how to create a simple code for secret messages. He stressed the need to stay fit during captivity and the importance of having a compass in order to reach the border. All of these lessons he framed within the context of his own story of crash-landing into the sea in 1917, fifteen miles from Zeebrugge, the Belgian port controlled at that time by the Germans. After he and the plane's pilot had drifted in the downed craft for almost an hour, a U-boat surfaced beneath them and its crew seized the two men.

Bennett illustrated his account with slides showing his aircraft, the camps in which he had been imprisoned, coded letters, and tools used in various escape attempts. He spoke about Holzminden, the most notorious POW camp of the Great War, and the tunnel he and his fellow inmates had dug to escape its walls — how, over months, they had scraped away dirt, clay, and stone to burrow an underground passageway, inch by inch. He chronicled their preparations for the treacherous 150-mile journey through Germany to reach the Dutch border, how they had smuggled in supplies and hidden them in fake ceiling beams.

Although Bennett had delivered this lecture many times, his voice still conveyed the range of emotion he had experienced during the breakout from Holzminden. No doubt his audience was riveted as he described the events of that night: The thrill of the call to go. The first moments moving into the tunnel on his belly, clawing his way forward in the darkness without enough space overhead even to raise himself up on his forearms. The stalled advance. The rats scampering over his arms and legs. The muffled grunts and panicked breaths of the men in front of him and those behind. The straps of his escape kit getting caught on a rock. The hour it took to travel a distance he could have walked in a minute. The tunnel roof that was slowly collapsing on top of him, threatening to entomb him and all those who remained. The terror of possibly facing a rifle when he surfaced at last . . .

The sense of responsibility Bennett felt made his retelling all the more visceral and electric. The young men gathered before him were running defensive patrols against German raiders and participating in offensive sweeps over France. There was a good chance that some of them would soon find themselves behind enemy lines, held as POWs or on the run. Given the Nazi reputation for torturing, and sometimes hanging, captured airmen, Bennett knew that his story, the story of the leaders of the 1918 Holzminden breakout, might well save the life of a pilot in that hall.

PART I

Capture

One

The sky lightened from gray to pink as the No. 70 Squadron of the Royal Flying Corps prepared to take off from its base. Already the din of shelling sounded in the distance. It was August 7, 1916, at Fienvillers, twenty miles from the Somme battlefront. "Contact, sir!" called the mechanic, his hand on the black walnut propeller of a Sopwith 1½ Strutter biplane.

"Contact!" answered its pilot, Cecil Blain, from the fore cockpit, pushing the throttle open halfway, allowing fuel to rush into the nine-cylinder rotary engine. The mechanic jerked the propeller downward counterclockwise. With a belch of blue smoke, the Sopwith sputtered to life, the rush of air from the spinning propeller flattening the grass on the airfield behind the tailplane. As the engine warmed, its castor oil lubricant filled the air with the odor of burned almonds, nearly overwhelming Blain and his observer, Charles Griffiths. Seated in the aft cockpit, the observer's role was critical. His various tasks included radio communication, aerial reconnaissance, and manning the guns. Once they finished their flight checks, Blain waved his arm fore and aft, and the mechanic yanked out the wooden chocks securing the biplane's wheels in place.

All of nineteen years of age, the youngest pilot in his squadron, Blain might well have stepped straight off a Hollywood silent-movie screen. With his square shoulders, handsome boyish face, sweep of ruffled blond hair, and the perennial glint in his eye, he was well suited for the part of troublesome rascal. In the cockpit that morning he looked like he might have been playing the role of Arctic explorer. Over a woolen pullover and a double set of underclothes, he sported a heavy leather jacket with fur-lined collar. He wore heavy boots and thick gloves. His neck was sheathed in a white silk scarf, and his face was slathered with whale oil and covered by a balaclava and goggles. He would need all that protection to withstand the blistering cold at ten thousand feet.

After his squadron commander's plane took off, Blain moved his Sopwith onto the runway. Following a quick look over his shoulder to check that Griffiths was ready, he directed the biplane forward. Its red, white, and blue roundels stood in sharp relief to the mud-green fuselage. Throttle full open now, engine buzzing, the Sopwith picked up momentum. Blain fought against the crosswinds buffeting the wings and the inclination of the biplane's nose to lift up too early. Of the many accidents these rudimentary machines suffered, takeoffs accounted for almost half. Finally at flying speed, Blain pulled back the control stick and the Sopwith's wheels lifted gently free from the ground. Banking eastward, they soon left behind their tented camp, in an orchard next to the aerodrome, then the bundle of thirty ramshackle cottages and the simple church that constituted Fienvillers.

Once assembled in a V formation, the five Sopwiths set off eastward, the sky emblazoned bright orange ahead. Their mission was reconnaissance of Maubeuge, deep behind German enemy lines, to locate some munitions factories and an airship base housing Zeppelins. For a limited spell, Blain and Griffiths could enjoy the thrill of soaring through the open air. The horizons stretched out in every direction. Mist clung to the low hollows of the hills, and chimney smoke rose from the surrounding villages. Compared to their maps — main roads clearly delineated in red, railways in black, forests in green — the French countryside was an endless patchwork of colored fields threaded with gray lines and shadowed by clouds. In such a setting, pilots often found themselves as bewildered as a hiker in a dense forest, wandering in circles, trying to find a landmark.

But as they approached the trenches of the Western Front, there was no mistaking their position. "It looks from the air as if the gods had made a gigantic steam roller, 40 miles wide and run it from the coast to Switzerland, leaving its spike holes behind as it went," wrote one airman of the field of battle. Another described it thus: "Open for us to inspect were all the secrets of this waste of tortured soil, a barrier along which millions of armed men crouched in foul trenches . . . Below us lay displayed the zigzagging entrenchments, the wriggling communications to the rear, the untidy belts of rusty wire." Few accounts told of the innumerable dead soldiers rotting in no-man's-land, but they would have been visible to pilots that passed over the cratered chalk soil.

On July 1, 1916, shortly after Blain arrived in France, seventeen Allied divisions had begun a massive offensive to break through German lines on the upper reaches of the river Somme. At "zero hour," 7:30 a.m., to the sound of whistles blowing, lines of khaki-clad British soldiers and their blue-gray-uniformed French counterparts rose from their trenches and attacked the Germans through no-man's-land under the withering chatter of machine-gun fire.

On the offensive's first day, the Allies took but a bite out of the enemy's ruined line — at the cost of almost twenty thousand British dead and double that figure in wounded: the greatest loss of life in a single day in the country's military history. In the weeks that followed, wave after wave of attack and counterattack resettled the lines largely to where they had started. While continuing to attempt to wear down the enemy with small offensives, the British and French prepared for their next major move.

For the No. 70 Squadron, there had been no pause from the unrelenting schedule of patrols and reconnaissance missions. Just the day before, Blain had helped thwart a run by ten German bombers over Allied trenches, harassing them in the sky until they retreated.

As the five Sopwiths traveled across no-man's-land, the sky went thick with sudden coughs of black smoke. Before the smell of cordite stung their noses, the same thought ran through the whole patrol: *Archie!* Innocuously nicknamed by pilots after a popular London music-hall song, whose refrain went, "Archibald! Certainly not!," these shells delivered death in many ways. A direct hit would crumple a plane in an instant, sending it in a precipitous drop from the sky, like a bird downed by a shotgun. The explosion alone could hurl a plane into an irrecoverable spiral. And Archie shells could kill an entire aircrew with a 360-degree spray of shrapnel that tore through flesh and the fragile structures that kept the planes aloft.

On the port side of their formation, a shell rocked one Sopwith, but its pilot recovered. Another cut confetti-sized slits into the wings of Blain's biplane, and shrapnel pinged against his engine cowling. As the *wouft, wouft, wouft* of Archies pounded in their ears, Blain inspected his controls. Everything looked OK. He glanced back at Griffiths, and they exchanged a thumbs-up. As quickly as the barrage began, it ended.

Onward they flew toward Maubeuge to continue their reconnaissance. Now that they were beyond enemy lines, Blain knew that German fighters were likely to attack their formation, and he noted that there was little cloud cover in which to hide. Griffiths readied himself at his mounted Lewis machine gun, and they both searched the sky. Seconds later, their flight leader wiggled his wings, a warning signal. In the far distance, Blain saw a colorless dot framed by the sun. The British formation remained tight, waiting to see if this speck in the sky would take the shape of a German patrol airplane.

Nerves tight, prepared to separate from the formation for an aerial fight, Blain waited. He soon picked out the black crosses of a lone two-seater German reconnaissance plane. Some pilots likened the sensation of first seeing the enemy to "plunging into a cold bath."

One aggressive move from it and the Sopwiths would engage. Instead, the enemy plane swept past them in a straight westward line, no doubt on a scouting mission of its own in Allied territory. The Sopwiths continued east, no other planes in sight. The Germans might well wait to ambush their formation on its return toward Fienvillers. The airmen would be tired, dulled by the bitter cold, short on fuel, and slowed by the almost constant west wind that blew across northern France. Sixty miles behind enemy lines, they sighted the glint of sun off the river Sambre and reached Maubeuge. The ancient city had been besieged and sacked many times over the centuries, handed between French, Spanish, and Austrian dukes and counts almost too many times to count. Yet it had never suffered the kind of heavy-artillery bombardment unleashed by the Germans in their advance toward Paris in August 1914. When Blain descended toward Maubeuge, he saw that its fortress walls were spilled piles of rubble.

The Sopwiths broke away from one another to begin their reconnaissance. Cutting over the city, Blain and Griffiths looked for the airship base marked on their maps. They passed the train station, the puffs of steam from a departing locomotive rising into the air. Up ahead, the mammoth gray sheds were easy to spot. On his first pass, Blain saw nothing of note, but the Zeppelins could well be inside. He banked around and descended low for a second look.

Approaching the sheds again, he eased back on the throttle. In that moment, a spout of blue flame burst from the Sopwith's rotary engine. Determining that one of the intake valves might be jammed, Blain increased throttle again. More flames flashed out of the engine. As he tried to regain altitude, the engine's rhythmic, continuous drone became an irregular stutter. The Sopwith began to vibrate around him. A glance at the revolutions-per-minute counter confirmed the fear that had already shot through him: engine trouble. The best he could hope for now was to get his plane out of enemy-occupied territory. There was a chance. He turned westward.

One cylinder was definitely cutting out. Any attempt to alter the carburetor mix or clear the stuck valve failed. Blain pushed to maintain altitude. The acrid stench of hot metal filled the air, and the Sopwith bobbed slightly up and down in the airstream as it slowed. Blain continued to woo some effort from the engine, mile after precious mile. Then, with a frightening shriek, a piece of metal ripped through the engine cowling and flung off into the air behind them. Flames flared from the broken intake valve and, all of a sudden, the propeller stopped dead.

Its violent arrest rattled the Sopwith. Blain feared the whole engine might come loose. When its bearings held, he finally faced the realization that they remained far from home. They were going down. The best he could do now was get himself and Griffiths onto the ground alive.

When Orville Wright performed the first flight in a powered airplane on December 17, 1903, he declared it to be "the introduction into the world of an invention which would make further wars practically impossible." Hyperbole aside, Wright was correct that airplanes would bring a revolution in war, but not in the way he imagined. Instead of an instrument for peace, the airplane became a multipronged weapon in a conflict that would envelope the world.

The British military establishment was slow to this realization. In 1910 the chief of the Imperial General Staff, Sir William Nicholson, regarded aviation as "a useless and expensive fad advocated by a few individuals whose ideas are unworthy of attention." The First Sea Lord, Sir Arthur Wilson, followed up by stating that the "naval requirement for aircraft was two." Nonetheless, given developments in aviation, popular fascination with cross-channel flights, and the rise of air forces on the European continent, the Royal Flying Corps was founded in April 1912.

Many remained unconvinced, including Douglas Haig, future commander in chief of the British Expeditionary Force. Four weeks before Kaiser Wilhelm II sent German troops into Belgium, Haig declared to a roomful of generals, "I hope none of you is so foolish as to think that aeroplanes will be able to be usefully employed for reconnaissance in the air. There is only one way for a commander to get information . . . and that is by the use of cavalry."

With such lack of support, the new branch of the British Army entered the war a fledgling force staffed mostly by enterprising, well-heeled amateurs. The aircraft they brought to France were made from wood, wire, and canvas. They had only seventy-horsepower engines, sped barely over seventy-five miles per hour, and took almost an hour to climb to their ceiling height of ten thousand feet. Pilots carried rifles for weapons and grenades for bombs. Soon after fighting began, however, many credited their bird's-eye role tracking troop movements with staving off the German envelopment of British troops and an early knockout blow in the war. A dispatch to London from the field commander praised the RFC's "skill, energy and perseverance."

Beyond reconnaissance and artillery observation, squadrons started bombing German targets, tracking U-boats, battling the enemy for control of the skies, and defending the home front from Zeppelin and other attacks. An ever-widening war and increased duties demanded the RFC mint faster, more maneuverable, better-armed, and more stable planes. Further, they needed to recruit thousands of pilots to fly them.

By summer 1915 there were only two hundred trainees at flying stations. The force did little to shake its preference for individuals of means, pedigree, and attendance at the best schools. Applicants abounded from Harrow and Eton, Oxford and Cambridge. After first asking why a potential candidate wanted to be a pilot, some interviewers followed with, "Do you ride?" The director general of military aeronautics stated that "flying is perhaps a little easier than riding a horse because you sit in a comfortable armchair in a quiet machine instead of a slippery saddle on a very lively horse." Candidates were also asked, "What is your favorite amusement? Who is your favorite poet? Do you mind solitude?" According to a journalist who reported on the selection process, "Kipling or Stevenson was supposed to indicate greater promise than Shelley or Meredith. A football player stood better with the examiners than a pianist." It also did not hurt if applicants rode motorcycles, fast.

Notwithstanding the desire for gentleman pilots, Hugh Trenchard, the RFC's commander in France, looked for other characteristics as well: "High spirits and resilience of youth . . . They should be under twenty-five, and unmarried. Athletic, alert, cheerful, even happy-go-lucky, the paragon would also reveal initiative and a sense of humour. The greatest strength was an incurable optimism."

In temperament and background, Cecil William Blain fit the bill perfectly. Born in 1896, he was the eldest son of a wealthy cotton merchant in Bromborough, a village on the Wirral Peninsula south of Liverpool. His mother, Mary, was a descendant of Sir Joshua Reynolds, the painter and founder of the Royal Academy of Arts. Blain attended the Loretto School, the Scottish institution that had churned out its share of famous bankers, politicians, judges, and clergymen. The boarding school was also known for its sporting prowess, and like his younger brother, Harry, Cecil excelled at cricket, rugby, and golf.

On graduation at seventeen years of age, he did not join his classmates at university. Instead, he journeyed to South Africa, where his uncle owned a large ranch and pineapple farm. Rather than follow his father into business, he intended to be a farmer, where he could tend a field, ride horses, and spend his days in the sun. The outbreak of war foiled these free-spirited plans. Blain felt compelled to return to fight for his country. With connections and letters of reference, he secured a spot in the RFC. Its glamour and gallant reputation made it an attractive service for most young men.

To start his training, Blain ran the gauntlet of School of Military Aeronautics lectures on everything but the practical aspects of flying. Then, in mid-December 1915, he traveled to Northolt aerodrome outside London for flight school. Hours after his arrival he was climbing into a Maurice Farman Longhorn biplane for his first spin in the air. He stepped carefully as he boarded so as not to put his foot through the canvas wing.

With a fifty-foot span and powered by a V8 engine, the Longhorn looked as unsteady as the first plane flown by the Wright Brothers. "The whole contraption was held together with piano wire," one trainee described. "Lift wires, landing wires, drift wires, bracing wires: we used to say you could safely cage a canary in a Longhorn without fear of losing it."

For his maiden flight, sitting in the toe of the shoe-shaped cockpit with an instructor behind him, Blain did not have command of the Longhorn's dual controls. His instructor simply wanted to see how he reacted to the flight — and if he lost his wits when the instructor staged a planned stall in midair.

Blain passed the test. Then he had a few lessons in the Longhorn, where he learned to fly the aircraft himself. He took off, performed left-hand and right-hand circuits, and landed, all the while suffering the shouts and kicks to the back of his seat from his instructor, who would take over the controls only if they were at the precipice of a crash. After too few hours of flying experience, he was charged with his first solo.

Blain was not following a set syllabus or instruction technique. Neither existed, nor were his instructors professionals. Most were simply RFC veterans on leave from the front, some washed out from trauma. At Northolt, crashes were frequent, often deadly. Of the roughly nine thousand men who died in the RFC over the course of the war, one in four was killed in training. Planes pancaked on rough landings or overshot the runway altogether, smashing into trees. Midair collisions occurred. Planes overturned and spiraled out of control. Engines died. Petrol ran out. Wings became untethered. Rudders stuck. Pilot inexperience or mechanical failure — or both — delivered death equally. On a typical day of training, it was standard fare for a cadet to witness a dozen crashes. Often the wreckage was so grisly the ambulance did not have to hurry. The flight school took up collections to pay for funerals, and trainees often found themselves serving as pallbearers.

When Blain took his first solo flight, pilots stood at the aerodrome perimeter, a last will and testament held aloft in their hands. The gallows humor was meant to cut through the tension, but Blain would have to have been made of stone to be unafraid. In his memoir, *Sagittarius Rising,* World War I pilot Cecil Lewis best described the terrifying thoughts that sprinted through a cadet's head when first flying solo. At the takeoff: "Rudder — Elevator — Ailerons . . . God! Who said they wanted to fly . . .

She's lifting away! She's away." At midflight: "Try a right turn now. Now . . . Oh, she's shuddering. There's something wrong. Straighten! Quick! Straighten . . . No, it's all right." At landing: "Throttle back and nose down together . . . Shall we get in? Yes. No. A bit more engine. That's it . . . You're flying into the ground! Pull her up! Up! Not too much . . . Bang! Bounce! Bounce! Rumble! . . . We're down . . . I've done it. I haven't crashed!"

Blain survived his fifteen-minute solo. After a test flight on January 14, 1916, that included a pair of figure-eight turns, a climb to nine hundred feet, and a pinpoint landing with the engine cut off, he was issued his wings. Donning the double-breasted, high-collared uniform that pilots nicknamed the "maternity jacket," Second Lieutenant Blain had no more than a handful of hours in the air.

Over the next five months, he continued training in England, a benefit many new pilots missed before shipping off for a squadron in France. At Northolt and reserve squadrons elsewhere, Blain witnessed more crashes, more death, all the while growing to be a steady hand in Avros, Blériots, and Sopwiths. Although no pilot could avoid his share of surprise stalls or strut-smashing landings, Blain proved himself a natural in the air.

In June the RFC assigned him to the newly formed No. 70 Squadron, responsible for long-range offensive patrols in enemy territory. He left for France in time for the launch of the Somme offensive. Eight weeks later, of the thirty-six original pilots and observers in his squadron, Blain was one of only nine who remained. Some dropped out from nerves, others were severely wounded, and the rest had been killed or captured by the enemy.

"No use! Got to land!" Blain called back to Griffiths. "Throw your gun overboard!" With the propeller stopped, and the altimeter reading 3,000 feet, they were going down. The lighter the plane, the more distance Blain might be able to eke out of their glide. Five miles was likely the maximum, far from the safety of Allied lines. At best, they had made it two dozen miles from Maubeuge.

As Griffiths tossed out drums of ammunition, then the Lewis gun, Blain performed a delicate dance in the air. He alternated between leveling the nose of the plane and pointing it downward. Too much of the former, they would lose height quickly. Too much of the latter, they would stall, the wings not producing enough lift to keep the Sopwith in flight. He played by feel, by the sound of the biplane's wires moving through the air. Whenever the wires started to vibrate at a high pitch, he needed to pull back on the control stick and level out some. When they went almost quiet, he angled the nose down again. With the engine dead, the cockpit was unnervingly silent but for the singing of the wires and the rushing wind.

At last, there was nothing Blain could do but land. They sailed over a French village, low enough to see its inhabitants looking up at them with incredulous faces. Blain spied a level pasture dotted with cows, and he aimed to land on a path between the beasts. He set the plane gently down, and its wheels rumbled to a stop in the high grass.

Alone but for the cows, Blain and Griffiths scrambled out of the plane. If they were able to fix the engine quickly enough, they could get themselves back in the air and out of harm's way. A quick inspection dashed their hopes. The crankcase was a shred of metal. One of the nine cylinders of the rotary engine was loose and its piston was crushed. Knowing full well they were stuck, Blain and Griffiths set upon their plane, putting fists and feet through the wings. Of the few instructions their commanders gave them in the event they were shot down, the first was to destroy their machine so the Germans could neither use it nor learn from its advances. In this new battlefield in the sky, every advantage in developing technology might prove the difference between defeat and victory.

By this time a crowd of women and young children had crossed the pasture toward them, shouting and gesturing frantically at the two Englishmen. Blain understood them to be saying that they had landed near Caudry, far on the wrong side of the line. He smiled and shook their hands repeatedly — the Allies were winning the war, he reassured them. The women urged the two aviators to return into the sky. "Les Boches arrivent," they said.

Griffiths opened the fuel tank and soaked a cloth with some petrol. He then circled the biplane, smearing petrol across the wings, while Blain moved the crowd away. Then he set the biplane on fire with his lighter. Flames ran across the fuselage and wings as the first German soldiers marched into the pasture, weapons drawn.

The heat from the spreading inferno reached several bullet cartridges that Griffiths had not thrown out of the plane. The crack of exploding bullets stopped the advancing soldiers. Blain and Griffiths kept their hands high in the air. The soldiers started forward again, one with an Alsatian dog on a leash. They were almost upon the two airmen when the petrol tank burst. The shock sent the Alsatian dashing away in fright, its handler sprinting across the uneven field after him. For a moment, as the villagers laughed at the absurd scene, Blain could push away the crushing truth that he was about to become a prisoner of war.

The patrol seized the two Englishmen and marched them into Caudry. Blain, who during his time in South Africa had learned Cape Dutch, similar to German, was able to decipher some of the soldiers' orders. The town did not have a jail, so they were held in its post office. An hour later, a German officer named Röder, who spoke English, arrived on the scene. He had the two searched and took away some personal letters and money in their possession. Blain managed to hide his silver cigarette lighter. Then Röder and a guard took them away in his car. On the road to Cambrai, they passed columns of worn-out soldiers followed by a line of horse transports. The old French fortress town stood on a slight hill, its stone ramparts stretching fifty feet high. Guards stopped the car at the edge of the old moat. Röder barked at them and was allowed to pass across the drawbridge and under the massive archway of the fortress.

Blain and Griffiths were directed into a sliver of a cell. The stifling heat hit them first, then the foul smell. Two straw mattresses covered what little floor there was. When they tried to sleep, they found their threadbare, soiled blankets alive with lice. In the morning, a guard brought them some square hunks of sour black bread, their first meal in twenty-four

hours. Lunch and dinner was cabbage soup that resembled filthy bathwa-
ter. It was served in slop pails. When briefly let out of their cell, they found
the citadel crowded with other prisoners and plagued by dysentery. Blain
saw a wounded soldier lying on the stone floor, his upper arm a fetid gob
of open flesh, dried blood, dirt, and straw. Guards forbid anyone from
helping him. The cruelty made Blain seethe.

Night after night the airman lay on his mattress, too troubled to sleep.
Thoughts of escape crept around the edges of his consciousness, but the
shock of his capture overwhelmed him.

Two

Early on August 17, 1916, under the red glow of a falling flare, Second Lieutenant Will Harvey made his way through the front line trench. The narrow passages were sunk a few feet into the earth, then built up with sandbag walls that rose high over his head, resembling crenellated battlements. Duckboards covered the trench floor, but the slick planks were not enough to prevent his boots sinking into the river of mud beneath as he pushed through the mass of soldiers who inhabited this bleak underworld.

Those on sentry duty stood up on the fire step, rifles in hand, peering into the dark for any hint of a German advance. Others worked to shore up crumbling walls, hauled supplies, rebuilt parapets destroyed by shelling. Some clambered back down into the trench after fixing a patch of barbwire in no-man's-land. Those who were off duty huddled along the passageways, smoking cigarettes, brewing tea on charcoal braziers, or trying to catch a couple of hours of restless sleep amid a scurry of rats.

Harvey continued through the trench, checking on his platoon in the 5th Battalion, Gloucestershire Regiment. He did not look like the typical decorated officer. "I never saw anyone less like a hero in my life," one soldier wrote. "Imagine a small, dirty, nearly middle-aged man, wearing glasses and an apologetic air, trudging along the pavé under a huge pack ... He looks as if he stuffed birds in civil life." At twenty-eight years of age, Harvey was hardly middle-aged, but his short, sturdy frame and soft round face made him easily forgettable. Few have better proved that a book is best not judged by its cover.

Only the day before, his battalion had moved into the Fauquissart sector. Near the village of Neuve Chapelle, site of a fierce onslaught by the British across two thousand yards of no-man's-land in March 1915, the area was now in a state of relative calm. They were far north of the Somme, the latest fixation of the Allies in their attempt to break the stalemate of the Western Front.

Before dawn came the chilling call of "Stand to!" Soldiers scrambled to take their positions along the parapet wall with fixed bayonets, knowing well that the rising sun often brought an enemy attack. In the silence that followed, Harvey and his men stared across the tangled hedges of barbwire for any sign of movement. Minute after minute passed, but the only assault came from the swarms of fetid, blue-bellied flies that thrived in the summer heat and flesh of the dead. An hour later, "Stand down" passed through the line, and drams of rum were given out.

The morning looked to be the usual start of another day in the trenches. Harvey tried to get some rest in a dugout, but he could not shake loose his thoughts about the patrol he was tasked to lead that evening. He had more experience — and success — with such dangerous missions than anyone in his battalion, but this did not ease his mind.

The British command wanted to ensure that the Germans did not divert resources from other areas to the Somme, and ordered sporadic raids up and down the line to keep them on edge. For the upcoming raid by Harvey's battalion, a reconnaissance of the German trenches was considered necessary.

The more Harvey thought about it, the more determined he was to check out the terrain himself before venturing out with his men. This action might well save one of their lives. Once he had resolved to go out alone first, Harvey was able to shut his eyes and sleep for a couple of hours.

Later that morning, he searched out his friend from home, Ivor Gurney. Although they were in the same regiment, they rarely saw one another, given the shifting schedules of the trench. The two shared a love for poetry, music, and books. Harvey gave Gurney his pocket edition of *The Spirit of Man* by Robert Bridges, and they spent a few moments in conversation about Britain's poet laureate, whose latest work urged his fellow countrymen to face the "intolerable grief" of war by training their minds to "interpret the world according to [their] higher nature."

In the early afternoon, Harvey sent word of his proposed scouting mission to his company officer, then alerted the British sentries about the same, to avoid being killed by friendly fire. At 2:00 p.m. he readied to go, a mud-stained copy of Shakespeare's sonnets in his pocket as always. A sentry pulled aside the sally port in the parapet wall. Mouth dry from nerves, Harvey climbed through it. As the soldier returned the defense into place, Harvey wriggled across a stretch of tall grass that had somehow avoided being burned or destroyed by shelling.

Three hundred yards away stood the German lines. The next few hours were typically the part of the day when both sides rested before the long pitch of night. Few were on duty apart from the sentries — and even they were not at their keenest. Harvey hoped to reconnoiter a forward sap, a span of trench that ran out perpendicular from the enemy's front line that was used as an observation post. He believed the sap was lightly defended or altogether unoccupied. If it was, it might serve as a point of attack in the upcoming raid.

An unsteady wind blew, rustling the tall grass, camouflaging Harvey as he moved forward on his stomach. When he came upon twists of barbwire, he either crawled over them or brushed them aside with the wooden bludgeon he always carried on such patrols. At times, he was hidden in shell holes or in the shadow of a short hedge that ran through this former farmland. Other times, he was all but exposed if he lifted up too high on his forearms.

Every move risked detection. If his equipment rattled, if he knocked into an unseen tin can or other piece of litter, he was lost. Although he held his bludgeon in one hand and an automatic pistol in the other, he knew that neither would serve much purpose if a German sniper spotted him. All the way forward, he made note of where the barbwire was thickest as well as any shell holes that might serve as temporary shelters from machine-gun fire.

He crawled down into a drain that ran toward the German parapet. Very close now. At this point, if he had been there with others, he would have turned back. Alone, confident in his ability, he inched onward until he reached the front line trench. Resting in the shadow cast by the stacked sandbags, he held his breath and trained his ears for any sound beyond: a cough, a whisper of conversation, a footfall, a cleared throat, a rifle stock shifted into place. There was nothing. Lifting his head slightly, he peered left and right along the parapet, searching for a spying German periscope or the top of a head. Nothing. After a few seconds, he rose slowly onto the parapet, then popped up to look down into the trench. It was empty.

There was no doubt he should return to his own line. He had scouted a path through no-man's-land and had found a potential access point for the raid on the German trenches. Although his objective was fulfilled, he wanted to explore further, to see how much of this section was undefended. Every yard of weakness in the line he could scout would save many lives. He'd already come this far. "Be damned if I go back," Harvey muttered to himself.

He heaved himself up and over the parapet wall into the trench. Unseen, he moved down the sap toward the adjoining traverse and peered down the path, finding it also to be empty. Creeping onward, pistol at the ready, he thought about hiding out in the German lines throughout the night, to scout their mortar placements and machine-gun nests. If he found an exit gap in the back wall of their trenches, he could lie in the grass until early morning. With this idea in mind, he searched for such a gap but found none.

Reaching the next turn in the line, he heard from behind him the sound of advancing soldiers. There was no going back. He continued on ahead, glancing left and right, urgently needing an exit now. The walls were uni-

form, tall, and without a break. On the next traverse, he turned the corner
to discover a dugout braced with iron — a mortar shelter. He could hide
there until whoever was coming from behind had passed. Rushing toward the doorway, he was suddenly confronted by two German soldiers
on their way out. In his shock, Harvey did not have time to raise his pistol.
The two men seized the poet-soldier of Gloucestershire with little trouble.

· · ·

> *When earth was a chalice*
> *Of wonder, not malice,*
> *And time but a palace*
> *Built for a boy.*

So had written Frederick William Harvey from the trenches, in a poem
about his childhood home, the Redlands. Constructed by his father, a
farmer and horse breeder, the Georgian house sat amid gardens, orchards,
and water meadows on the banks of the river Severn. The eldest of five,
Will enjoyed a happy middle-class childhood, mucking about in the duck
pond, riding ponies in the surrounding countryside, and sporting against
other kids in nearby Minsterworth village, west of the city of Gloucester.
While their father tirelessly worked the farm and bred shire horses, their
mother was the gentle but firm hand that ran the household. Laughter and
love surrounded the Harvey dinner table at night.

Within the bounds of this normal, pleasant life, Will stood apart from
his siblings. He was almost a head shorter than his younger brothers and
shared none of their stark good looks. Although he liked the rough-and-
tumble of cricket and hockey, he was equally content reading a book. At
seven, he could recite by heart whole poems by Shelley and Browning,
and he loved to sing. Prone to mood swings, he was never quite at peace
within himself. He was also cavalier about risk, whether handling unbroken horses or engaging in a rugby scrum. He measured danger with a
different yardstick than others did.

As the eldest, Will carried the greatest weight of his parents' expectations. Good school, proper job, proper life. After his eighteenth birthday in 1906, he began the study of law in Gloucester at the urging of his mother. He found the subject dry and soulless. While in the city, he befriended Ivor Gurney and a host of others whose passion was the arts rather than the rule of law. Harvey began writing lines of verse and despaired that he was not being true to the "real me." His father's unexpected death, then the failure to pass his law examinations after four years of study, only heightened this feeling that he was being caged into a life he did not want.

The same rumbling against convention roiled all of Britain at that time. Queen Victoria died in 1901 after almost sixty-four years on the throne, espousing throughout her reign the virtues of order, class, duty, and Empire. Her death unmoored the country, and her son and successor Edward VII ushered in a new age while putting a much lighter hand on the helm. Those insulated from change — or blind to it — looked forward to the first decade of the twentieth century as a languid stroll through a comfortable afternoon. The economy was stable, incomes and trade were up, and there was peace between most nations. Regardless, the modern age was steaming into the station, with all its possibilities and pitfalls. Workers unionized, women demanded the right to vote, parents clamored for better schools for their children, and the poor for opportunities for a better life.

In the House of Commons, upstart politicians promised that they better represented the people's will than the bluebloods of the House of Lords. The Irish raised to a fever pitch the right to home rule. Playwrights like Bernard Shaw fought to stage stories of life as it was, not as moralist Victorian censors wanted it to be. Novelists and poets published works with the same intent. The Church fell exposed to advances in science and technology. The secrets of the atom revealed by Ernest Rutherford called into question the very nature of the world, while the invention of radio, the telegraph, motorcars, airplanes, and turbine-powered ships showed the power of humankind to bridge expanses once unimaginable.

Despite these reverberations of change and his own unease, Harvey tried to remain dutiful to family and a stable career. After renewed study in London, he managed to pass the law exams and began working as a solicitor, writing business contracts, settling will disputes, and the like. Now with a steady salary, he aimed to marry a young Irish nurse, Sarah Anne Kane, who went by her middle name, whom he had met during a short stay in hospital for a minor infection. Everything was falling into place as it should in terms of familial expectations, yet Harvey longed to devote himself to poetry.

One afternoon in 1914, bored with the law, believing he was helping industry at the expense of the worker, Harvey walked away from his solicitor's job. He returned to the Redlands, hopeless and unsure of his future in every way but for his love of Anne.

Then, on June 28, Serbian nationalists assassinated Austrian archduke Franz Ferdinand in Sarajevo. Although the death of the heir to the Austro-Hungarian Empire may have lit the fuse of war, any number of acts could have stamped it out before the explosion, but hapless diplomats, and the leaders they served, failed to do so. Indeed, many never tried, giving in to the suggestions of battle-hungry generals. Hastening the disaster was an assembly of ossified empires, tangled alliances, inflexible war plans, massive standing armies, and the views of Germany, most prominently those of Kaiser Wilhelm II, that the country must choose "world power or downfall."

At its outset, the march to war looked often like a celebration. In capital cities throughout Europe, crowds poured into the streets, waving flags and singing national anthems. Czar Nicholas stood on the balcony of the Winter Palace in St. Petersburg, and thousands kneeled to pay him homage. Kaiser Wilhelm appeared in field uniform and spoke to the German people of the sword "forced into our hands." Mustering in the millions, soldiers prepared for war by sharpening swords, cleaning pistols, polishing their boots, and readying the saddlebags for their cavalry horses. Flowers garlanded their paths to trains and ships, and words such as "honor" and "glory" were spoken with reverence. In his poem "1914," Rupert Brooke wrote of his thankfulness for this fine hour:

> To turn, as swimmers into cleanness leaping
> Glad from a world grown old and cold and weary.

Many believed the war would be over by Christmas. Swept into this patriotic tide, Harvey and two of his brothers, Eric and Roy, enlisted in the army, while their sister Gladys volunteered as a nurse. The youngest, Bernard, stayed at home to help their mother run the farm. Before leaving for training, Harvey wandered the lane that led to the Redlands. In farewell, he embraced each of the trees along its border.

While Private Harvey was learning to be a soldier, the true nature of the war manifested itself. Under the Schlieffen Plan, Germany intended a swift march through Belgium, followed by a broad sweep south to envelop Paris; this decisive thrust would allow its armies to focus their attention on defeating Russia. They made quick early progress. Their huge artillery took mere hours to level Belgian forts that had stood for centuries. To forestall future local resistance, they torched villages and executed their inhabitants. It was a first shiver of the horrors to follow. As armies of a scale never seen before engaged one another — marshaling rifles, machine guns, high-explosive shells, and even poison gas — deaths mounted at an alarming rate.

In the west, the British and French slowed the German advance on Paris, then pushed it back. A series of flanking offensives and counteroffensives followed. In the east, the Russians threw themselves against German and Austro-Hungarian troops with abandon. By winter, any chance of a swift victory was lost. Hundreds of thousands of soldiers were already dead, on both sides, and the murder mill of the trenches had only just begun. Now this struggle became what some predicted it always would be — a war of attrition and wholesale annihilation — that enveloped countries around the globe.

On March 29, 1915, Harvey disembarked in Boulogne, France. After a frigid night bivouacked on a hillside, he climbed into a cattle truck packed with soldiers, and a train carried them toward the front in Belgium. Marching to reach Plug Street — or, more formally, the Ploegsteert sector — his battalion passed a hastily dug graveyard whose rotting stink made them retch. Later, they dashed through woodland, threatened by gunfire. Finally, they scrambled into trenches pooled with the heavy April rains. A sniper's bullet soon took the left eye of a private in their battalion. Another killed one of their lieutenants. At Plug Street, and across the Western Front, death came from everywhere, every minute of every hour, up close.

Most horrific of all was the shelling. "I must say it is a devilish affair altogether," wrote one soldier, who arrived at the front at the same time as Harvey. "You sit like rabbits in a burrow and just wait for something to come and blow you to hell." Jack Johnsons, whizz bangs, woolly bears, Minnies — each type of shell had a name, each a distinctive sound, but there was little to do about any of them except tighten into a ball against the trench walls and hope. In spells of heavy shelling, the world erupted into flashing lights, mad screams, and concussive waves of sound that had an almost physical presence. The British lines alone suffered approximately seven thousand casualties daily. "Wastage" was how staff headquarters referred to the number of dead and wounded in their ledgers.

Harvey managed to survive three months at Plug Street, then more in other nearby sectors. One trench looked the same as another. The battles were alike too. He preferred patrols to "waiting . . . passive" for shellfire in the trenches. Affectionately nicknamed the Little Man, Harvey was an expert scout. On August 3, 1915, he participated in a nighttime patrol led by his good friend Raymond Knight. They discovered a German listening post hidden in some bushes. Knight attacked first, Harvey followed. He shot two men with his revolver and then chased after a third. Near the German lines, he knocked down the fleeing man with his bludgeon and grabbed his collar to take him prisoner. At that moment, a spray of bullets from the enemy trenches whistled past Harvey. Appearing out of nowhere, Knight yanked his friend to safety. For the incident, Harvey and Knight were awarded the Distinguished Conduct Medal for "conspicuous gallantry," recommended for a commission, and won a short leave home, where Harvey reunited with Anne.

Throughout his time in the trenches, Harvey found comfort in the act of writing poetry in a small notebook he always kept on him. On trudging toward the lines:

> *This route march is a blighted thing — God wot.*
> *The sun —*
> *How hot!*
> *No breeze!*
> *No pewter pot!*

On the death of the poet Rupert Brooke:

> *Joy diadems thy death to all*
> *Who loving thee — loves beauty more,*
> *Since in thy death thou showest plain*
> *Though Songs must cease and Life must fall*
> *The things that made the songs remain.*

On Gloucestershire:

> *I'm homesick for my hills again —*
> *My hills again!*
> *To see above the Severn plain*
> *Unscabbarded against the sky*
> *The blue high blade of Cotswold lie.*

With his poems, Harvey found a welcome audience, initially with his mates in the trenches, then in the *5th Gloucester Gazette.* The first of its kind, the regimental journal aimed to entertain and raise morale in the battalion. Harvey contributed many poems and other writings to it, and they were reprinted in newspapers far and wide under his initials "F. W. H." Their acclaim won him a publisher in Sidgwick & Jackson, which planned to release a collection entitled *A Gloucestershire Lad,* a couple of months after Harvey arrived at the front lines in Fauquissart.

When Harvey failed to return from his daytime scouting mission, most in his battalion thought him dead. A grieving Ivor Gurney wrote home: "His desire for nobility and sacrifice was insatiable and was at last his doom, but his friends may be excused for desiring a better ending than that probably of a sniper's bullet in No Man's Lands." Back in Gloucester, newsboys announced "Local Poet Missing."

"How did you get here?" one of the German soldiers asked Harvey, his hand forcing him against the trench wall.

"Over no-man's-land, of course," he answered.

"What were you doing?"

"Patrolling."

"Where is the rest of your patrol?"

"There wasn't one."

Suddenly, Harvey began to laugh. It was a mad kind of chuckle, born from shock and the uncanny resemblance of one of his captors to a Redlands farmhand. The two enemy soldiers stared at their prisoner, confused, then took him away. Harvey's reaction may have well saved him from a quick bullet to the head.

At the rear of the trenches, a senior officer interrogated him on British artillery positions and the reasoning behind a recent attack by two divisions. "Oh, we have plenty of men," Harvey said casually. With that, he was delivered to the barracks in nearby Douai. Alone in a small room, the spell of adrenaline broken, Harvey started to realize the truth of his situation, something he had never imagined possible: he was a prisoner. He feared his battalion would send out a search party and that his friends might die looking for him. He worried that Anne and his family might believe him lost forever. "By God," he declared. "They've got me."

In his mind, he ran through the events leading to his capture, picking at what he could have done differently to avoid his ill fate. If only he had turned back after meeting his initial objective. Should he have assumed the dugout was occupied? Should he have fired his revolver and fled? He found no good answers, only a merry-go-round of more questions. Finally he ceased that line of thought. He was where he was, and that was the end of it.

Hungry, harassed by lice, he opened his pocketbook Shakespeare and read several sonnets to pass the time. Soon the light grew too dim to read, but he continued to recite the lines from memory. When sleep eluded him, he took a small dose from the vial of morphine he always brought with him on patrols in case he was wounded in no-man's-land. Soft dreams followed, but he awakened a prisoner all the same.

In the morning, he wrote a poem called "Solitary Confinement" on the flyleaf of a dusty French book someone had left in the room. It began:

> No mortal comes to visit me to-day,
> Only the gay and early-rising Sun
> Who strolled in nonchalantly, just to say,
> "Good morrow, and despair not, foolish one!"

For ten days Harvey remained in Douai, surviving by the motto: "Shakespeare for the light, morphia for the night." Then he and several other prisoners were sent by train across the border into Germany. Left to sit on the floor of their fourth-class carriage, they endured cross looks from soldiers who occupied the single row of benches in the compartment. At station stops, some civilians on the platform shouted, "Nein! Engländer!" through the windows. For the most part though they were treated decently along the way. Harvey even befriended one of the guards, who spoke some pidgin English and had earned an Iron Cross on the Russian front. When he asked when the war might end, the guard said, "Krieg. Nix gut. Deutschland kaput. France kaput. Russia kaput. England kaput. Alles kaput."

Their journey concluded in the middle of the night, with a screeching halt, at Gütersloh, an industrial town in Westphalia, Germany. From the station, they trekked to the town's outskirts, where a boot-shaped assembly of buildings stood ringed in light and pine trees. Built as an insane asylum a couple of years before the war, the Gütersloh facility was now a prison camp for twelve hundred officers.

Harvey and the others were led into a building block painted with a big letter *H*. Guards searched them one by one, placing all their belongings on a long table — keeping whatever items suited them. Then each prisoner was interrogated and given a piece of black bread as compensation for the grilling. Afterward, they were stripped and their clothes taken away for fumigation. Once deloused and showered, the prisoners sat in an empty room until guards finally returned their clothes. Then came inoculations, injections into the chest and arm for a litany of diseases.

They remained in quarantine in Block H for several days, removed from the hundreds of other British, Irish, French, Belgian, and Russian prisoners who gathered outside in the sandy grounds during the day. Harvey met a pair of RFC pilots, one of whom told him about being paraded naked through Ostend after he was shot down at sea. "Bad sportsmen," the pilot said. He had informed his captors as much. When they were finally allowed into the main prison, Harvey and the pilots quickly came to learn what most prisoners knew about their German captors. "Frontline troops have some respect for each other," noted one British officer. "But the farther from the front you get, the more bellicose and beastly the people become."

Three

T here is to be a big push shortly . . . Every bit of energy must be con- centrated on the task." General Hugh "Boom" Trenchard spoke in the thunderous voice — and with the hard-charging attitude — that had earned him his nickname. It was the second week of September, 1916, and he was traveling from aerodrome to aerodrome delivering his message to the RFC squadrons. The British were bringing a "new engine of war" to break through the lines: the tank. The RFC would be critical to the suc- cess of the offensive. "We must shoot all Huns on sight and give them no rest. Our bombers should make life a burden on the enemy lines . . . Re- connaissance jobs must be completed at all costs." In essence, Trenchard repeated the simple tactical directive sent earlier by one of his squadron commanders: "Attack everything!"

At Le Hameau aerodrome in northern France, Captain David Gray ac- cepted these orders with his usual aplomb. A flight leader in the No. 11 Squadron — the RFC's first fighter group and home of several of its finest aces — aggression in the sky was his specialty. Trimly built, with an erect posture and a neatly pressed uniform, he was every inch the military man. His stern glance, accentuated by a ruler-straight part in his hair, high fore- head, trim mustache, and hatchet nose, marked an officer who brooked no compromise with himself or his command.

On September 15, after a half hour of heavy-artillery bombardment of the German lines that one pilot likened to a "solid grey wool carpet of shell bursts," British soldiers rose from their trenches in a major offensive. Aided by tanks clearing a path and providing gunfire cover through no-man's-land, the troops overran a nine-thousand-yard stretch of the first line of German trenches and some of the second.

Gray, his observer, Leonard Helder, and scores of other RFC aircrews flew day and night, both before and after the initial ground attack. Beyond the threats of Archie and mechanical failure, they also faced reinvigorated attacks from German fighter squadrons — who brought a new type of plane into the fray. One British pilot later described in his diary the speed of this new German aircraft: "The next moment I saw a Fokker biplane coming toward us. It gained on us so quick and was so infinitely superior that I made for a cloud and got to it just in time."

Since the war began, there had been a back-and-forth struggle between the Allies and the Germans over who ruled the skies over western Europe. Part depended on the quality of aircrews, their tactics, and the latest aeronautical developments. Part hung on the combatants' sheer force of will.

At the start of 1916 Trenchard made clear that he wanted to overwhelm the Germans, best planes or not, with nonstop patrols and deep penetration behind enemy lines. Throughout late spring and summer, he largely had his way, but at the severe cost of exhausting his men — and of losing many of them. The RFC was increasingly seen as a "suicide club," and a pilot who lasted a few weeks on the front was considered an "absolute master." Air crews were not issued parachutes, and when they prepared emergency kits, with rations, maps, and other gear to allow them to survive if shot down, their commanders castigated them for showing an unwillingness to fight to the bitter end.

With the big September push and increased German resistance, the butcher's bill steepened rapidly. The RFC now approached the most gruesome wastage rate of the entire war, when pilots and observers could expect to survive only seventeen and a half hours in the air before becoming casualty statistics. It was "bloody murder," one fighter leader said. New pilots arrived almost daily to take the place of crews who did not return.

What the British command did not yet know was that Oswald Böelcke, the fearsome German ace, was back on the Western Front. An aggressive, practiced pilot, the twenty-five-year-old Böelcke was also a keen tactical thinker. In the first half of the year, he shot down thirteen planes. The German air force had sent him to the East for the summer, but in late August, with the RFC again holding supremacy in the skies, they ordered him back in an effort to turn the tide.

Böelcke started a new squadron, the Jagdstaffel, whose purpose was to hunt British planes. He recruited the best pilots, including the young Baron Manfred von Richthofen (the future Red Baron). Böelcke demanded that his squadron be fully supplied with the new Albatros D.III, a fast, easily handled biplane with two fixed guns. He had already experienced its effectiveness over the Somme. With the imminent arrival of these planes and his soon-to-be-tested tactic of coordinated assault, his Jagdstaffel promised to be a vicious force.

Back at their aerodromes in France, Allied pilots chronicled the rising threat in flight logs, diaries, and letters home. However, they mostly tried to relax between their flying missions. They took walks, rode horses, drank French port, played bridge, listened to music on the gramophone, and sang songs. There was comfort in the farmhouses and chateaus they inhabited, where they tried to forget the *wouft, wouft, wouft* of antiartillery and the sight of friends plummeting in corkscrews to the earth, their planes on fire or split in two.

Even so, at breakfast on September 17, Gray could not help but notice the pair of empty seats and the dark mood around the tables in the Le Hameau mess hall. The men drank their tea and drew heavily on cigarettes. Their hands shook, their eyes glazed over in a thousand-yard stare, and their faces were fixed in a rictus of tension from the constant cold, wind, and threat of death in the sky. Two members of their squadron had been shot down the day before. With dawn approaching, it was soon time to go back into the deathly fray.

Gray reviewed his morning mission, pinned to the noticeboard: lead a six-plane fighter escort on a bombing run to the Marcoing rail junction to disrupt the German resupply of men and ammunition at the Somme. He suited up in preparation for the attack ahead. At thirty years of age, Gray was the "old man" in his squadron. Few, if any, had his military experience, including action under fire. His fighters, and the bomber crews they were protecting, would need every bit of it.

David Gray spent the first seven years of his life on a tea plantation hewed out of the dense Indian jungles of Upper Assam. It was a land both beautiful and perilous — of misted rivers and dense canopies of palm trees; of insufferable heat, monsoons, malaria, cobras, and leopards that preyed in the dark.

In the late eighteenth century, explorers for the East India Company discovered tea trees growing in the jungle, and an industry was born to rival Chinese tea production. In 1874 newlyweds Dr. Edward and Helen Gray took a six-month sea voyage from England, then journeyed by paddle steamer up the swirling brown currents of the Brahmaputra River to Assam. Edward had been recruited by the Jorehaut Tea Company to run a medical clinic for the British staff and the hundreds of locals who worked the estates. In addition to his doctor's salary, he was paid a percentage of the company's profits.

In a bamboo-framed thatched bungalow, set amid fifteen acres of hillside tea garden and surrounded by jungle, Edward and Helen started their family. David was born in 1884, the seventh of nine children. Two of his siblings died from the many fevers that plagued the area. When David was almost eight, the family returned to England. Dr. Gray opened a surgical practice in London, and they lived in a townhouse in the well-heeled neighborhood bordering Regent's Park. The culture shock was profound, but David adapted quickly. Instead of hide-and-seek in the jungle, he now played cricket and polo with great élan.

He settled early on an army career — perhaps in rebellion against his father, who had a penchant for practical jokes, business schemes, and too much sherry — and attended the Royal Military Academy in Woolwich, in the southeast of London. Founded by King George II and known as the Shop, the academy's students were destined to be sappers — combat engineers who built roads and bridges and laid and cleared mines — and artillery officers. A shrill trumpet called reveille daily at 6:15 a.m. After a parade, cadets attended lectures in the ivy-clad redbrick buildings on everything from history and mathematics to electricity, fortifications, and explosives. They built wooden mountings for eighty-ton artillery guns and soldered shell casings. They surveyed hills using three-legged plane tables and dug long tunnels with pickaxes and shovels across the campus grounds. Upon graduation, Gray was commissioned as a second lieutenant in the Royal Garrison Artillery and stationed in a fort on the Red Sea. He was nineteen.

Two years later, wishing to return to the country of his birth, Gray joined the 48th Pioneers of the British Indian Army and was based first in Bareilly, then Allahabad, in the northern reaches of the British raj. Although an infantry regiment, the Pioneers specialized in constructing bridges, fortifications, and roads in the often impassable Indian landscape. Gray was well liked both by his soldiers and by the officers above him, and was promoted to lieutenant. His record read: "A capable and efficient officer. Good eye for country. Has tact and judgment. Energetic and self-reliant." Positions as quartermaster and adjutant followed, then a promotion to captain.

Despite his quick advancement and military bearing, Gray also had the understated air of an adventurer. He sank himself into the varied cultures in which he lived. Languages came to him as easily as bad habits did to others; his nickname in India was Munshi, "teacher of tongues." Besides

English, he spoke serviceable French, German, Russian, Bengali, Hindi, and Arabic, as well as a healthy smattering of several others.

Soon after the outbreak of World War I, the 48th Pioneers embarked from Bombay with the 6th (Poona) division of the British Indian Army. Their transport ship steamed up the Persian Gulf and anchored at the mouth of the Shatt al-Arab, the river created from the confluence of the Tigris and Euphrates. The British needed to ensure a steady supply of oil from Mesopotamia. For that, they had to maintain dominance in the region, first by wresting control of Basra from the Turks. Within days of the Pioneers' arrival, Gray led a machine-gun company in a fierce fight to take Kut-az-Zain, a fort manned by forty-five hundred Turks that protected the advance toward Basra. Although slowed by torrential rains and a mirage that confounded the artillery, the British division cleared the fort. Gray thrived in his first test of combat. The division then forced-marched thirty miles across the desert to take Basra from the fleeing Turks.

The town of sixty thousand Muslims and Christians, located amid palm groves and tidal waterways, was essentially a level patch of land that flooded twice a day. There was little potable water and no infrastructure to encamp an army. Between sporadic fights with the Turks, the 48th Pioneers labored against the alluvial mud to make Basra habitable — and secure — for their division.

In spring 1915 Allied biplanes of the newly founded Indian Royal Flying Corps soared over Basra, scouting Turkish movements in the deserts to the north. Like many others in the army, the sight inspired Gray. Here were masters of the air, flying engineered marvels able to evade or engage the enemy on their own terms. As an RFC historian noted, the war most soldiers were fighting fell far short of the heroic tales of old. "There were no gleaming rows of Lancers, no saber charges of Hussars and Dragoons, no epic stands of the Thin Red Line, no stirrup charges staged by the Scots Greys and Black Watch . . . It was drab khaki, mud, blood, and apparently there was no end to the carnage. Only the bright-blue sky seemed worth fighting for."

Later that year, Gray returned to London to claim a spot in the RFC flight school at Hendon. The air force was desperate for men of his background, and he was able to answer a definitive yes to the question "Do you ride?" After earning his wings in January 1916, he distinguished himself flying for a Home Defense squadron, then another in France, before the elite No. 11 recruited him to its fighter ranks. He was schooled in dogfighting by Albert Ball, Britain's most famous ace. Soon he became a flight leader, known in the squadron for his preternatural calm.

After a dismal breakfast in the mess hall, Gray and Helder took off in their trusted Farman Experimental FE2b. Helder, who had been slated for a musical scholarship at Cambridge before the war, was an experienced observer, and he and Gray made a fine team. Their British-built two-seater, with its V-shaped structure, stab of a tailplane, and 160-horsepower engine, had served them well on numerous missions. It carried colored streamers on the tail to mark it as the escort leader.

Minutes after clearing the aerodrome, the plane's engine began to knock, and Gray signaled the five other escorts to return. Ground crews prepared another FE, this one new, fresh off the factory line. To the RFC, though, "new" meant untested and prone to fault. Gray ascended into the air again, this time without much confidence in his machine, but because of a low fog the run was postponed again, and they returned to base.

At 9:30 a.m. he lifted off from Le Hameau for the third time. His friend Lionel Morris, with whom he had learned to fly, was second lead. The sky was now clear and bright. As they circled at ten thousand feet, awaiting the arrival of the bombers, they could spy the white cliffs of Dover in the distance. Although it was wonderful to see their homeland, the clear skies guaranteed attack from German fighters, and the lack of clouds meant an absence of places to hide.

To the north, Helder sighted the dozen bombers from the No. 16 Squadron. They were slow but sturdy BE2cs carrying 20- and 112-pound "eggs" under their carriages. Gray waggled his wings, the signal for Morris and the other escort pilots to tighten into a diamond formation. A red flare from the lead bomber indicated the mission was a go. With Marcoing thirty-five miles away, the journey would be short.

Before crossing the front, Helder fired his Lewis gun to warm up its action. No sooner had their ears stopped ringing from their own gunfire when bursts of Archie surrounded them. All the planes sailed unharmed through the barrage. As they continued eastward, no German attackers materialized, and after a short time they spotted the sun's reflection shining from the railway track that ran to Marcoing. Perhaps fortune was shining on them and the run would come off without interference.

The bombers were below them, at six thousand feet, and they now zeroed in on the railway junction. Gray maintained his escort's position above, where they could prevent any diving attacks from the enemy. All his crews kept a sharp eye out.

The eggs dropped one after the next over Marcoing. Explosions rocked the air and sent up mushroom clouds of black smoke. One must have hit an ammunition dump, because the resulting blast jolted its bomber upward in a column of smoke and flying debris. The pilot recovered and — job well done by all — the bomber squadron turned back toward the west.

Gray and the other escorts circled over the junction one last time, and seeing no fighters, turned to follow the bombers home. Then: "Fokkers!" Helder screamed through the rush of air. Suddenly the sky was alive with planes emblazoned with the black Iron Cross, swooping in from the blind of the sun. Flying their newly arrived Albatros fighters, Böelcke and his Jagdstaffel drove home the surprise attack. One British bomber was ripped to pieces before it could take evasive maneuvers.

Gray banked, then dove downward to protect the others, thinking nothing of his own safety. Watching the Fokkers for any change in their direction, he gauged his angle of descent to maximize the FE's arc of fire. Knees braced against the sides of the cockpit, Helder stood on his seat to man the Lewis gun. Its spit of bullets, and those from other FEs, cut through the air. An Albatros exploded into a ball of flame. Gray and Helder's quick and courageous actions gave the other bombers the seconds they needed to escape to the west.

Now the scarlet-and-black Albatros formation cartwheeled around to focus on the six escort fighters. Assembled in batches, they swarmed the British with the bewildering force and speed that would later earn the Jagdstaffel its sobriquet, the Flying Circus. A close-quarter rake of bullets from Böelcke ripped through Gray's engine and shredded an aileron. Propeller stopped, balance control lost, the plane plummeted into a spin. Böelcke hounded them as Gray tried to recover, and Helder hung on to a strut to avoid being flung out. The German ace continued to target the escort leader, the quickest way to throw the British into disarray, and emptied his drum on the falling plane. Bullets punctured the petrol tank and shredded a wing. The plane rendered useless, its pilot having little chance to survive such a stalled plunge, Böelcke swung away to single out another fighter. The others in the Jagdstaffel swerved and sideslipped through the air in an elegant but deadly pursuit. One of them, Richthofen, aiming for his first victory, chased after Morris, the second lead of the British squadron.

Meanwhile, ground approaching, the world a dizzying swirl of sky and black smoke, Gray fought the unwieldy controls of his FE to recover from the spin. Nothing worked. The altimeter quickly spun downward: 4,000 feet . . . 3,000 . . . 2,000. Gray wrenched the stick back and forth and pressed on the foot controls to adjust the rudder, yet the plane spiraled toward the ground as petrol sprayed from its punctured tank: 1,000 feet . . . 500 feet. Still Gray struggled to regain control.

With a sudden calm, the plane stopped its corkscrew and Gray leveled out. He attempted to restart the engine, but it was shot dead. Moments later, he crash-landed into a field crowded with German infantry and a reconnaissance balloon. Face lacerated with cuts, arm broken, he crawled out of the plane. Helder also survived the crash. A match ensured the FE, already soaked with petrol, quickly lit up in flames. A safe distance from the blaze, soldiers encircled the British airmen. A gray-haired officer approached, his Luger leveled at their heads. Gray and Helder raised their arms. "You are my prisoners, gentlemen," he said in proper English as their plane broke apart in the flames.

At that moment, overhead, Richthofen put one last burst of bullets into the plane flown by Morris. It fell sideways and crashed behind some trees, five hundred yards from where Gray and Helder stood, unable to do anything but watch. Their German captor kept his pistol trained on them, seemingly confused over what to do next. "Mind if we put our hands down?" Gray asked, too much in pain, too distressed over seeing his friend go down, to care much about the danger his words might put him in.

Once reassured they were unarmed, the officer directed them to lower their arms. He introduced himself as Müller and asked them some questions, then led them to a truck at the edge of the field. They were driven off toward nearby Cambrai. On the way, they came upon Morris's FE, half-buried in a road embankment. A crowd of German soldiers had gathered around the plane, which was now a grim tangle of wire, torn cloth, and splintered wood.

Müller told his driver to stop the truck. Gray could not see Morris, but his observer was still in the cockpit, clearly dead. Gray insisted on knowing the pilot's fate. Müller made some inquiries and learned that an ambulance had taken a severely injured Morris to hospital. With that, the truck continued to the citadel.

Gray remained quiet for the short ride. He blamed himself for the devastation of his squadron. As much as he had prepared them for the mission, as much as he had tried to do everything right, the Germans had bested him, and his crews had paid a dear price. For a man like Gray, raised in the army tradition of "Fix bayonets and die like British soldiers do!" capture was a black mark of shame akin to desertion or a self-inflicted wound. He had no choice except surrender, but that did not lessen the blow.

At Cambrai, a medic set Gray's broken arm, then soldiers hustled him and Helder through the stone fortress, down a narrow, dark stairwell to the cellars — just as they had done with Cecil Blain six weeks before. "The war is over for you," one said in English. Other soldiers spoke to Gray in German, but not once did he let on that he understood them. Ever present of mind, he knew his proficiency in the language would be an advantage if it remained hidden. The soldiers put him and Helder into a large cell with double-tier wooden bunks. It was already occupied by several crews from the Marcoing run and also, to their great relief, the two No. 11 Squadron officers who had not returned from their mission the day before. At least they were alive.

The next day, the interrogations started. Neither Gray nor his countrymen gave away any information despite questions about their squadrons, their planes, aerodrome locations, how they communicated target positions with artillery battalions on the ground. Afterward, they were returned to their cells to stew.

The following morning, waking up on a straw mattress, the fastidious Gray was disgusted to find his shirt populated by lice. Later, several Jagdstaffel officers visited the British crews to gloat. The Germans' bandbox blue-gray parade uniforms struck a contrast to their own soiled, bloodied outfits, further darkening the mood in the cell. Their demoralization turned to despair when more RFC crews arrived, having been shot down by the Jagdstaffel. Then the news came that Lionel Morris and another pilot had died in the hospital. Their deaths came as a terrible blow to Gray.

On September 26 he and the others were marched out of Cambrai and onto a third-class train carriage headed for Germany. They stopped in Douai, Valenciennes, Brussels, Liège, and other towns, the battered ruins affording them a close look at the effects of war. Everything looked shrouded in a veil of gloom, and the streets were crowded with pale-faced widows dressed in black. At Aachen, they knew they were finally across the German border. During a particularly slow crawl from station to station, one pilot made an effort at humor, joking, "Why do so many stations have the same name? I've seen several called 'Ausgang'!" In Cologne, they

were allowed to disembark and follow those exit signs from the train platform, but only to sit for hours in an underground waiting room while
German civilians eyed them as if they were a pestilence.

Finally, another train brought them to Gütersloh. In the quarantine
building, Block H, Gray surveyed his new surroundings, which were
suitably better than Cambrai and much less secure. From what prisoners
working in the building said, the commandant was reasonable, the food
decent, and they were even allowed to play tennis. Gray drew Helder aside
and, in an even tone, suggested that the time was right to plan an escape.
The thought of remaining a prisoner through to the end of the war was
something Gray could not abide.

But on September 29, before their ten-day quarantine period ended,
soldiers escorted Gray and Helder back to the local railway station. Already corralled on the train were twenty-six other Gütersloh prisoners, all
of them RFC. Demands to know the reason for their assembly — and their
destination — were met with silence.

The train clanked its way northward. Gray was seated across from a
young pilot he had never met: Cecil Blain. Gray watched as Blain engaged
in a whispered conversation with his seatmate. A guard, suspicious of their
conspiratorial tone, stomped over and began haranguing the two prisoners in German. Blain pantomimed both innocence and incomprehension,
as if involved in an elaborate game of charades. The guard attempted to
silence him, but Blain continued to gesticulate wildy until finally bursting
out in laughter. The vexed guard slammed his rifle butt between the pilot's
feet, shouted a few words of warning, and strode off. Blain then shared
with his seatmate the gist of what the guard had said. Gray took note of
all of this, appreciating Blain's cleverness in hiding his understanding of
German. The man had spirit.

Several hours later, the train pulled into Osnabrück station, and the
airmen plodded through the streets in a cold downpour to the edge of
town. Guards drew them up in a line beside a twelve-foot-high brick wall.

A gate cut into the wall was opened from the inside, and they were led into a narrow graveled courtyard. Before them stood a four-story barracks.

Once inside, Gray and the others learned that their party comprised almost the sum total of British POWs held there. The others were French and Russian. Locked together in a single room, its windows painted white and nailed shut, the twenty-eight men awaited what was to come. They were segregated from the other prisoners, and the condemnatory looks of their guards, who brought the sparest of meals — raw fish and gherkins — began to fester worry.

When Gray, the senior British officer among them, asked why they were not in the general barracks with the other prisoners, and when they might be joining them, he was told simply, "I don't know. Tomorrow perhaps." Rumors, then information supplied to them by the prison commandant, Captain Blankenstein, proved they had just cause for concern.

On September 3, RFC pilot William Leefe Robinson had destroyed a Zeppelin airship flying high over North London — the first time a German airship had been downed on such a bombing raid. Its sixteen crew members, young men mostly in their early twenties, went down with the flaming ship. In retribution, the German high command intended to put twice that number of British airmen in front of a firing squad.

Four

O ctober 9, 1916. It was to be a short flight, his first in France. Caspar Kennard intended only to feel out his BE2c reconnaissance plane and get his bearings around Saint-Omer. Air mechanic Ben Digby, whose oil-smeared face looked barely old enough to manage a beard, accompanied as observer — and guide, since he had been fixing planes at the RFC's main aerodrome for several months and knew the area well.

Minutes after takeoff, Kennard was already in trouble. The engine was rattling as they headed southeastward; he could not coax the plane to climb higher than two thousand feet. From the forward cockpit, Digby turned to signal they were crossing over the trenches at an altitude that put them in range of small-arms fire. They needed to circle back. As Kennard banked around, the plane was consumed by a huge cloud. Wisps of murky white vapor blinded him and he lost all sense of direction. Again he throttled up the engine, hoping to climb into clear skies, but the plane would not respond.

Then, in an instant, they were free of the cloud only to discover themselves straight over the enemy trench lines, low enough to see individual German soldiers. There was no escape. Black shell-bursts surrounded them. Fragments tore through the fuel tank with a terrible hiss. One shell exploded directly under the port-side wing, tipping the plane over on its side before sending it into a nosedive. Kennard fought to regain control. Still, they plummeted.

In the frenzy, Digby was sure his pilot had been hit. He began to climb from his seat to take over the stick. Kennard waved him away. As they fell, more Archie boomed around the plane, followed by cracks of rifle fire from the lines. Then, with a shuddering jolt, they hit the ground. The tail of the plane almost sheared off. They bounced and careened through a field before coming to a halt. Rooted in their seats, Kennard and Digby were both stunned that they had actually survived the crash. In the last moment, Kennard must have righted the plane enough to avoid hitting the ground head-on, but he could not recall how he had done it.

Kennard had been flying solo for only two dozen hours. Seven months before, he had been living in the Argentine Pampas, working as a hand on a twenty-thousand-acre ranch. It was a long way from his homeland, Kent, England, where he was born into the landed gentry. The Kennards owned a large estate outside Maidstone and produced hops. Caspar spent his early years in the family's stately home, Frith Hall, then attended Felsted School in Essex, a private boarding school.

On graduation, he decided against university. With his older brother Keith set to inherit the estate, there was little future for him at Frith Hall. He decided to make his own way in the world and left on a steamer ship for South America. Through his extended family he gained an introduction to J. C. Douglas, the owner of an expansive ranch in Argentina. Soon after, he found himself speaking pidgin Spanish and spending all day in a saddle, herding cattle.

By April 1916, with newspaper accounts and letters from home chronicling the German advances at Verdun, Kennard could no longer remain on the sidelines. He returned to England and joined the RFC. Twenty-five years old, tall and big-boned, he looked like he could wrestle a steer to the ground with little trouble. A bushy mustache, dark slicked-back hair, and bronzed skin — and the carved wooden pipe perpetually stuck between his teeth — added to the overall South American cowboy effect. After earning his wings in late June, he served in a reserve squadron before being sent to Saint-Omer in October. It had taken him less than a week to be shot down.

A company of German soldiers surrounded Kennard and Digby before they could climb out of the plane. They took them to a holding camp — "Somewhere behind the German lines," Kennard wrote to his parents three days later. Although "lucky to be alive," he described being consumed by "one big feeling of disappointment . . . You can imagine how we feel. It was my first flight to the lines, and to have to come down without ever having had a decent scrap of it."

Days later, their captors took Digby to a German camp for common soldiers and sent Kennard to Gütersloh.

The airman did not remain there for long. Hungry for more than bitter soup, bristling against his imprisonment, and desperate to be back in a fight he had only just joined, Kennard looked for any opportunity to escape. When a guard making the lunch rounds came to his cell, Kennard hurled him against the wall, sprinted through the door, and turned the key, locking the guard in.

He found himself alone in the hallway, with no plans for where to go next. If he stepped out of the building and tried to make a run for the gate in broad daylight, he would be shot by guards. If he hid out until dark, he would be found missing at roll call and a search would ensue. Resigned to his rash mistake, he sat down and waited to be discovered.

As a consequence of his action, the Germans delivered him straightaway to Osnabrück, where Commandant Blankenstein had him thrown in a solitary cell, giving no indication when — or if — he would be allowed to join the general barracks. Kennard was beginning to understand that the Germans had no intention of abiding by the international agreements governing the treatment of prisoners of war.

"Those vanquished in war are held to belong to the victor," stated Aristotle, and indeed for most of the history of humankind, death or enslavement awaited soldiers captured on the battlefield. Often their families suffered the same fate, and homes and entire villages of those defeated in battle would be razed. Egyptian, Greek, Mongol, Persian, Viking, Aztec, Slav, Roman — the only difference was location. Brutality was strength; mercy, weakness. To warn against further resistance, a Byzantine emperor blinded fourteen thousand prisoners and sent them home in columns led by the one man out of every hundred from whom he had taken only a single eye.

Neither philosophy nor religion made any provision in how an enemy combatant was treated. Christian crusaders and Muslim conquerors alike routinely killed those who surrendered to them.

During the Middle Ages, there was a stir of change, albeit not a benevolent one. Knights serving their kings bore the brunt of the cost of war, bringing men-at-arms and horse archers into battle with them. To offset the expense, these "noble warriors" took many prisoners — to hold to ransom. The captives' chances depended on their status and bloodline, an early signal that a soldier's rank decided his treatment. Seeing an opportunity, merchants opened shops to trade in ransoms. In 1347 a good French knight listed in Calais for fifteen hundred pounds. Of course, captors had to pay a share to their lords, if the latter did not simply take the best prizes for themselves.

Enrichment did not, however, supplant the bloodthirsty rage of some conquerors during this epoch. At the Battle of Agincourt in 1415, Henry V of England set his army loose on his surrendered enemy, the French. Later, a historian chronicled the brutal fate of these vanquished soldiers: "sticked with daggers, brained with poleaxes, slain with mauls, others had their throats cut, and some their bellies panched."

In 1625 the Dutch legal theorist (and former prison escapee) Hugo Grotius published his seminal work, *On the Law of War and Peace,* demanding that nations commit to a set of international rules between warring parties, including for those captured on the battlefield. A short while later, during the English Civil War, Parliament stated that "None shall kill an Enemy who yields and throws down his Arms." Of course, without agreement from both sides or consequences for violation, these regulations and norms amounted to empty promises.

Slowly, however, there was cause for hope in the event of surrender. The Age of Reason put a value on the individual above how he might serve the state. Prisoners were "merely men, whose life no one has a right to take," declared Jean-Jacques Rousseau. With the rise of professional armies in the eighteenth century, internment and POW exchanges became more standardized. France's King Louis XV instructed his officers to treat the vanquished British "like your own."

Nonetheless, the British and French, particularly during the Napoleonic Age, ran a race to the bottom in their handling of the captured, many of whom were interned in the dark, sodden underbellies of moored ships, or "hulks." Some American soldiers in the Revolutionary War died in these same "sinkholes of filth, vermin, infectious disease and despair" as prisoners of the British outside New York City. On the heels of the formation of the International Committee of the Red Cross in Geneva in 1863, Abraham Lincoln made a marked leap forward by codifying some principles of prisoner treatment in an army field manual, not the least of which stated that POWs should be given the basic needs of shelter, food, clothing, and medical attention.

In 1899, and again in 1907, delegations from across the globe gathered in The Hague, the Netherlands, to "civilize war." Beyond stipulations on diplomacy, naval warfare, and restrictions over the use of poisonous gases and hollow-point bullets, the two international conferences set out clear rules about the treatment of prisoners. It was forbidden to kill or wound an enemy combatant who had surrendered his arms or who could not defend himself. Prisoners must be "humanely treated" on the "same footing as the troops of the Government who captured them." Enlisted soldiers (but not officers) could be used for labor, but the tasks were not to be excessive, nor related to the war. Finally, relief societies were to be allowed to channel aid to prisoners.

Germany, Britain, France, Russia, Italy, the United States, and Austria-

Hungary, among many other nations, agreed to these conventions. Such was the laundry list of dos and don'ts, a British international lawyer stated in 1911 that the future POW (a "spoilt darling") could expect "a halcyon time to be nursed fondly in memory, a kind of inexpensive rest-cure after the wearisome turmoil of fighting."

None of the diplomats gathered in The Hague in 1899 or 1907 could have anticipated the vast populations of prisoners that would come out of industrialized total war — nor the challenges this would involve. In the first six months of World War I, 1.3 million soldiers became POWs across Europe. Combatant nations struggled to confine and maintain this tide of men, and there was no sign that it would ebb anytime soon. By mid-1916 Germany held 1.65 million men in an archipelago of prison camps across the country. Its treatment of the British, let alone the French and Russians, was far from the high standard of "civilized war" promised by the Hague Conventions and the like.

In the act of surrender on the Western Front, one in five British soldiers was shot or bayoneted. The moans of wounded in no-man's-land were often silenced the same way, or men were simply left to die on stretchers behind the lines. Those who reached field hospitals often perished from neglect, as German doctors would frequently carry through on their Hippocratic oath only after attending to their own countrymen. Individual acts of kindness occurred in these first hours of captivity, but they were far from the general rule.

Before being brought to Germany, soldiers were carefully relieved of watches, money, cigarettes, wedding rings, and even boots. More out of tradition than adherence to the Hague Conventions, officers were separated from the rank and file, who were to suffer the worst in captivity. At the start of the war, their camps were overcrowded cities of mere tents surrounded by sentry boxes and barbwire fences. Some held thirty thousand to fifty thousand prisoners. Wood-slatted huts eventually replaced the canvas shelters, but the improvement only offered an excuse to pack in more men.

Lack of food, threadbare clothes, poor sanitation, and bitter winters meant that disease ran rampant. In winter 1914–15 an outbreak of typhus at Wittenberg camp prompted the Germans manning the facility to abandon its interior and restrict patrols to the perimeter. Supplies were delivered in by chute. Eventually six British doctors volunteered to enter the camp to tend to the unfortunate men, a mix of their own countrymen and French and Russian prisoners. Three of the doctors died. Those who survived reported unlit rooms where the sick wandered around delirious or shared a mattress with the already dead. "The patients were alive with vermin," one report stated. "In the half-light, [a doctor] attempted to brush what he took to be an accumulation of dust from the folds of a patient's clothes, and he discovered it to be a moving mass of lice."

Roughly 80 percent of enlisted men taken prisoner were forced to work for the Germans. Small numbers of fortunate ones, often the recovering wounded, served as orderlies in officer prison camps, cooking meals and cleaning rooms, like Jeeves of old. Volunteers for these positions were easy to find. The majority of enlisted suffered hard labor in *Arbeitskommandos* (work parties). They dug in the salt and coal mines, plowed fields, cut peat, split rocks in quarries, laid railroads, emptied barges, and worked in factories. They were treated little better than slaves — and flogged and abused the same. For a period, their death rates were greater than those on the front lines. According to one historian, some fifty thousand Allied troops and civilians perished under such conditions.

In comparison, captive officers had it much better. They inhabited less crowded, solidly built prisons. They did not have to work and were even afforded the services of rank-and-file prisoners to perform basic manual duties. An officer who pledged not to escape might be allowed to take parole, or temporary leave, typically for walks outside the camp. Such was the currency of a gentleman's word being his bond and the vestiges of the old class system that once dominated all of Europe.

Imprisoned officers and rank-and-file men alike were subject to a German high command that connived against the Hague Conventions. At the outbreak of war, Kaiser Wilhelm gathered his generals at his army headquarters in Koblenz and urged them to "take no prisoners." The old general Paul von Hindenburg declared that a German triumph depended on war production; to turn this "screw up the most," Germany needed prisoners to do the work. The army issued a handbook to its troops that called attention to the Hague pledges but included amendments about how prisoners could be put to death for insubordination, for attempting to escape, in reprisal for similar measures by the enemy, and the very broad "in case of overwhelming necessity."

Other nations were far from blameless in their treatment of prisoners. The British and French were known to employ captured Germans near the Western Front, in direct violation of the Hague Conventions. Early in the war, Britain imprisoned some POWs and interned civilians in over-crowded ships that likened to the hulks of yesteryear, yet despite accusations of widescale abuse from Germany, the majority were maintained in decent conditions. Russia was one of the worst caretakers of POWs, who died in vast numbers from neglect, exposure, and hard labor, many in Siberia.

The political leadership in each country may have set the standard for POW treatment, but in Germany, at least, the individual army district in which a prison camp was located was the most important factor. The general in charge of each district, and the commandants tasked to run individual camps, had the autonomy to do mostly as they pleased. Diplomats, led by James W. Gerard, the American ambassador to Germany before the United States entered the war in 1917, tried to alleviate the worst of the abuses, but with 165 POW camps scattered throughout Germany and orchestrated efforts by their commandants to deceive inspectors, diplomats who succeeded in shutting down one camp faced the opening of another of equal — or worse — conditions to serve the same population. Their rights under the Hague Conventions ignored or abused, prisoners in Germany were largely left to fend for themselves.

• • •

In mid-October, Gray, Blain, and the other RFC officers brought from Gütersloh to Osnabrück were led out of their room one by one to meet with a civilian investigator from Berlin. He harassed each of them with repeated questions on the latest British planes, including their guns and types of ammunition. The airmen were circumspect in their responses, no matter the yelling and threats from their interrogator. The next day, guards moved the lot of them into the camp's general barracks. Commandant Blankenstein offered no explanation for the reprieve of their death sentence. Nor would he comment on a rumor circulating among the men that another RFC pilot was being held in isolation at the prison. Several days later, however, that rumor was confirmed.

When Kennard emerged from his segregation, he had decided that escape was his best shot at survival. While he was being led into the gravel yard for his first evening roll call, he noticed that the few straggly trees around the yard's edge had all but lost their leaves since his arrival. They looked as haunted and gray as his twenty-eight fellow airmen, who now stood with two hundred Russians and ninety French in the cold dusk chill. Blankenstein arrived, and one of his lieutenants shouted out the roll call. Though he answered when his name was called, Kennard otherwise distanced himself from the quiet chatter among the airmen, his unlit pipe stuck firmly between his lips. Once all the prisoners were accounted for, Blankenstein stepped forward and singled out Kennard in the line, warning that any further attempts at escape would bring the harshest of punishments. Then he dismissed them.

A guard brought Kennard to a second-floor room, where seven of his countrymen, including Blain, were already installed. There were beds for each of them, two chairs, a single table, and a stove — with no supply of coal. A Russian orderly, who spoke no English, cleaned the room and made the beds each morning.

Beyond the schedule of roll calls and meals, there was little to do. Some of the British made friends with their fellow Russian and French officers, and they started language lessons between them. Others organized boxing and wrestling matches in the small yard. The airmen also spent their time writing home. They were allowed to send only two letters (of four pages maximum) and four postcards each month, so these missives were often written in minute script, covering the front, back, and margins of the paper. Most letters included requests, for food, clothing, money, books, and a host of other items.

The British Red Cross helped facilitate these deliveries and sent its own fortnightly parcel of food to every British captive. The German high command was more than happy to allow the enemy to sustain its imprisoned troops. Osnabrück also ran a brisk business out of its canteen, which supplemented the meager, often putrid, meals served by the Germans. Prisoners paid for items with *Lagergeld,* specially issued camp money funded either from their military pay in captivity (per an agreement between the British and German governments) or through transfers from their own banks in England.

Throughout his first days after leaving solitary, Kennard continued to keep himself at a remove from the others. His roommate Blain tried to befriend him, but Kennard was too preoccupied brooding over his capture and stalking Osnabrück, looking for a means of escape. In early November he discovered a window with a missing latch at the end of the second-floor hallway. The window faced a twelve-foot-high wall topped with barbwire. In his mind, a plan fell into place: he would drop out of the window at night, cut through the short fence that surrounded the barracks, climb over the wall and onto the street below. From Osnabrück, he would take a train to a town close to the Dutch border, some seventy miles away. Once in the Netherlands, a neutral nation, he would be free to return to England and to the fight.

First he would need to learn a few words of German. His fellow prisoners at Osnabrück knew that Captain Gray spoke fluent German, despite his efforts to hide it. Going to the room to which Gray was assigned, Kennard asked his countryman to teach him the phrases he would need to buy a train ticket in German. And fast. Gray was reluctant, especially when Kennard refused to explain what he was up to. Disciplined and uncompromising, Gray was not one to involve himself in any foolhardy schemes. Having no other choice, Kennard divulged his plan. It was probably the most he had spoken in weeks.

Gray thought the idea had promise but suggested there was no way a few phrases in German would be enough to secure Kennard a railway ticket. Kennard would have a better chance, Gray maintained, getting to the border on foot. For that he would need a compass, food, and a map, and it would be best if he had help. Together with a couple of men, he could more quickly gather the essential supplies. He would have help on the night of the breakout and during the journey to the Netherlands. Before Kennard could ask, he had a partner.

To round out the group, Gray recommended a third man join them. Helder, his former observer, had shown little interest in risking an escape during their earlier conversations, so Gray suggested Blain. The young pilot had also come to him for tutoring. Although his knowledge of Cape Dutch enabled him to understand some German, as Gray had witnessed on the train to Osnabrück, Blain was unable to speak the language with any proficiency. But he had guts to spare. Before Kennard went to bed that night, the three were a cabal, with Gray decidedly its leader. For the first time since his capture, Kennard felt his dark mood lift. Now, there was hope.

They started with milk. Any schoolboy worth his salt knew that milk could be used as invisible ink. Take a milk-dipped fountain pen, scrawl a message on a blank sheet of paper, write a note on top of that in ink, then send. The recipient runs a hot iron over the paper and the fat in the milk below burns through, revealing the hidden words. Message delivered.

On the inside of an envelope addressed to his mother, Blain wrote in milk that he needed a compass, which could be smuggled in to him in a parcel. He also wanted some warm clothes, but these could come in an ordinary package. To alert her to a hidden message, he included a simple code in his letter. It began: "My deaarest Mother, I am so sorry I am unable to account for the los of my letter home to you but I hop that this one will rive soon telling you that I am very fit and well. I ccannot tell you how I long to get ome again." With the additional and missing letters, the code spelled out: "Search." Gray and Kennard prepared similar messages.

"Will they twig it?" Blain wondered to his coconspirators. Even if his letter cleared the censors, he feared that his mother might not decipher the code.

At any other prison, a month or more might pass before they knew. But Osnabrück, they had learned, served as a main censoring depot for northwest Germany. Every package and letter sent throughout the surrounding area was routed through the city. Delivery came faster than they might expect from the Royal Mail.

While they waited, the three men acted like they were settling into Osnabrück for the long haul. They befriended some Russian officers, and at night they would have tea together and listen to concerts by balalaika and guitar players. They even participated in a theater show with some fellow RFC pilots, twisting themselves together and acting the part of an automobile racing across the stage. The crowd roared with laughter.

Not all was easy diversion, especially for Gray. As senior British officer at the camp, he needed to cajole Blankenstein at every turn into providing better conditions. The floor of the latrine was like an ice-skating rink in the cold, so Gray demanded coal for its stove. He also pushed for bigger exercise grounds. Blankenstein, who turned out to be a reasonable man, acceded to both requests. Gray also led a protest against a spike in canteen prices. When a French pilot, Captain Allouche, tried to stop it, saying the Germans were only passing off a rise in costs, Gray threatened him into silence. Always trying to curry favor with the Germans, Allouche had few friends. Even his own countrymen despised him, a martinet who dressed every day with his crowd of medals on his uniform. Some even thought him a German spy.

When not handling such concerns, Gray labored over letters to the families of those who died on the Marcoing run. Writing to the mother of Lionel Morris, Gray praised her son for his "stout heart and steady nerve" and explained how he had been shot down after bravely circling back to protect another plane. Morris's death weighed on Gray.

Preparing for escape and the hope that came with it brought solace. Every day, Gray, Blain, and Kennard checked the parcel room for word from their families. Finally, Blain received a package from home. As required, a guard closely watched him open the box to make sure he did not slip something into his pocket before its contents were inspected. Inside was a handful of soft candies wrapped in wax paper and a sealed tin containing a nutcake flavored with crème de menthe. At first blush, Blain feared there must have been a mix-up with the parcels. His mother would never have sent such a dessert — she knew he hated mint. In the next moment, he realized what it might actually contain.

He passed the tin to the guard, who shook it in his hand like a child rattling a present to guess what was inside. Blain had to remind himself to breathe so as not to give away his nervous expectation. If suspicious, the guard would surely pry open the lid and look more closely. If the contraband were discovered, Blain could face time in isolation or a beating — or both. Then the wait was over. The guard handed the tin back to Blain and waved him away.

Sitting on his bed, Gray and Kennard hovering beside him, Blain removed the lid of the tin. Wafts of mint rose from the sugar-coated dessert. When he lifted the cake from the tin, he noticed that its weight was off. He dug his fingers into it and pulled out something wrapped in oilskin cloth. "Dear old Mum. God bless you," he said, his hands trembling as he uncovered a compass. He was overcome with thoughts of his family, how much they supported him, how much they must miss him — as much as he did them. Tears pooled in his eyes. Leaving him to be alone, Gray and Kennard no doubt felt homesick as well.

Over the course of the week, Gray received a map, hidden at the bottom of a box of chocolates, while Kennard uncovered a small flashlight and file in a parcel of his own. They also collected clothes and a week's worth of tinned meat, chocolate, Oxo cubes, and milk tablets for the run to the Dutch border. Overjoyed at their bounty, the three almost danced a jig.

But not everything they needed could come by mail. One day, the canteen had a manicure set on sale. The Germans must not have considered how sharp it was, nor how well made: the nail clippers sliced through wire like it was paper, perfect to cut a hole in the fence. From some scrap canvas, they sewed haversacks. From parcel string, they wove a rope to lower themselves from the window.

In early December, their preparations complete, the men were set to go. First an unexpected snowfall stalled them. No matter how dark the night, guards would have easily spotted their figures in the light reflected off the snow. Then a rumor came that Blankenstein had got wind of an imminent escape attempt. According to the prison grapevine, which the British called the Poldhu (after the wireless station in Cornwall where Guglielmo Marconi sent the first transatlantic radio transmission), Blankenstein had placed six sharpshooters in the streets outside the barracks to pick off anyone who managed to make it outside the wall.

At first, Gray, Blain, and Kennard did not believe it. There was always scuttlebutt of every sort passing through the prison. The men planned to keep careful watch for the next few nights on the movements to and from the barracks. When they spotted some figures with rifles stalking in the dark outside the walls, they decided to put the escape on brief hold. The Germans would surely not maintain such vigilance throughout the long winter. Then, on December 17, guards informed Gray that he was to be moved to another camp. Immediately. The three were shattered by the news. Their cabal was broken.

Five

Gütersloh was a Tower of Babel, holding prisoners from almost every Allied country, but the British associated mostly with the Russians. Will Harvey, a lover of music, savored the Russian songs and dances that echoed through the camp at night. They gave him a momentary lift away from the "pine-shadowed cage" in which he was being kept. Before Christmas, the Russians had been secretly engaged in constructing a balloon in the unused top rooms of their block. They somehow collected enough scraps of paper — everything from old envelopes to brown paper from parcels — to paste together to create an inflatable in which to escape. Extending like sausage links, it filled several rooms. Just before they sailed away — or at least made the attempt — the German guards discovered their plot. The balloon was deflated, folded in sacks, and burned in a furnace.

Crushed by this failure, the would-be escapees had only a dreary dinner to look forward to on Christmas. Of all the POWs in the camp, the Russians received the least number of parcels from home and so had meager holiday fare. Wanting to do a good turn for their fellow captives, Harvey and his countrymen shared with them some of the cheese, meat, and desserts they'd collected for a Christmas feast. Together they sang carols and toasted to a better year ahead with a punch Harvey brewed from "bad German wine, tinned fruit, and smuggled cognac, raisins, cloves, cinnamon, and a spot or two of Worcester sauce — for bite."

A few days later, a newspaper was smuggled into camp. Woodrow

Wilson, the American president, was asking the warring parties to make peace, but the prospects for a negotiated settlement appeared dim. The daily infliction of casualties across the Western Front promised to continue without end, both sides clearly believing they would win the war of attrition. The mighty Russian bear had awakened, pushing back against the earlier Austrian and German advances, though at a steep price of over a million casualties. Retrenchment guaranteed a frigid winter on the Eastern Front.

Also printed in the smuggled newspaper was King George V's Christmas address. In it he extolled the continuing bravery of Britain's soldiers and sailors and praised the men and women on the home front who labored to keep their country in the fight. Nowhere in his speech did he mention those who had been taken prisoner — not a word. Their struggles, their sacrifices, had seemingly been forgotten.

When Harvey first arrived at Gütersloh, he imagined he would be welcomed by his British countrymen already in the camp. Instead, he felt abandoned by the veteran prisoners, who left him and the other arrivals to find their own place. Every day, alone, he walked the perimeter fence — a distance of about half a mile. On weekends, local civilians gathered outside the wire to gape at him and his fellow captives. The only inmates who paid him any mind were Russians, who were often looking for tutoring in English. He wrote a poem, "Gütersloh," about the time, which concluded:

> *Walking round our cages like the lions at the Zoo,*
> *We see the phantom faces of you, and you, and you,*
> *Faces of those we loved or loathed — oh, everyone we knew!*
> *And deeds we wrought in carelessness for happiness or rue;*
> *And dreams we broke in folly, and seek to build anew —*
> *Walking round our cages like the lions at the Zoo.*

In his second month, Harvey dashed off lyrics set to the tune of an old drinking song and belted them out to the delight of his bunkmates. He started writing more songs, sharing his own poems, and lecturing on the arts. Notably, he delivered a lacerating critique of playwright George Bernard Shaw, whose theories on "life force" and "supermen" Harvey found "less important than a single sunset, less worthy of deep, thoughtful consideration than the scarlet cup of one poppy." Soon prisoners were calling Harvey "the Poet" — an epithet reinforced by the success back home of his first book. Over time, he found a place for himself in the camp and felt less marooned.

Despite all this, the gloom of captivity clung to him like a sickness. It was not the boredom, though, that was profound. Every day followed the same routine: it started with morning roll call, followed by black bread for breakfast, queues for the parcel room, yard time, lunch, yard time, tea, dinner, evening roll call, and lockdown for the night. It was not the hardship, either. Commandant Gröben, a grizzled veteran of the Franco-Prussian War, who shouted "Achtung!" as a standard greeting, brooked no compromise with the rules, but if prisoners abided by them he left them to themselves.

Harvey missed the Redlands and his family. He also longed for Anne, penning a poem, "Loneliness," in lament. But even their absence was not the source of his greatest despair. What plagued him most was a feeling of uselessness, one shared by many of the prisoners. Try as he did to throw himself into poetry and music, he could not help but think it was for nothing. While he sat in Gütersloh, his battalion mates, his friends, and his brothers were risking death. "He cannot help them," Harvey blistered, regarding the circumstances of the prisoner of war. "He cannot join any more in the dreadful and glorious fight for England and her liberty. Yes, he is futile. There is no more terrible reflection for a man . . . Her enemies are still unbroken. He is idle. That is the essence of his trouble, the true agony of the prisoner-state."

If he would only seize it, Harvey had plenty of opportunity not to be idle. His bunkmates, and close friends, infantry captains Joseph Rogers and Frank Moysey, were leading an attempt to break out of the camp. A former coal-mine engineer, Rogers was well suited to the task. They nick-named their band the Pink Toes, likely due to the state of their feet after burrowing through the ground underneath the camp. They accessed their sap, located in a disused cellar, through a shaft that opened up behind a stairway on the side of their barracks. Rogers had engineered the bottom step to slide on greased wooden runners, allowing an easy, albeit tight, entrance and exit.

Throughout the winter, during the couple of hours the guards were at dinner, they scraped out a tunnel through the sandy ground, using table-spoons. At each session's end, Moysey, Rogers, and their fellow Pink Toes scattered the excavated debris in the exercise yard from bags hidden under their Burberry trench coats and then returned to their room exhausted and dirty as chimney sweeps. Harvey nicknamed Moysey "Mossy" after the earthy smell emanating from him.

By mid-March 1917 the tunnel's mouth extended beyond the wire. Another ten yards and they would reach a slight hill shadowed by pine trees that would serve as the perfect exit. Then Gröben announced that all British prisoners were to be transferred to a camp in Crefeld. Rogers and Mossy made a last-ditch attempt to finish the tunnel but failed. Their tireless work, excavating an exact 2,553 bags of sand and earth for a thirty-five-yard stretch, had been for naught.

In their months together in Room 65, Harvey never threw in his lot with the Pink Toes. A German guard had told him, when he first arrived at the camp, that many had tried to escape but had never made it. The Russians, the guard called "foolish." The French, "occasionally so." As for the British, "Ah, they are good — so — like sheep." Harvey had shown himself almost recklessly courageous in the trenches, but at Gütersloh it was not sheepish fear that stopped him from joining the tunnel plan. In-stead, prison was eating at his will to be free.

Some thirty miles north of where Harvey languished at Gütersloh, Cecil Blain and Caspar Kennard were eager and ready to implement their own breakout plan. Two months had passed since their partner Gray had been transferred from Osnabrück. Suspicion over an escape attempt had abated, and sharpshooters no longer patrolled outside the prison wall. The two men decided upon February 22, 1917, as their getaway night. They both acknowledged that they would be better off with Gray still on their team, but they had resolved to make do.

When the designated time had at last come, Blain and Kennard slung their haversacks over their shoulders. Peering out of their room, they surveyed the hallway and, assured it was empty, began to make their way down the corridor. Before they could reach the broken window, though, they heard the whine of a door closing at the corridor's end. Someone had seen them — perhaps the French pilot Allouche, whom Gray had threatened months before. His room was located in that direction. Both Blain and Kennard knew that the Frenchman was not to be trusted.

The two men turned back to their room. To be safe, they would delay another day. But before they awoke the next morning, six guards roused them from their beds, and Commandant Blankenstein stood in the doorway as a search of the room began. The guards found their rope, their haversacks, every tool of their escape. They shoved the two Englishmen into the hallway, then down to the solitary cells in the basement. The airmen's dreams of getting back to England were dashed.

Neither had any doubt that it was Allouche who had given them up. Doing his punishment in solitary for two weeks, Blain had only plots of vengeance against the Frenchman to keep him warm. Upon his release, he found that Kennard had been consumed by the same thoughts.

At the first roll call after their emergence, Blankenstein announced that the Germans were instituting a new policy of separating prisoners of different nationalities into different camps. Accordingly, the British would be moved. Blain and Kennard welcomed the transfer — a new prison might offer better opportunities for escape — but they had no intention of leaving Osnabrück without first exacting retribution on the "evil swine," Allouche. Several of their fellow British officers wanted to participate as well.

After lights-out on March 7, a dozen men tiptoed to the end of the second-floor corridor. They carried chamber pots that sloshed with the most vile concoctions of ash, urine, excrement, water, jam, and rotting food. Blain was proudest of all about his preparation: a one-pound tin of Morton's Black Treacle, courtesy of his mother. Allouche would be tasting molasses and scrubbing it from his skin for weeks.

At the door, Kennard turned to the others. "Ready?"

"Not half," Blain whispered back.

The two burst into the room, followed by the rest of the men. They pinned Allouche to his bunk and stuffed a blanket into his mouth to cut off his protests. Then they poured their awful brews over the traitor as he thrashed about with fright. At one point, Allouche freed the gag from his mouth and howled "Au secours!" Seizing the moment, Blain dumped a fair measure of the treacle into his mouth. Revenge exacted, the British ran from the room. Allouche staggered down the hallway. "Help! The English have tried to murder me," he shouted. "Strike a match quickly. I am covered with blood!" Awakened by the ruckus, other prisoners emerged from their rooms. One lit a match beside Allouche, and the hallway erupted in guffaws at the sight of him.

The next day, the French officer identified the perpetrators. When one of Blankenstein's lieutenants asked Blain and Kennard if they had indeed participated in the attack, the men, flashing proud smiles, admitted they had. Blankenstein decided to leave their punishment to the commandant at Clausthal, the new camp for which the British prisoners were now bound. The dozen culprits walked into the yard to cheers from all but the Germans. Shortly after, the rest of the British POWs were assembled to go, almost a hundred men with suitcases, mandolins, gramophones, bags of food, and even pots and kettles strung over their shoulders. They aimed to leave nothing behind.

A train carried them into the snowbound Harz Mountains, 150 miles due east, deeper into Germany. Blain and Kennard watched from their carriage as they passed high into the shadowed hills. The lights in the train flickered from the jarring movement on the rails. After midnight, the train halted at Clausthal station, and the guards shouted "Raus!" Snow was falling as they stepped down onto the platform with their belongings. They were told they would have to wait until morning to head up to their new camp.

After a couple of hours shivering in the snow, the men were allowed into the station restaurant, where the owner spread out some ham sandwiches and hearty soup. The British bought every bottle of wine behind the bar, reveling in particular in a fine prewar vintage. A raucous party broke out as the guards joined the festivities, effecting a temporary truce. At first light, feeling the worse for wear, the prisoners tramped two miles into the mountains, sometimes through heavy drifts that threatened to bury them. In the distance, they sighted the Brocken, the tallest peak in northern Germany. Finally, they arrived at Clausthal prison camp.

Set amid mountain lakes, the building had formerly been the Kurhaus Pfauenteichen (Peacock Lake Hotel), an expansive four-story holiday retreat. With its bulky wings, steeply sloped roofs, and stunted belfry tower, the structure looked like a wedding cake gone awry. Surrounding the retreat now was a twelve-foot-tall fence made of iron-wire torpedo netting with a two-inch mesh. Arc lights stood at intervals; so too did sentries with dogs.

Blain, Kennard, and the others involved in the revenge plot on Captain Allouche won only the briefest glimpse inside Clausthal before being shunted off to Hanover for court-martial. They passed the night before their trial in a garrison jail, each in a lone cell with a single, iron-barred window. There were so many rats that the prisoners sounded like a percussion band as they batted the vermin away with their boots.

Come morning, guards ushered them across a yard and into a courtroom adorned with a large crucifix. They stood before their judges, an assembly of German colonels all dressed in their blue-grays, buttons and sword hilts burnished. By comparison, the twelve prisoners, unwashed and wearing what was left of their now-threadbare uniforms, looked like street vagrants. It was altogether an intimidating scene until the court interpreter introduced one of the defendants as from the "Middlesessex" Regiment. Blain and Kennard could not suppress their grins.

The prosecutor read out the penal-code violations for the "cunning attack" against Captain Allouche. Of note, he detailed the tarring with treacle. The French major assigned to defend the twelve men tried to chalk up the whole affair to a petty squabble between prisoners of different nations. The judges would have none of it. After a brief adjournment, they sentenced the lot to fifty days in solitary or a five-hundred-mark fine.

Unwilling to give the enemy money that might be used to prosecute the war, the British officers took the time. They spent it at Clausthal in huts built behind the old hotel. Their cells grew so cold at night that the rags they were given to wash with became stiff as boards. But never for a moment did Blain or Kennard regret taking their revenge on the despicable Allouche.

Captain David Gray regarded himself in the mirror. Mustache trimmed. Suit fitted. Forged pass in jacket pocket. Wallet stuffed with marks. Folded map, secret report, and some provisions in his valise. Time to go. He stepped out of his room at Crefeld barracks. With its warm stove, real beds, and chintz-covered walls, Crefeld was a dream compared to Osnabrück. He shared the space with several captains, including Douglas Lyall Grant, of the London Scottish Regiment. A blueblood through and through, Grant was a sybarite of the highest order. On his capture, a day after leave back in Britain, the officer had simply remarked, "I wish I had gone to the dentist when I was at home." His teeth were no doubt in need of attention, considering the endless flow of wine, fowl, pudding, candied almonds, and other sweets supplied by his well-heeled parents.

Holding some eight hundred British officers and a scattering of other nationalities, Crefeld had hallways so wide you could throw a party in them, barracks blocks with views for miles, and a rectangular courtyard with tennis courts. Built in 1906, the expansive grounds originally housed a renowned Hussar regiment. Kaiser Wilhelm II spared no luxury for the young German cavalrymen, who were celebrated as much for their courtly dancing as for their horsemanship. Neither, however, were of much use after their dispatch to the Eastern Front. Crefeld itself was a prosperous town, enriched by the silk trade. Linden trees and stylish houses bordered its cobblestone streets. The prison's Commandant Courth, a local, was a gentleman with the bulbous red nose of an imbiber, who allowed his charges long walks on parole in the surrounding woods.

Despite the camp's relative comforts, Gray remained desperate to escape. He wanted to get back to the fight, of course, but he was also eager to right a wrong, having collected testimonies of abuse that had been witnessed — or suffered — by his fellow officers before they arrived at Crefeld. Particularly concerning were the accounts involving those in the infantry who were captured earlier in the war. Gray planned to travel to London personally to deliver his report. His government needed to know the extent of the German crimes against his countrymen, including dreadful beatings and the cold-blooded mowing-down by machine-gun fire of soldiers surrendering on the front line.

With Crefeld only eighteen miles from the Dutch border, Gray knew there was a good chance he could reach the frontier — and freedom — once he got outside its high walls. Disguised as a German businessman, he intended to stroll past the suite of guards at the double-arched front gate. His impeccable German and forged pass indicating he had met with the commandant should do the trick. He was undeterred by the signs posted around Crefeld warning prisoners against "evading your fate by escaping" on account that "the guards are earnest men, knowing their duty."

Gray left the barracks entrance and paid no mind to the prisoners eyeing him in his civilian clothes. Civvies were strictly forbidden among the inmates, and he had made his from a stripped-down uniform and several smuggled items. Acting like he had not a care in the world, he timed his walk to arrive at the gate just as a truck pulled up. The "earnest" guards, accustomed to the traffic in and out of the facility and busy checking the driver's credentials, barely gave the suited Gray a look. In a perfect accent, he offered a few words of greeting to them and flashed his mocked-up stamped pass. They waved him on. With a *Danke schön*, Gray walked straight out of the prison. Crossing Bissingstrasse, he glanced sideways to see if there was any sign of pursuit or any need for alarm. He detected neither. He was just another local on the sidewalk, going about his afternoon with what leisure the war allowed. He reached a tram stop and waited for the next streetcar.

In the months since separating from Blain and Kennard and arriving at Crefeld, Gray had been devising a way out. Two Russian prisoners had tried to hide in a rubbish cart, but they were caught before it was taken away. A Frenchman tried to get past the guards by mimicking the skittering, hunched gait of one of Courth's lieutenants (a man known as the Crab). The guards almost let him past, but when they asked in German for his papers, he did not understand their request and thus could not comply. Another scheme saw a dozen RFC officers building a glider plane to fly over the walls. Ultimately, the makeshift craft did not prove airworthy. Most escape efforts, though, were focused on tunneling under the barracks. So numerous were these attempts that the ground beneath Crefeld resembled a busy ant colony. The discovery of each burrow seemed only to embolden others to try. Commandant Courth and his guards had shown themselves effective in rooting out the honeycomb of tunnels by knocking on every wall and floor in the prison, listening for the sound of a hollow space behind.

Of late, Gray had become acquainted with recent arrivals from Gütersloh, the Pink Toes. No doubt they would have liked Gray to join in their new tunneling effort at Crefeld, particularly given his Woolwich education and experience with the 48th Pioneers. But Gray did not much care for the dirty business of sapping; he wanted to try another way.

After a long wait, Gray boarded Tram 88 and paid his fare. He took one of the wooden seats hidden from the street by curtained windows. Though the drumbeat in his chest had yet to subside, he folded one leg over the other in an attempt to look every bit the casual passenger. The tram delivered him to Crefeld train station. There were trains headed due west toward Venlo, the closest Dutch town. But given that he had experienced no trouble as of yet, he figured that he was safe to journey farther to the north, to Nordhorn, where the border guards might be more lax.

He arrived at the small German textile town well after dark and left the station on foot, heading north over a series of small canals. Then he followed a road toward Neuenhaus, seven miles away. By his map, once the road intersected with a railway line, he would be a mile from the zigzagged border. A heavy rain was falling, which gave him the advantage of having the road to himself but made the going miserable. At the railway line, he turned west and started through some soggy fields. He did not have a compass, but he hoped there was little chance he would get turned around over such a short distance.

Half an hour into his hike, trousers muddy up to his knees, he reckoned he had reached the border. If there had been a demarcation, he had missed it.

He took out his map. Rain pelted his face and soaked his collar. Cold, wet, and potentially lost, he dared lighting a match to divine his location. If a German frontier post was nearby, the guards would see the flicker of light and converge on his position. After several attempts to strike a match in the downpour, one remained alight long enough for him to read the squiggles of lines. He had veered a little northward in his slog, but if he made his way due south he should reach the Dutch border village of Breklenkamp.

Minutes later, trekking through another field, he spotted the dim glow of a village. Then he came onto a road. He followed it a short distance before seeing a wooden signpost that read BREKLENKAMP. Elated, he headed down the road until he sighted an illuminated military post. A pair of soldiers in dark greatcoats sought shelter from the rain under its awning. Gray moved forward.

The two guards drew their rifles, but he figured they were simply startled by his emergence from the dark. In English, he explained that he was an RFC officer who had escaped from a prison camp. Saying nothing, the guards led him inside. Rising from a desk to meet Gray was a German officer. From behind Gray, the guards seized his arms.

There was not one, but two Breklenkamps, separated by the border, the officer explained later. Gray had the bad luck of having a map that showed only the Dutch town, which he had missed by a short walk. The knowledge of having come so close to freedom was crushing for Gray. The next morning, the soldiers returned him to Crefeld, his secret report still hidden in his valise.

Something was afoot. In mid-May, a hundred active-service soldiers in heavy helmets marched through the gate at Crefeld, doubling its regular guard of older reservists. They mounted two machine guns outside the high walls, and two atop the barracks buildings. The slightest congregation of prisoners after lights-out resulted in shouts to disperse, often at the prodding of bayonets. In one such incident, Douglas Lyall Grant stuck a hunk of ham upon the tip of an offending blade and was nearly run through for the gag.

Neither Harvey, in the general barracks, nor Gray, in solitary after his escape attempt, knew the cause of the increased presence of the guards. The Poldhu had it that the citizens of Crefeld, fed up by war rationing, intended to overrun the prison and steal the food supplies sent to the British. There was also a rumor of a mass escape planned from the camp, precipitated by an imminent Allied bombing of the town. Whatever the reason, all the prisoners and guards were on edge.

Finally, on May 20, Commandant Court announced that the prisoners were being separated and sent off to four different camps. They would be allowed to carry only one piece of hand luggage each. He offered no explanation for the move, and said he was sorry to lose them. Then his lieutenant, the Crab, started calling out names, assigning the men to one of four groups. Harvey and the Pink Toes were selected for Group B, as was Gray, although he was not there to hear his name called.

Early the next morning, the prisoners started preparing their bags. Many had spent several months at Crefeld; some had spent years there. In that time, they had accumulated a household of goods — and menageries of pet rabbits, canaries, and even spiders. They had built private cardboard rooms in the wide barracks hallways. Few wanted to abandon everything to start anew, and tempers flared as guards began eyeing what they wanted to take afterward — or steal there and then. The mood tensed even more when two of the prisoners attempted to smuggle themselves out in a van.

At the evening roll call, a riot was in the making, especially as the head count was off and the Crab needed to repeat the call of eight hundred names not once, not twice, but three times. Harvey and some others were throwing off the count on purpose, moving about to various positions in the assembly and answering to other prisoners' names. Mossy planned on hiding in a sap the Pink Toes had dug but not finished after their transfer from Gütersloh, and escaping from Crefeld once the camp had been emptied. The guards could not be allowed to know he was missing.

When the roll call finally ended, near midnight, some prisoners started tossing chairs, benches, tennis rackets, cardboard boxes, and other items out of their windows. One prisoner lit the bristles of an old broom and used it as a torch to start fires in the yard. More furniture and belongings followed. The blazes grew. As soon as guards snuffed out one, another flickered to life. Their shouts in the square had little effect. Finally, the guards announced that anyone left in the square in five minutes' time would be shot. Then they rushed the barracks in numbers. A British colonel received a rifle butt to his back. Others were shoved away from the windows. Miraculously, in quieting the bedlam not a shot was fired.

Harvey spent what little time he had left packing his bags. He would not miss Crefeld. Despite its relative comfort, the prisoners kept to their individual fiefdoms, and the camp lacked the camaraderie of Gütersloh.

To his mind, Crefeld had the "mouldy atmosphere of a club — a bad one." Courth was its only saving grace. He had allowed Harvey to send a manuscript of the poems he had written in captivity to England for publication, a kindness he suspected most commandants would have denied.

At 3:30 a.m. bonfires continued to dot the yard as Group B was led four abreast from Crefeld by almost as many guards as there were prisoners. Weakened by his time in solitary, Gray was slow along the path to the train station. At one point he dropped his bag, and a guard booted him to the ground from behind. He got up again, picked up his bag and, resisting the urge to start a fight, continued on.

Guards herded them into third-class carriages, shut the windows, and posted themselves at either end of the cars before the train clattered down the track.

When the sun came up, the carriages became hot as stoves. The train was headed east, over an iron bridge that spanned the Rhine; the men were uncertain of their destination. To pass the time, they played poker and bridge. There were whispers that they should try to rush the guards and jump from the train, but nobody risked the effort, especially since their watchers were keen to any movement.

Along the route, they passed a long line of factories, their blast furnaces roaring bright orange, no doubt producing weapons of war. They also saw massive assemblies of soldiers waiting at stations to be sent toward the front. "Cannon fodder," the prisoners remarked, loud enough for their guards to hear. Late that night, the train stopped at Hademstorf. Few had heard of the small town between Bremen and Hanover in northern Germany. They remained there for the night, the guards pitching a cordon around the train.

At dawn, the guards ordered the prisoners out of the car and marched them away from the station. Dehydrated from the train ride, hauling heavy bags, the prisoners tramped through a pine forest. The air was thick with heat. After they crossed over a swiftly moving river, the path leveled and the trees grew more stunted. They reached a broad, barren heath that stretched as far as the eye could see. Their guards led them down a sandy cart track that made a straight line into a swamp.

For a couple of hours they struggled to continue on this track, bordered by peat hags and water dark and viscous as oil. When one man who was walking beside Gray and Grant asked a guard where they were being sent, the German replied only that he "thanked his God" he would not have to join them there.

Finally they came to the end of their eight-mile march. Located on a four-and-a-half-acre patch of dirt in the middle of the swamp, Schwarmstedt camp was nothing but four long wooden barracks with tarred felt roofs, a scattering of single-room huts, and an oblong ring of barbwire. Guard towers stocked with machine guns loomed over the starkly empty grounds, which were crisscrossed with open ditches that drained the constant seeping of swamp water. The exhausted prisoners cursed their bad fortune as they dragged themselves inside. Then the gate closed behind, and they were silent with worry.

Six

May 25, 1917. Jim Bennett scanned the rolling gray seas for any sign of an enemy U-boat breaking to the surface. Twenty-five years old and an observer in the Royal Naval Air Service, he was perched in a Sunbeam seaplane flying alongside the Belgian coastline. They were near Zeebrugge, the German-controlled port, and almost finished with their patrol, when Bennett spotted a conning tower break through the waves. His pilot swooped down for a closer look, but the U-boat submerged again. Bennett believed it was headed toward the English Channel to lay mines, and on his return to the Dunkirk sea base informed his commanding officer about it.

At midday, their plane loaded with bombs, another crew left to hunt the U-boat. It returned without having made a sighting. Bennett convinced his commanding officer to let him go up again, even though he was beyond his scheduled hours in the air for the day. He wrangled Lieutenant Colin Laurence for the mission, and off they went in another Sunbeam to scour the sea.

Bennett had every reason to be charged to action. Three months before, the Germans had returned to an unrestricted campaign of sinking merchant fleets supplying the Allies. Each month, U-boats were sending almost six hundred thousand tons of precious resources for the war to the bottom of the sea. On land, the French had suffered a string of defeats on the Western Front that now embroiled their armies in near mutiny, and uprisings in Russia had seen Czar Nicholas II toppled from his throne, leaving a power vacuum that threatened the country's will to continue the fight against Germany.

The only bright spot for the Allies was the recent declaration of war by the United States. The German U-boat campaign had sunk one too many of its merchant ships for President Wilson to bear. However, it would take some time before American forces were mustered. Britain was heading into the most perilous moments of the war, and its forces needed to redouble their efforts until help arrived.

Leonard James Bennett was a doer. His family had toiled the land in Somerset for hundreds of years. His father, William, had done so too until he'd been crippled after falling from his horse. William's wife, Harriet, tended to her husband while also raising Jim and his four siblings and continuing to run the farm. Jim took after her. In 1904 the Bennetts moved to north London, following the many others who were leaving their farms because of mechanization. Jim left school at fourteen and took a job with a carpet installer, pushing a wheelbarrow through the city streets. Other such jobs followed, then work as a draper. For fun, he ran races and proved a fast miler.

After his twenty-first birthday, he signed up for the Royal Naval Reserve to earn a few more pounds. At five feet ten inches tall, with dark hair, a round face, and an easy smile, he looked like any one of the hundreds of young men from modest means who joined. A little over a year later, Germany invaded Belgium. Since there were not enough ships for men, some of those in the naval reserves became part of infantry battalions. Bennett fought in the defense of Antwerp in September 1914 and earned the Mons Star. He was one of the fortunate ones to survive the devastating battle.

By spring the following year, he was aboard the HMS *Riviera* as an able seaman. During his next posting, on a seaplane carrier, he served as a gunner and radio operator. One day, he stopped a plane from sinking off the side of the carrier and rescued its pilot. Afterward, Bennett asked the captain to recommend him for a commission in the RNAS. The captain agreed straightaway. When Bennett arrived at the service's training head-quarters at Crystal Palace in south London, he alone wore the uniform of an enlisted sailor. The other recruits, most of whom were from private schools, wore suits. After months of training to become an observer, Tem-porary Sublieutenant James Bennett left for Dunkirk to hunt U-boats. He proved very good at his job.

The Sunbeam raced over the sea, roughly fifteen miles off Zeebrugge. Bennett was thinking they might well return empty-handed when he fi-nally saw a submarine. "There it is!" he shouted. Laurence pushed his stick forward. Before Bennett could prepare a bomb, there was an alarm-ing grinding of metal, and the Sunbeam's engine seized up. A second later, the propeller shaft ripped loose. Helpless but to land, Laurence put the plane down on the water. Bennett quickly tossed his lead-covered wire-less-signaling book overboard, and he and Laurence emptied their pock-ets of any papers. Bennett dispatched a hastily written note by carrier pi-geon to inform Dunkirk that they had gone down — and to give them the submarine's location.

They drifted toward Ostend for about an hour, Bennett ready at his Lewis machine gun the entire time. He had three trays of ammunition — they could put up some kind of fight if the submarine approached. Then, without warning, the nose of the U-boat rose out of the water, right be-tween the plane's floats. They were trapped. For a moment, Bennett con-sidered dropping his Hales bomb onto the vessel, but he quickly decided against suicide. Armed crew emerged from the U-boat and led Laurence, then Bennett, down into the submarine, separating them into different quarters.

As the U-boat dove below, several explosions sounded overhead. An-other patrol must have spotted them. Speaking English, the submarine captain interrogated Bennett for information on British minefields in the Channel, but Bennett denied knowing anything about those. "Then we might all be blown up together," the captain warned.

"That suits me fine," Bennett said, unwilling to talk.

For the next nineteen hours, Bennett and Laurence remained in the submarine as it laid its own mines. Finally, they docked at Zeebrugge, and the men were transferred to a civil prison in Bruges. Bennett was questioned by a German intelligence officer who, in return for his cooperation, promised to send him to "a lovely seaside camp on the Baltic" to bathe, play tennis, and "generally have a wonderful time." All he had to do was share what he knew about the British fleet and a potential attack on the Belgian coast. Bennett divulged nothing.

Over the next week, these interrogations continued. He and Laurence were given very little food or exercise, and only a cache of chocolate provided any comfort. On May 30, the day his mother received notice from the Admiralty telling her of her son's capture, Bennett wrote her his first letter from captivity. It began, "As you see, I am a prisoner of War but you do not want to worry about me as I am quite all right . . . I must say that we are being treated very well here." He asked after her vegetable garden, sent his best to the family, and concluded, "I am your loving son."

From Bruges, Bennett and Laurence were sent by train to Germany. They were weak from hunger, idleness, and long hours of interrogation. The train stopped at a POW camp for enlisted ranks, and the next morning they were put into the fields to work with them. The two airmen learned that the Dutch border was only thirty miles away; it would have been an easy run into the woods, but such was their depleted physical condition that neither Bennett nor Laurence even contemplated such a move.

The next day, the two were put on a train, this time with little guard. The cars rattled down the track so slowly that had they excused themselves to go to the toilet, they could have jimmied open a window and jumped out without injury. Again, neither considered such a possibility. Only after Bennett found himself behind two rectangular sets of high, barbwire fences at the Ströhen prison camp, set in the middle of an empty moor, did he realize that his two best opportunities of escape had passed.

The doer in Bennett refused to sit in the dark, dilapidated hut where he was housed and wallow in regret. Straightaway, he started to prepare for escape, first by getting back into shape. His fellow officers, most of whom had been transferred from Crefeld, found his propensity to walk around the prison for hours on end somewhat odd. But the distance to the Dutch border amounted to three marathons, and with Ströhen quickly descending into a nightmare of abuse, Bennett would have to make his move soon.

Ströhen, Schwarmstedt, Clausthal, and several other camps under the remit of the 10th Army Corp Division were all now in the hands of General Karl von Hänisch, an ogre of a Prussian officer, as the prisoners would soon learn.

On Friday morning, June 8, 1917, David Gray awoke at Schwarmstedt. He shared the small matchboard-walled compartment with twelve other officers, their beds stacked like berths on a steamer ship. Through slits in the uneven, warped roof, they could see clear blue sky. These same slits allowed entry to a host of fleas, flies, and mosquitoes from the surrounding swamp, which mounted a nightly assault on the prisoners. Open latrines situated eight feet from the barracks also allowed the insects to flourish. The stench stung the eyes and nose.

Two weeks before, the prisoners had been welcomed to the camp by its commandant, Colonel Dietz. Close to seventy, Dietz was tall and dressed in a resplendently medaled uniform that barely buttoned over his overfed waist. "Gentlemen," he began in a courteous voice, "I'm sorry not to be able to welcome you to a better camp. I do not think it a fit camp to put officers, and I think the best thing would be for you to write home and see if you can't get both yourself, and myself, out of it."

He continued, with no apparent order to his thoughts: The rooms would be crowded, so they could be with their friends; he "knew all that was to be known about the English" because of a visit to Scotland; the water at the camp was not fit to drink. He then offered to sell the prisoners local maps so they could know exactly where they were. "You see," he said, "it would be quite useless for you to try to escape because the whole of this heath is surrounded by impassable bogs." Gray and the others did not know whether the jumbled speech was a calculated threat or simply the ravings of a mad old soldier.

The next day, two prisoners tested out his theory about the heath. They cut through the wire fence and ran off. Soon after, half a dozen others followed suit. Still weakened from his stint in solitary confinement and the journey from Crefeld, Gray did not make an attempt. Few made it out of the bogs; none made it to freedom. Soon enough, every prisoner at Schwarmstedt understood two things: they had been sent to "Swamp Camp" by the German command to suffer, and Dietz was its willing accomplice.

That Friday morning, General Hänisch, the fifty-six-year-old officer who had ordered them sent there, was to pay a visit. After a hurried wash at the two water pumps, the prisoners assembled for morning roll call, and Dietz presented the general. On looks alone, there was little to distinguish Hänisch from any other Prussian career officer in the Imperial German Army: cropped hair, humorless expression, all iron in the frame.

The prisoners knew, according to rumors that preceded his visit, that Hänisch had led divisions at the Battles of Arras and the Somme. At both, the British overran his lines to embarrassing effect, and as a result he had been removed from active command. In the early spring of 1917 he was sent back to Germany to run the 10th Army Division. The Poldhu also spread the information that Hänisch's son had been killed by the British, and from the moment he swaggered in to address the Schwarmstedt prisoners, it was clear he felt nothing but hatred toward them.

After a short speech in which he shared his recommendation that the prisoners be moved just behind German lines in order to be shelled by their own troops, Hänisch carried out an inspection of the camp. In one room, he found a British flag beside a bunk. He ripped it away, shouting, "There is only one flag in Germany." In another he discovered an unopened tin and chastised a guard, ordering him to inspect it immediately. When the senior British officer recommended that the food be improved and lights allowed in the barracks at night, Hänisch went on a tirade. If the prisoners wanted better conditions, they should send a letter to their prime minister to plead the end of the blockade of Germany. With that, he left the camp, in a storm of rage.

The next day, guards raided the barracks and confiscated any contraband — including area maps that had been bought by the prisoners. Gray managed to keep his hidden. Fearing that the visit from Hänisch would lead to an increase in patrols or camp defenses, he determined to make an escape attempt as soon as possible with two fellow officers.

Their plan was to open the gate by the parcel room. Gray would be disguised as a German private, his two accomplices as orderlies, the three of them setting off to collect wood. Schwarmstedt had a roster of men willing to help them out. One had stolen the gate key from a guard and created a mold of it. A key was then made out of melted-down *Lagergeld* coins. Another officer helped fashion their uniforms.

For the run to the border, another prisoner provided a makeshift compass through a particularly ingenious solution. He engineered the flywheel on a wristwatch to rotate freely on its mount. Then, by running a current from a disassembled light fixture through a sewing needle, he created a magnetized compass pointer. This was fixed onto the flywheel, and the watch face and hands were replaced. It looked like a normal timepiece.

While Gray readied their breakout, there were other attempts in the offing, including another Pink Toes tunnel, this one through soft peaty ground. Mossy, who had been caught in his tunnel hideout before the transfer from Crefeld, was leading the effort. Gray thought his plan had a better chance of success.

With clothes prepared, and an assembled kit of food, he and his two partners set off. They got outside the camp easily, but as they crossed toward the cart track, Dietz and his lieutenant emerged from their nearby quarters. Gray kept his cool, giving Dietz a firm salute, and the three continued on without incident.

They did not make it far. At evening roll call, they were missed, and

Dietz sent out a hunting party that captured them in the bog. A few days later, at sunset, a fire broke out on the heath. Its heat and gray plumes colored the sky in wondrous layers of pink and orange. Gray saw none of it. Confined to a thin-walled solitary cell, baking under its tarred roof, he could only choke on the thick smoke.

Seventy-five miles south, in Clausthal, Blain and Kennard endured their punishment for the revenge attack on Allouche. For almost two months, the two men were in solitary confinement, inhabiting ten-by-six-foot cells between a pigsty and a mechanic's shed on the northern end of the camp. The maddening squeals of the pigs bothered them more than the tight confines and the absence of windows. At the end of May, at long last, they were allowed out. They had not bathed or exercised in weeks. They had to shield their eyes from the piercing sun coming over the Harz Mountains, and the short walk to their rooms in the former Peacock Hotel was a trial.

Commandant Wolfe, or Pig Face — so called by the men for his bald round head, puffy face, and tiny, closely spaced eyes — had stripped Clausthal of everything that had once made it a tourist resort. Six officers crowded into each guest room, and the overflow was housed in wooden barracks. Mattresses were replaced with wooden planks and straw paillasses. Guards roused any prisoner sleeping past 7:00 a.m. and limited the 260 imprisoned officers to four shower heads whose pressure was little more than a trickle — they had a better chance of washing themselves by squeezing a damp rag over their heads. Flies infested the latrines, meals were rushed, roll calls were deliberately drawn out, and searches were frequent. Sentries and guard dogs patrolled the fence, and all parcels, including those from the Red Cross, were hacked apart to test for contraband. Hänisch instructed his staff, "Cut up their soap in pieces, cut up their bread in slices, and remember you are a German."

The prisoners made the best of the limited grounds available to them. They laid tennis courts and imported a net at their own expense. They built a six-hole golf course, staged boxing matches, and organized a theater troupe, bridge tournament, gambling den, and language instruction. When allowed out on parole, on the promise not to escape, they hiked through the pine-forested hillsides under a limited guard.

Compared to their solitary cells, the camp was a paradise to Blain and Kennard. As is the case in most such institutions, the prisoners tended to congregate with those of like mind. Some groups were content to do nothing but entertain themselves. Others passed their days reading and studying. Others were do-nothings. Blain and Kennard were a different breed — they fell into the small but distinct class of Clausthal men that one veteran labeled "escape fiends." They were indefatigable.

It began with tunnels. Kennard was invited to join a breakout effort underneath one of the wooden barracks; then he brought Blain into the fold. It was tough going. The sap needed to be only ten yards in length to reach beyond the fence, but the earth was a mix of granite and shale, and it took hours of digging to proceed just a few inches. The work also caused quite a din. During the noisiest stretches, the tunnelers tried to distract the guards by holding boisterous tennis matches.

Their effort would have continued, but Commandant Wolfe discovered a separate tunnel scheme in progress, initiating under the stage the prisoners had built for their makeshift theater. Any further digging would have been a fool's errand.

One of the other escape fiends, William Colquhoun, decided on a new course: directly through the wire. The Canadian lieutenant, twenty-eight years old and six foot six inches tall, had proved his mettle on the front, leading a platoon to take out German snipers and sapper teams. In early 1915 he earned the Military Cross while retrieving from the front line, under intense fire, a mortally wounded officer.

A month later, during a scouting mission in no-man's-land, he was knocked senseless — and half-buried in dirt — by an explosion. His platoon mates thought him dead. When his German captor brought him into the trenches, he looked Colquhoun up and down and asked, "Are all Canadians as tall as you?" To which Colquhoun responded, "Well, they call me Shorty."

One day, in broad daylight, Colquhoun cut a hole in the fence around Clausthal, stepped through it, and ran. Such was the brazenness of the attempt that the guards were oblivious to his flight. Some children playing in pine woods outside the camp spotted him on the run, but none of the guards believed their tale. By the time Wolfe determined that Colquhoun was gone, the Canadian was far away. A week into his 212-mile flight to the border, he was captured by a German soldier searching for an escaped Russian prisoner. Hours after being sent to the nearest internment camp, Colquhoun busted through a skylight in his cell. He was caught again three days later by some trackers with dogs. Undeterred, he used his long arms to grab the keys to his cell door through the spy aperture used by the guards. Starving and exhausted, he stole a bicycle and pedaled to the north. The bike broke, and while trying to fix it he was detained yet again. This time he was returned to Clausthal.

A squadron mate of Blain's, John Tullis, hatched a plot of his own. One afternoon, he dug a shallow ditch by the fence between the two tennis courts, ostensibly as part of his grounds-repair duties. Then, when the guards were distracted, he lay down in the ditch, flat on his chest and holding some wire clippers, and had a friend cover him with eight inches of dirt. He kept his left arm positioned near his head so he could read his luminous wristwatch. By breathing through a pipe shaped like a snorkel, camouflaged at the top with a tuft of grass, Tullis planned to remain there until nightfall. An accomplice would answer his name at roll call. Once it was dark, Tullis would climb out of the trench, then cut his way through the fence to freedom.

After the bugle of evening roll call, the yard cleared. In the silence, buried in dirt, Tullis wanted nothing more than to wriggle free or, at the very least, roll onto his side, but he knew he had to remain motionless. The time passed slowly. Finally, a check of his watch showed it soon would be dark. Only a few minutes longer now. Just as he was about to begin his escape, he heard a muffled chuckle coming from above him, then felt the dirt being scooped away from around his head. A guard, triumphant in his discovery, was looming over him. He had either spotted the tube, or some slight involuntary shift from Tullis had alerted him to his hiding place.

Blain and Kennard were just as bent on escape. Always on the lookout for opportunity, they had detected a vulnerability in Clausthal's defenses. There were a number of gates leading into the camp, which the Germans, confident that nobody could pick their locks, did not post sentries beside. Blain and Kennard managed to briefly obtain a set of keys from an unsuspecting guard, and an impression was made in a bar of soap. Using the mold, they then cut their own set of keys out of a sardine can. While Blain hid in a nearby shed, Kennard had a go at one of the gate locks.

But to no end. No matter his frustrated attempts, the keys didn't fit, and the two men were almost caught in the act. Following this failed effort, they tried to impersonate a pair of camp workmen and simply walk through the gate. They dyed black some clothes received from their families, to resemble the outfits worn by the workers. They also forged papers, using a typewriter for the text and an "official" stamp made with the lid of a small tin, a two-mark silver piece, and the ink from a toy printing set sold in the canteen, of all places. They had only made it a few steps past the gate when the guards got wise to their scheme and hauled them back inside. Wolfe confiscated their escape kit and sentenced them to solitary once more.

The punishment wielded at Clausthal for prisoners attempting escape was a far cry from the medieval practice of hacking off the feet of escapees or, during the American Civil War, branding with a *T* the foreheads of those caught tunneling out of captivity. The Hague Conventions offered sparse protection for escapees, since punishments were considered "subject to the military law of the host nation." The German "War Book," the handbook of the Imperial German General Staff, stated that prisoners could be sentenced to death for so much as plotting an escape, but allowed the commanding officer to decide if a "restriction of privileges" and "sharper supervision" was adequate punishment. Rumor had it that Hänisch had recently instituted a sentence of five months' solitary confinement for any officer trying to escape. Such lengths in isolation could break a man. Whatever the truth, Wolfe did seem to have some discretion on how to respond to escape attempts. Tullis received forty days; Kennard and Blain, fourteen. As well as these individual punishments, Wolfe made life at Clausthal collectively harder for its prisoners. Parole walks were stopped, and room searches became ransacks.

The commandant was aided by a host of willing lieutenants. Shooting Sam — as the prisoners called him — liked to pop off rifle shots to warn any inmate standing too near the fence. Whistling Rufus, a cross-eyed detective from Berlin, searched the camp for contraband with a dog he summoned with a piercing shriek. Then there was Windy Dick — Heinrich Niemeyer, by his Christian name — a boorish, bullet-headed figure with a square jaw who claimed he had learned to speak English while working for a time in America. He threw tantrums over the men's failure to properly salute him or for any infraction of the rules — and he constantly suspected the prisoners of plotting escapes, for which he threatened the severest of punishments. "Because I say, you know. That is enough for you," he would warn in one of his bedeviling English idioms.

Some of the prisoners believed the escape fiends were the source of all their troubles at the camp and began to frown on any breakout attempt. General Hurdis Ravenshaw, the senior British officer at Clausthal, warned his charges that he would have any potential escapee "court-martialed on his return to England." The War Office was as ambiguous about escape as the Germans were about punishment for same. According to its 1907 military manual, a British soldier faced court-martial if he failed "to rejoin His Majesty's service when able to rejoin the same." In law, the phrase "when able" was subject to interpretation.

Blain felt no duty to abide by Ravenshaw's dictate, nor did he feel compelled to escape because of what some military lawyers in London had written before the war. He simply wanted to be free and far away from his captors, whom he despised to his very core. Kennard felt the same.

Wolfe made sure the two inveterate breakout artists would not be teaming up together again. To their chagrin, the commandant removed Kennard to a different camp, breaking their partnership.

Undaunted, Blain partnered with Captain Edward Leggatt, whom he had known since Osnabrück. An RFC pilot, Leggatt had won acclaim shooting down two German Albatros planes on one of his first missions in France. He and Blain managed to break into an attic storeroom in the former hotel, where they discovered a bounty that included two bottles of 1811 brandy, crates of sausages, bacon, and chocolate, and an arsenal of rifles, revolvers, and ammunition. The weapons they left alone; the brandy they drank; the food they kept for their hike to the border; and the storeroom they used to forge new documents and prepare a new plan of escape.

PART II

All Roads Lead to Hellminden

Seven

Swamp Camp was no place to dig a tunnel. Underneath Schwarm-stedt's top layer of black sand, the ground was crumbly peat. Any effort to dig sufficiently deep left one kneeling in a small pool of water. To the amazement of Will Harvey, the Pink Toes made the attempt, starting their sap under the floorboards of a utility shed. The peat gave way easily to digging. Within a couple of weeks the tunnel stretched beyond the fence, but never at a depth of more than a few feet underground. It was so shallow that anyone digging in the tunnel could feel the footsteps of the men walking above.

Before dawn on June 27, they cleared away the last yard of dirt. The tunnel opened out into the main ditch that drained water from the camp. Mossy led the way out that same morning, followed by Captain William Morritt of the East Surrey Regiment. Four others were crawling down the tunnel when the first shot cracked out. Forewarned somehow about the escape, guards fired on Morritt at close range from the bridge, only five yards away. He tumbled into the ditch, a bullet through his lung.

As Mossy sprinted off, two more rifle shots sounded. He fell, too, hit badly in the arm. Guards seized him as the other Pink Toes crept backward in their tunnel before they were caught. Morritt died soon after, drowned in his own blood. Harvey called the twenty-four-year-old infantry officer "one of the bravest and gentlest souls I ever knew."

Two days later, Harvey and eighty other officers marched behind a cart carrying Morritt's coffin to a small church in a neighboring village. The Germans permitted a military burial, with a firing party and a bugler trumpeting out "The Last Post," but there was no British flag to drape over the coffin. Every officer present considered Morritt's death a murder, but there was little they could do about it. Their helplessness stung.

Mossy was sent to a hospital for treatment, then on to another camp. Life at Schwarmstedt continued on as if the shootings had never occurred: the dreaded routine of roll calls, meals cooked in sandpits, and interminable conversations centering on how long the war would last. The summer heat was relentless, and the men spent their days in shorts, singlets, and bare feet. Many shaved their heads in an attempt to stay cool and clean. There was never enough soap for washing, and their water supply was filthy brown and polluted by leakage from the open latrines. They had to pay for drinking water, which was the same filthy water, only filtered. At night, fleas and mosquitoes attacked them with abandon under the glare of arc lamps.

On July 9, Dr. Rudolf Römer visited the camp. Römer was the Dutch attaché assigned to inspect German camps for compliance with the Hague Conventions. Despite noting the need for netting on windows, better water, fresh vegetables, and clean latrines, he reported back to British officials that "there has never been a case of ill-treatment by the Germans . . . The officers looked healthy and were in good spirits." About Morritt's shooting, only the briefest mention was made.

After Römer left, the prisoners learned through the Poldhu that Germany and Britain had met in The Hague to review POW and civilian internment conditions. From what they could make out, officers from both countries who had been held for more than eighteen months would soon be sent to neutral Holland and Switzerland, where they would remain until the end of the war. In addition, the warring parties agreed that punishment for escape would be limited to a two-week maximum sentence in solitary — except in extreme cases. The timeline and numbers approved for transfer kept shifting, and Gray and the other officers in solitary confinement remained in their cells. The inmates who brought them meals made note of their poor condition.

Although physically fine, Harvey had fallen deeper into a desperate mental state that prisoners of the time referred to as barbwire disease. "The wearisome sameness of the days, the monotony of the faces, the unchanged landscape, the intolerable talk about the war, all these tended to produce the effect of complete and utter depression," one prisoner wrote. "This was far and away our worst enemy: whole days were drenched in incurable melancholia." Harvey likened the effect of barbwire disease to a green mold that grew thick on his mind, leaving him stale and incapable of joy. His poem "Prisoners" gave voice to this state:

> Laugh, O laugh loud! All yet who long ago
> Adventure sought in gallant company
> Safe in stagnation, laugh! Laugh heartily!
> While on this filthiest backwater of Time's flow
> Drift we and rot till something set us free.
> Laugh like old men with senses atrophied,
> Heeding no Present, to the Future dead,
> Nodding quite foolish by the warm fireside,
> And seeing no flame, but only I the red
> And flickering embers pictures of the Past—
> Life like a cinder fading black at last.

Determined to be rid of the feeling, Harvey was finally spurred to escape. He copied a map onto some paper from a biscuit tin, acquired a homemade compass, and sewed a knapsack to hold food. His idea, hatched on a visit to the parcel room outside the wire one day, was simple. He would sneak into the second floor of the building, hide out until after dark, then leap from its lone window onto an adjacent telegraph pole. A quick slide down to the ground and he would be off. He was almost ready to go when a friend alerted him to the fact that the guards had recently wrapped the base of the pole with barbwire. Looking for another opportunity to escape but growing moldier by the day, the Poet found himself struggling to write anything other than letters home. In these, he lamented his loss of ability to craft the work that gave meaning to his life.

There was a new commandant at Ströhen, Captain Karl Niemeyer. He was the twin brother of Heinrich "Windy Dick," stationed at Clausthal, and of similar bent. Karl Niemeyer intended to show the roughly four hundred prisoners in his charge that order and obedience would be paramount under his watch. In his previous role as camp adjutant, he'd been loathed by his charges, Kennard and Bennett among them. His elevation to commandant only deepened the men's contempt for him.

Tall and stout, Niemeyer was built like an upright rectangle. Except for his muttonchops and bushy eyebrows, his bowling ball of a head was pasty-white and cleanly shaved. Typically he wore a military cap perched at a rakish angle. A bully of the first order, he had a rash temper and a thin skin. He often skulked bowlegged about the camp in his starched uniform and high cavalry boots, chomping on a cigar while looking for trouble like a dog would a bone. No slight from a prisoner — a weak salute, a roll of the eyes, an impertinent remark — went unnoticed or unpunished.

Such was his character that there were few pejoratives not cast his way by the prisoners in their diaries and other accounts. He was a "cad," "a low-bred ruffian," "the personification of hate," "a bloated, pompous, crawling individual," "a man of unbridled ferocity and bravado," "a cheat," "a plausible rogue," and "a coward with all the attributes of one: he deceives, he is cruel, he blusters, he is dishonest, he cringes." Prone to apoplectic fits of rage, typically while brandishing a large revolver or his knobbed walking cane, Niemeyer scolded and threatened prisoners with a zeal that left him red-faced and panting for breath.

The root of his grievances was unclear, and given his propensity to tell lies, his background was in question. Although born in Germany, he and his twin brother spent seventeen years living in the United States. He might have tended bar in Milwaukee. He might have built billiard tables in New York. He might have done both. His stories changed as often as he told them. He had learned enough English to slaughter the language wholesale.

After President Wilson declared war — or before, if one cared about logical timelines — Niemeyer fled across the Atlantic. Such was his perilous escape that he was awarded the Iron Cross, though there was no proof of this, nor of his claim that he had worked undercover in England as a spy for the kaiser. Despite being in his sixties, he had also fought at the Somme — for one week, he said, which "had been enough for him." There was no doubt, however, that the Niemeyer twins were exactly what Hänisch was looking for, and he elevated them both to key positions in his network of prison camps. They followed his instructions assiduously when it came to the treatment of POWs.

On his first day in command, August 4, 1917, Niemeyer proved how capable he was of malevolence. Newcomers were frequent at Ströhen, and the prisoners typically congregated by the fences to watch them arrive and welcome them. These arrivals were boisterous affairs, complete with shouting and festive reunions. Niemeyer declared that such gatherings would no longer take place, effective immediately. In the early evening, guards brought fifteen British officers to the eastern gate, and they were made to enter one at a time. Ignoring Niemeyer's order, a group of prisoners approached the fence to cheer those arriving and warn them to expect an intensive search.

The new commandant watched the scene unfold through his office window, as the number of men forming a semicircle by the gate continued to increase. He stamped from his office to the nearest sentry box, waving his cap at his guards and screaming for them to "make use of their arms" to drive the men away. Bayonets fixed, four guards moved toward the prisoners. "Los! Los!" Niemeyer yelled for them to charge.

The prisoners began to back away from the fence, but not quickly enough for the guards. Lieutenant Downes, a former medical student who had come out of his hut to see what the commotion was about, received a bayonet in his back for his curiosity. In shock, he turned toward the guard, who then plunged the blade into his side, narrowly missing his kidney. Two other prisoners were also stabbed, one of them deflecting with his arm what might have been a mortal blow. As Downes staggered and fell to the ground, blood pouring through his singlet, mayhem was unleashed in the camp. More guards moved forward, and those stationed in the sentry boxes readied their machine guns. With roughly a hundred guards and four hundred prisoners, there would likely have been a massacre were it not for the coolheaded thinking of one British officer, who began singing "God Save the King" at the top of his voice. Other prisoners added their voices to his, and soon the whole camp was standing to attention and belting out the song. The guards backed off.

When the yard quieted down, the prisoners carried Downes and the other two wounded officers to the camp hospital. They survived, even though they were without medical attention for almost three hours. When the senior British officer went to see Niemeyer about the attack, the commandant had already departed for the day. Later, when asked to account for his order, he declared, "I had nothing to do with it all. I was not in the camp. I did not give the order." Such was the men's introduction to the leadership of Karl Niemeyer.

After Niemeyer became commandant, prisoners could not beat a quick enough path from Ströhen. Bennett was chief among those determined to escape. By his third month in captivity he was back in shape, involved in a tunneling scheme and collecting an escape kit from parcels sent by his mother. Beyond sentiments of "making the best of a bad job," his letters home always included a list of items he needed, ostensibly for his life as a POW but especially intended for a run to the border. These included "easy to pack" dried fruits, hard biscuits, a traveling rug, strong boots, warm clothes, and a canvas kit bag. Since arriving at Ströhen, Bennett had made his intention to escape clear to his fellow officers. After only a few weeks there, some veteran prisoners asked him and his New Zealander bunkmate Roy Fitzgerald if they would be interested in digging a tunnel with them. Started by some Russians who had since been moved to another camp, its entrance was underneath the barracks hut that Bennett, Fitzgerald, and twenty-six other recent arrivals now occupied.

It was a risky proposition. The moorland meant any sap would be a shallow affair, with walls that collapsed easily. Niemeyer knew well the allure of the border, only seventy miles away, and he pressed his guards to remain vigilant to any breakout attempt. He offered a twenty-mark reward and fourteen days' leave for thwarting any such escape, as well as the threat of transfer to the front should his subordinates fail to do so. The heightened alert did not dull the feverish digging efforts of Bennett and his fellow tunnelers, nor the handful of other schemes in the works.

Bennett carefully observed and learned from all their methods, most notably those of Lieutenant Gerald Knight. Knight had been part of the gang at Osnabrück that carried out the revenge attack on Captain Allouche. At Ströhen, he'd concocted a plan to build, and eventually hide behind, a false wall in an alcove in the bathhouse that stood outside the wire. To match the color of his cardboard wall to the real one, he made a paste of cornstarch mixed with dirt and cobwebs. His deception worked, and Knight made a successful lone run to Holland.

Bennett and his fellow tunnelers had no such luck. Only a week after the assault on Downes, a heavy rainstorm flooded the Ströhen moor. When a guard on patrol crossed over the sap, his boot sank right into it. Niemeyer ordered the tunnel dug up to determine its starting point. Some of the officers congregated to watch, yielding one of them a jab with a bayonet. The tunnel led to the floor underneath where Bennett and Fitzgerald bunked. Of the twenty-eight in the barracks, they were the only two involved in the scheme, but when they attempted to give themselves up to save the others from punishment, the senior officer in their barracks ordered them to remain silent.

Niemeyer threw the lot of them into solitary. Day after day, the Germans interrogated them, trying to trick them into revealing who had participated in the digging. The guards told them that several others had already confessed, and they only wanted to cross off the names on the list of those who were innocent. None of the British officers took the bait, and Niemeyer grew more incensed by the week.

After the discovery of the tunnel and a rash of other escape attempts, Niemeyer was forced to bring in reinforcements. Even though he was stewing away in a cell, Bennett found comfort in the knowledge that in order to assist Niemeyer, young, fit German soldiers were being drawn away from the fighting on the front lines.

David Gray had very little left to give. Pale and listless, he emerged from his isolation cell at Schwarmstedt into the bright summer day. A guard led him to one of the water pumps to bathe, and a crowd of prisoners gathered around him, his poor condition stirring them to emotion. "What is it like?" one called out. Gray barely managed to look up. He knew better than to speak while out for his twice-weekly bath, but wanted them to know. "Very bad," he uttered, almost broken. Then he returned to his cell.

The space measured only a few square feet. There was a single barred window, too high up to see anything but an angle of the sky. Since the window was never opened, the only fresh air he enjoyed came through the uneven slits in the roof. He spent most days and nights baking in the heat of the cell, whose tarred roofs and thin walls acted like a furnace. He sweated constantly, and his body was pocked with insect bites. The only respite from the heat was during the occasional thunderstorm, when rain leaked through those same breaks in the roof.

The guards permitted him no books, no pen and paper. One hour of exercise was allowed a day. Meals were the only other interruption, and these were pushed through a slot in the door. On occasion, a fellow prisoner bringing his soup or a donated tin of food would offer a kind word of encouragement. Then Gray would return to his solitary plight. Life in the regular camp was conveyed to him in the distant summons to roll call, the indistinct voice of a passing guard, or a muffled tramping of feet, perhaps signaling a breakout.

A good military man, Gray would have made the effort to remain in shape while in his cell. But as July staggered into August, he was a shadow of his former self. Even so, thoughts of escape burned inside him. He determined to make his next attempt his final one. Any successful escape, he understood from his failures, would need to be a four-stage event: intense preparation, a foolproof breakout, an evasion scheme, and a bid to cross the border. At any of these stages, the entire effort could fall apart. One was no less important than the other, and each demanded thorough planning, resolve, quick wits — and a measure of good luck.

Toward the end of August, Gray was led out into the yard, free from his confinement. Guards led him and several others who had languished in solitary on foot to Hademstorf, five miles away, then onto a train bound for Ströhen. He was there only a short while before Karl Niemeyer was replaced by another commandant.

Hänisch was forming a new camp in a town called Holzminden, intended to hold the most troublesome, escape-prone British officers in Germany. He needed an iron fist to oversee them.

Eight

C harles Rathborne looked out into the dark night of September 11, 1917, from a train headed northward from Heidelberg. Crowded into his carriage were two dozen other British officers. They passed town after town, but except for a brief stop in Kassel, the train never slowed, thwarting a plan by several prisoners to leap from a window. They were all destined for Holzminden, the first group to be sent to the new camp.

Although a student of German, Rathborne could be forgiven for never having heard of the town south of Hanover in Lower Saxony. Founded in 1245 at the edge of the river Weser by Count Otto von Eberstein, it had little of which to boast. Its medieval timber buildings had been leveled by fire during the Thirty Years' War, a seventeenth-century struggle that only World War I would top in terms of cataclysmic destruction across Europe.

In the centuries that followed, the town had been home to iron foundries, a monastery school, some craftsmen guilds, and, most recently, a fragrance company — specialists, by some accounts, in the manufacture of the scent of vanilla and violets. At the onset of war, Holzminden was little more than a garrison town of roughly ten thousand people. The inhabitants of the red-roofed village had the benefit of a picturesque location, set on a broad plain cut through by the silver-dappled Weser, surrounded by small farms, extensive beech and fir forests, and rolling hills.

Rathborne and the others saw none of this during their nighttime approach, but expectations about their future camp were high. According to the Poldhu, it was to be a "prisoner's Mecca — fine, brand-new buildings, spacious grounds, good scenery, good air." They had no way of knowing whether this was true, but the very possibility fostered much debate, both skeptical and hopeful. Rathborne did not have enough experience of the German archipelago of camps to know which side to agree with.

Just months earlier, on April 14, the thirty-one-year-old pilot and RNAS wing commander had led a fighter escort providing cover for a bombing raid on Freiburg. The attack on the city center was in retribution for a number of unanswered atrocities by the Germans, including the death by firing squad of Edith Cavell, a British nurse who helped scores of Allied prisoners escape from occupied Belgium; the treatment of POWs, notably the many who died of typhoid at camps such as Wittenberg; and the recent torpedoing of a hospital ship. After the bombers dropped their eggs, Rathborne turned to escort the squadron home. Suddenly, a pack of German Albatros fighter planes struck. In the flurry of gunfire, Rathborne's engine was hit and his observer killed. Forced to land behind enemy lines, he was quickly seized. He was a great prize for the Germans — a lieutenant colonel and the Freiburg killer. They paraded him through the streets and pasted his photograph in the national papers.

Broad-shouldered, thickset, and of medium height, Charles Rathborne had soft features and a welcome smile. One likened his visage to "the face of an archbishop," a description that belied his natural grit and ambition. Private-school-educated and fluent in German and Italian, Rathborne joined the Royal Marine Light Infantry on his eighteenth birthday. He quickly rose through the ranks, his superiors remarking that he was "keen," "energetic," and "very good in taking charge of men." Frequently applied to him was the word "zealous." In 1912, sensing that air flight was the future, he trained to become a pilot. At the outbreak of war, he was named a flight commander, then a squadron commander, then placed in charge of an operational wing. The mission that saw him shot down was likely one he could have ordered subordinates to perform.

As a POW, Rathborne proved no less ambitious. In May he arrived at a camp in Karlsruhe, where he assumed the role of senior British officer. He fielded pleas from his fellow officers for better conditions and persuaded the commandant to provide them. Escape was a high priority, but his first effort, in which he planned to walk straight out of the gate in civilian clothes, was foiled by a spy who gave away the hiding place of his escape kit. Before he could concoct a new plan, the order came for transfer to the new camp at Holzminden.

It was after midnight when the train finally stuttered to a halt, and Rathborne and the others disembarked. In the twenty-one hours it had taken to travel from Karlsruhe they had been given nothing to eat and had slept only a few halting minutes in the overpacked carriage. They dragged themselves and their few belongings a mile east to the edge of the town.

At last, they arrived at the Holzminden officers' camp. The former infantry barracks, built a year before the war, was ringed by tall stone walls and lit by electric arc lamps. Guards directed them through the arched main entrance on the camp's western side. Directly to their right, they passed a small house that served as a guard room and then entered the main prison grounds through a gate in a barbwire fence. To their left stood a monolithic stone barracks they would come to know as Block A. A seventy-yard gap separated it from its twin, Block B.

Although exhausted and desperate for food, they were made to assemble in rows on the cobblestone path in front of the barracks. Beneath the glare of arc lamps, they were forced to wait in the chill of the night. Finally, a tall, beetle-browed German officer smoking a cigar strode to the head of the assembly to address them: Captain Karl Niemeyer. None of the prisoners had heard of the camp officer, a position second only to the commandant, and they were surprised when he addressed them in a cheerful, albeit off-kilter, American accent.

He opened by saying, that he was happy to see them, as he was always "glad to see any Englishman," many of whom had been his "great friends" before the war. He hoped this would be the case again, but, "in the meanwhile, war was war." He advised that they would be best served, "y'know," to write straight away to their families and friends "for your thickest clothes, y'know. It is very cold here in winter, y'know." He concluded, "So now, gentlemen, I expect you will be glad to go to your bedrooms. I will wish you good-night. You will be searched in the morning."

With that, the guards took them to the third floor of Block A, a four-story whitewashed building with a mansard roof covered in slate. As Rathborne and the others climbed the steps, they wondered if Holzminden might well live up to what the Poldhu had promised. Some imagined "bedroom candles and a comforting nightcap" awaiting them in the barracks. They were divided into three rooms with high ceilings and bare walls. Each room had a stove, but no coal or wood to fuel it. For furniture, each officer had a small cupboard, a stool, and an iron-framed bed whose mattress was filled with straw, wood shavings, and paper. Although they were desperately hungry, the guards offered them no food, and the doors clanged ominously shut when they left. Still, the prisoners continued to hope for the best.

In the morning, Rathborne succeeded in keeping hidden the compass he had bribed from a guard at Karlsruhe. He got a good look at Holzminden from the windows, then later, before roll call, on a walk around the grounds. The prison was a series of secure enclosures, one smaller than the next, like a Russian nesting doll. On the outside was the rectangular stone wall, eight feet high, topped in places with a barbwire palisade angled inward at 120 degrees to prevent climbing. Within this was a half oval — in the shape of the letter D — protected by a twelve-foot-high fence of thick mesh topped by another barbwire palisade. A chain of sentry boxes was positioned directly outside this fence. Six feet separated this enclosure from another barrier, which was the same shape and made from a simple three-strand wire fence strung on low wood posts. The space in between these two fences was a no-man's-land. Prisoners were allowed only within the inner enclosure, which contained the barracks and Spielplatz (a dual parade ground and exercise yard). In a sense, Holzminden was a prison within a prison within a prison, all set 150 miles from the Dutch border.

Beyond the security, and the buildings themselves, Holzminden was ill prepared to accommodate the hundreds of POWs sent there and the guards who oversaw them. The cookhouse lacked any dishes, and there were only three cauldrons. There was but a handful of taps, and no showers. Nor was there a parcel room or a canteen from which to buy goods. In the light of day, it became clear to the men that Holzminden was no prisoner's Mecca.

At morning roll call, the twenty-five officers gathered on the Spielplatz. Having not eaten in almost thirty-six hours, they were nearly faint. Beside Niemeyer stood the titular head of the camp, the elderly Colonel Habrecht, who stood by passively as his camp officer addressed the new arrivals. Niemeyer asked if they had breakfasted. The men answered no. Niemeyer promptly ordered his guards to prepare a meal, the likes of which, he promised, "you wouldn't get in Regent Street or Piccadilly." The famished British officers salivated at the thought of bacon and grilled sausage. Once dismissed, they hurried into the dining hall on the second floor of Block A, only to be served some tepid acorn coffee. Nothing else.

When Rathborne, senior among them, complained, Niemeyer feigned surprise over the men's purported dissatisfaction. Rathborne continued to press him on the men's treatment, reminding him that they were British officers.

"You damn well do as I tell you," the camp officer finally said, shutting down further discussion. "If you think you can get out, try." Then he and Colonel Habrecht marched off. They had other prisoners to welcome. As day after day passed, the officers were allotted little more than cabbage soup and small portions of bread to eat. Malnourished and harassed at every turn, they quickly grew to despise Karl Niemeyer.

On September 20 a storm swept across Schwarmstedt, with sand invading every crevice of the camp's huts. The prisoners hunkered down, covering their mouths and noses with wet cloths to help them breathe amid the onslaught. After the storm passed, the men were just beginning to clean up their quarters when the commandant assembled them for an announcement. Following a series of complaints to the British government about conditions at the camp, the men learned, Schwarmstedt was to be emptied.

Prior to the transfer, a search for contraband ensued. As the guards began opening trunks and pawing through their belongings, Will Harvey grew nervous. After being informed about the camp closing, he had procured a civilian suit in which he might cross the German countryside without arousing suspicion. Civilian clothes were prohibited in the prison, and if the guards found the suit, there would be hell to pay. His plan to jump from the train on the way to the new camp and make his way to the border on foot would be foiled.

Moments before the guards arrived at his barracks, Harvey came up with a bold solution: he would don the civvies under his Burberry trench coat, hiding his compass and map in the pockets. Standing just a few feet away from the guard who was meticulously inspecting the contents of his box, Harvey stifled an anxious laugh. If only the guard knew, he thought, that his escape kit was hiding in plain sight. Finding nothing of interest in the box, the guard moved on to the next prisoner and resumed his search.

The following day, the weather clear and fine, Harvey and over two hundred other officers prepared to leave the camp. The commandant gave an incomprehensible speech, praising the prisoners as "men of honor." Then they headed out of the swamp, leaving Schwarmstedt.

Once in the woods, three prisoners made a dash for it. Guards fired after them, but the men got away. Closer to Hademsdorf station, another prisoner broke free. Bullets fired by the guards tore at tree stumps but missed their mark. But then the fugitive stumbled in a ditch, and the guards giving chase successfully tackled him.

Harvey bided his time. He figured the train offered the best chance of escaping undetected, while giving him the advantage of a head start. He had his route to freedom carefully planned, thanks to Captain Godfrey Phillimore, who had escaped Schwarmstedt only to be captured just shy of the border; after twelve nights on the run he was returned to the camp. He'd shared every detail with Harvey and the Pink Toes, from the route he had followed to advice on when to travel (after midnight to avoid chance encounters), the best cover growth (rye), and places to avoid (damp woods — and mosquitoes that "rob you of vitality"). Finally, he cautioned them to abandon all roads and circumvent all villages within thirty miles of the frontier.

Once he and the other men had boarded the train, Harvey stashed his knapsack, filled with some tins of meat and several slabs of Canadian hardtack for his journey to the border, in a lavatory in the corridor. Then he entered his carriage and took a seat. The guard in his compartment was positioned at the door with a rifle between his legs. The opposite door was locked.

Harvey planned on waiting until after dusk, excusing himself to go to the lavatory, exiting through the window, and jumping, preferably when the train was on a slow uphill course. His compartment mates, wise to his intentions, made several trips to the lavatory in the first few hours of the journey, returning to the compartment without event, lulling the guard into a sense of complacency. He was an old soldier, with rheumy blue eyes and a slumping posture, who occasionally nodded off, spit bubbles forming on his lips.

After a time, Harvey stood and made his way to the lavatory to inspect it. Once inside, he pulled down the window. Fresh air rushed through the open gap, but it was too narrow for him to crawl through. The corridor outside was lined with windows, but none of these opened wide enough either. He returned to his carriage, this time with his knapsack.

He had one other option: soon after setting out from Hademsdorf, the men in his compartment had convinced Spit-Bubble to open their windows; these definitely allowed enough space for a grown man to climb through. He would have to make the leap without the guard seeing.

More hours passed. Harvey and the others offered Spit-Bubble some of their food and wine, which he gladly accepted. The meal, and the metro-

FE2b biplane
(Imperial War Museum)

Captain David Gray,
"Father of the Tunnel"
(Patrick Mallahan)

Second Lieutenant
Caspar Kennard
(Diana Gillyatt)

Second Lieutenant
Cecil Blain
(Hugh Lowe)

Karl Niemeyer, Holzminden commandant
(Patrick Mallahan)

Holzminden, "the Black Hole of Germany"
(Clouston Family)

Holzminden bedroom

(Clouston Family)

662

Ich gebe mein Ehrenwort, für den Fall meiner Beteiligung an einem Spaziergange, während des Spazierganges, d. h. vom Verlassen des Lagers bis zur Rückkehr in dasselbe nicht zu entfliehen, während der gleichen Zeit jeder Anordnung des Begleitpersonals nachzukommen und keine Handlungen zu begehen, die gegen die Sicherheit des Deutschen Reiches gerichtet sind. Ich weiss, dass nach § 159 des M.-St.-G.-B. ein Kriegsgefangener, der trotz abgegebenen Ehrenwortes entflieht, der Todesstrafe verfallen ist.

ich gebe auch mein Ehrenwort, diese Karte nur für mich zu gebrauchen und sie keinem anderen Gefangenen zu geben.

Holzminden, den 16. 2. 18.

I, herewith, give my word of honour that I shall not, in case of my taking part in a walk, make an attempt of escape during such walk, i. e. from the time of leaving the camp until having returned to it, at the same time strictly obeying any orders given to me by the accompanying officer an not to commit any acts that are directed against the safety of the German Empire. I know, that according to § 159 of the M.-St.-G.-B. a prisoner of war, who escapes in despite of the word of honour given, is liable to death.

I give also my word of honour to use this card only myself and not to give it to any other prisoner of war.

Name: L. J. Bennett
ob Sub Lt. RN

Buchdruckerei Otto Ebers, Holzminden.

Holzminden parole card, James Bennett

(Laurie Vaughan)

Tunnel entrance underneath the stairs

(© RAF Museum)

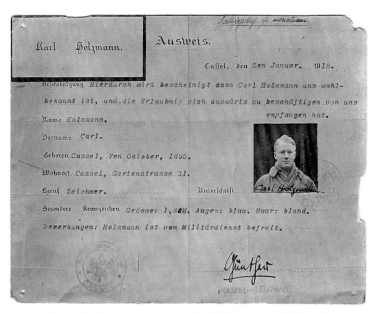

Forged identity card for "Carl Holzmann" (Blain)

(Hugh Lowe)

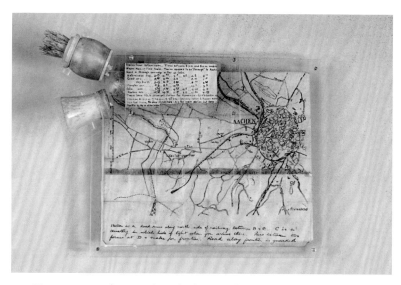

Escape artists' contraband: shaving brush with hidden map
(Imperial War Museum)

Escape contraband, including compass, hidden in a tin of tongue
(Imperial War Museum)

Block B, Holzminden,
and the dug-up tunnel
(Patrick Mallahan)

Lieutenant Edgar Garland,
hero of the collapsed tunnel
(Patrick Mallahan)

The escape artists in free Holland

(Patrick Mallahan)

Congratulatory note to James Bennett
from King George V

(Laurie Vaughan)

Recaptured tunnelers at Holzminden

(Clouston Family)

Achtung!

IT IS PROPOSED TO HOLD A

RE-UNION DINNER

on Saturday, 23rd July, 1938, at Ye Olde Cheshire Cheese, Fleet Street, London, to celebrate the 20th anniversary of the

HOLZMINDEN TUNNEL

Air Commodore C. E. H. RATHBORNE, C.B., D.S.O., will be in the Chair and the Orderlies who helped in the escape will be the Guests of Honour. Lounge Suits—6.30 for 7 p.m. The Committee cordially invite you to attend.

You will greatly assist by replying **AT ONCE** to—

L. James Bennett, 39, Maddox Street, London, W.1

SUBSCRIPTION FROM OFFICERS 10/-

Invitation to celebrate the 20th anniversary of the Holzminden escape

(Keil Tullis)

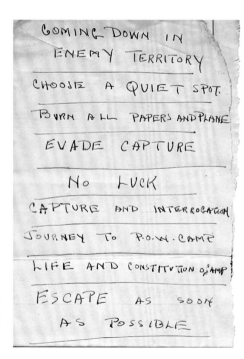

COMING DOWN IN
ENEMY TERRITORY

CHOOSE A QUIET SPOT.

BURN ALL PAPERS AND PLANE

EVADE CAPTURE

No LUCK

CAPTURE AND INTERROGATION

JOURNEY TO P.O.W. CAMP

LIFE AND CONSTITUTION OF CAMP

ESCAPE AS SOON
AS POSSIBLE

James Bennett's notes for his MI9 lectures

(Laurie Vaughan)

nomic back and forth of the train, lulled the old guard into sleep, but time and again he would jar awake, eye his charges, then drift back to the spit bubbles.

The train passed through Hanover, then down through the countryside toward Holzminden. They were making fast progress, and the sun had yet to set. Another guard passed through their carriage, announcing they would disembark within the hour. Harvey knew he had to go. After handing his knapsack to a fellow officer to hurl out after him, he waited for Spit-Bubble to drift off again. Then, with two of his compartment mates standing in front of the guard in case he awakened, Harvey climbed onto his seat, gripped the hanging arm-strap with one hand, and half-swung, half-pitched himself through the open window. The strap supported his weight. For a brief moment he stood on a railing outside the carriage car, buffeted by the wind, the countryside passing in a blur below his feet. Then, as the train rounded a bend, he leaped.

He hit the ground fast and hard. His knapsack followed, striking him in the back and spilling open. Stunned by the fall, he lay supine between the track and the embankment, forgetting for a brief second that he was a prisoner who had just jumped from a moving train crowded with armed German guards. In the next moment, wits returned, he collected his knapsack and scrambled away from the tracks as the last carriage left him behind. There were no shouts from the guards, nor any sudden braking of the train.

Soon enough, however, Harvey heard cries of alarm coming from a nearby field. He turned to see a surge of men, women, children, and even a dog pursuing him and calling out in German. They must have spotted him leaping from the train. Harvey hurried off. In the distance he spied some woods in which he could hide, but he would first have to pass a small village. He slowed his pace as he rounded it, not wanting to arouse suspicion.

In the meantime, his pursuers caught up to him, yet none of them attempted to detain him, perhaps fearing he posed a danger to them. Once beyond the village, he determined to run for the woods. But as he came to a crossroads, a teenage boy, no older than seventeen, grabbed him. Harvey tried to pull away, but the boy was all determination, and Harvey did not want to risk hurting him to free himself.

Emboldened by the boy, several in the crowd seized the fugitive by his arms and collar. Harvey surrendered and was led to the local police station. There he was accused of being a saboteur who aimed to blow up the nearby train tunnel. As evidence, a police officer brandished his Canadian hardtack, believing the concrete-like biscuit to be an explosive. Knowing that this misconception could get him shot, Harvey pleaded, in his best pidgin German, that he was in fact an unarmed British prisoner attempting to escape. Only after the officer contacted Holzminden was he convinced that this was true. Commandant Habrecht ordered the police officer to escort Harvey to the camp on the next available transport.

In the meantime, the other Schwarmstedt prisoners arrived at Holzminden. The train ran nearby the camp as they approached it in the late afternoon, and the men gathered at the carriage windows to look out. The two barracks gave the impression of a welcoming hotel, and they saw a number of prisoners waving from the rooms on the top floors.

After a walk from the station, the newcomers entered through the main gate. Their hopes of better treatment were summarily crushed when their brethren shouted down from their barracks windows that this was the "worst camp" they had ever known — and to prepare for an intensive search. One prisoner, nearly hanging out on the sill, shouted down at them in an Irish lilt to hide their money: "Bury your notes! They strip ye mother naked!"

Once in the parade ground, the prisoners sat down, some of them hastily burying compasses, money, maps, and other contraband in the dirt before the inspection began. It was intensive: the men were stripped naked, and their clothes and belongings were rifled through with great care. While this was under way, other guards unearthed the newly buried treasures in the yard. When they were finally allowed to get dressed, the prisoners were each issued a round metal tag stamped with a number. Their names were meaningless now. Then they were locked into their rooms for the night.

Harvey arrived into Holzminden on the late train. He winked at Spit-Bubble as he passed, and was delivered straight into a solitary cell in the basement of Block B. The door clanged behind him and was bolted shut. He sat down on the floor. On the wall, he scrawled the letters *D*, *A*, *M*, and *N*, and tried to think of a four-line poem, each line starting with one of the letters. Nothing came.

Nine

Wire cutters in hand, Cecil Blain and Edward Leggatt crawled toward the northern end of the fence surrounding Clausthal. It was a misty September night. They were only a few yards from a watch post, and a light was shining on their position, but for whatever reason there were no guards in the area at that precise moment. The two aimed to take advantage of that fact.

Blain was, as he wrote a family member, "mad keen" to make it home by his twenty-first birthday and return to the air with the RFC. Besides the news brought to the camp by recently captured prisoners, much of what Blain knew about the progress of the war came from the *Continental Times*, an English-language paper published in Germany — ostensibly a "Journal for Americans." The officers rightly called it the "Confidential Liar," but there was just enough hint of fact in the paper to cause them unease.

One recent headline read, "Utterly Hopeless Conditions Existing in Russia — Military, Economical and Civil Situation Has Come to Pass Where Collapse and Ruin Threaten." Baron von Richthofen and other German aces ruled the skies, according to the paper, and on both major fronts the kaiser's troops were crushing the Allies, including the devastation of the latest British offensive against the "Flanders Position" in August. Sweeping victory was close, especially as a "peace movement" in the U.S. government was working to remove America from the war before the nation joined in earnest.

Blain could not know for certain what was true, but if the paper's intention was to sap his will to escape — and make him, like every other British POW, according to one editorial, a "relentless critic of his own government" — then the propaganda rag failed. Blain's time in Germany had only heightened his desire to return to the fight against the Huns.

The fence was proving uncooperative. For fifteen minutes Blain hacked at the metal with his cutter, but he had yet to create a hole they could crawl through. They were running out of time. Leggatt kept a close eye out for the guards, who would likely return at any second. After one more clip of a link, Blain managed to create enough of a break in the fence to push through it. Leggatt followed with their two knapsacks. They wriggled their way forward until they were out of the glare of the arc lights, then dashed into the dark woods.

Dressed in civilian clothes and carrying forged documents identifying them as Belgian laborers, they headed west. When it was daylight they hid out in woods and fields. At night they marched as fast as they could through the countryside. They aimed to cross the Dutch border outside Venlo, two hundred miles from Clausthal as the crow flies. With streams to navigate, farms to circumvent, and all-too-frequent mistaken turns, their trek was an arduous one. The steady rain, cold nights, rationed food, and constant fear of discovery made the journey all the more trying.

By the fifth day, they had managed to cover only a quarter of the distance to the border and had started to snipe at one another — about the sluggish pace, or a turn down the wrong path — to vent frustration. They had been fast friends at Clausthal but they were both headstrong and hot-tempered, and the pressure of the escape was getting to them. As dusk fell on September 21, they mistakenly set their watches forward to account for daylight savings instead of back.

The rain had stopped as they ventured off again from their hiding place in an abandoned barn. According to their map, after traveling across some fields, they would soon reach the river Weser. The sky, marvelously lit with color from the passing storm, had gone almost black by the time they neared a village. Believing the hour to be later than it was, they figured the road would be clear, allowing them to pass undetected. To their dismay, as they made their way down the road they saw a band of German farmers and their families coming out of the fields to head back into the village. Committed to their route, Blain and Leggatt continued ahead.

The locals followed the men, but seemed unconcerned by their presence. When they came to a small lane, Blain and Leggatt turned onto it, and the farmers continued down the road into the village. The two Englishmen next found themselves in a field, lost, their shirts drenched with sweat from exertion, the warm evening, and not a little fear. Unsure of where they were, they circled back, only to be confronted in the village, this time by some youths carrying flashlights, who then drew the attention of their elders.

Blain stopped and turned, commenting in rough German on what a beautiful sunset they had enjoyed that evening. A muddled conversation in French, then English, followed, with the officers identifying themselves as Belgian workmen who had somehow gotten lost. The locals pointed them in the direction of the Weser, and off they went. Misfortune averted, they continued out of the village and through another stretch of countryside, finally reaching a well-built bridge over the river. On the opposite side was a large town. Short of swimming across the river farther downstream, they could not avoid it. With heavy beards and soiled clothes, they would surely arouse suspicion.

Once they were over the bridge, they crossed paths with a group of German officers carousing in the streets. Blain and Leggatt tipped their hats at the officers and made off without event. They might not be so lucky next time. Soon after, a young prostitute approached them from a street corner and put her hands on Blain, who managed to extricate himself from her solicitations before drawing even more attention to their presence. The two men then veered south, straight out of town and down to the river. There they took a break. Wanting to wash away the dirt and grime of almost a week of travel, they undressed and took a cold dip in the Weser.

As they started off again along the road, a flashlight suddenly shined in their faces and a German policeman approached, asking, "Wohin gehen sie? Wohen kommen sie?" Blain responded in his best French where they were going and where they had been — hoping their story of being Belgian laborers who had gotten lost would once again put them in the clear. The policeman examined their papers but remained unconvinced. Some thieves had been working the town lately, he said, and any strangers required investigation.

Once at the local jail, having exhausted their attempts at subterfuge, the unfortunate airmen gave up their real identities and soon found themselves back at Clausthal. Heinrich "Windy Dick" Niemeyer proved worthy of his name, ranting at the top of his lungs that they would face a court-martial that most assuredly would see them shot by firing squad. "Shot, shot, shot!" he screamed.

Over the course of its first month in operation, officers poured into Holzminden in the hundreds, many of them inveterate escape artists from camps across Germany, including Ingolstadt, Freiburg, Augustabad, Schwarmstedt, and the dreaded underground prison Fort Zorndorf. With every influx, Holzminden descended further into disarray. There was not enough food to eat and not enough fuel to heat the stoves; the shelves in the newly opened canteen were almost empty; the parcel room remained closed; British enlisted ranks who were to serve as orderlies were just arriving; and the German administration was a mess.

The elderly commandant Colonel Habrecht was overwhelmed. Try as Karl Niemeyer might to set some order, he spent a good share of his efforts maneuvering his ineffectual boss out of the way or lambasting the Feldwebels (noncommissioned officers) and Landsturms (reserve militiamen), who served as the camp's staff and guards, respectively.

They were a motley bunch. A man called Gröner, who had been re-cruited from Schwarmstedt, ruled over Block A. Many of the prisoners knew him well — and despised him. One described him as "a saturnine, sallow, heavy-mustachioed fellow, reputed a schoolmaster in civil life." He liked to rail at his charges almost as much as Niemeyer did. The man in charge of Block B, Ulrich, alternated between obsequiousness with re-spect to his superiors and a self-important authoritarianism in relation to the prisoners. The men had a feeling he would do anything to stay away from the front. Feldwebel Welman was head of the canteen. He had a whiny voice and a penchant for theft. Then there was Mandelbrot, a short, rigid figure, a walking rulebook on everything from what the officers were permitted to wear to how they should keep their rooms.

Prisoners practiced in the art of escape knew that the best chance of-ten came in a camp's early life, before the chinks in its security had been discovered. The chaos at Holzminden added to this opportunity. Two of their number, recently arrived from Fort Zorndorf, were particularly keen to find a way out. Canadian infantry officer John Thorn, captured on the front in April 1915, had made several breakout attempts at previous camps, one of them dressed as a German war widow, black crepe veil and all. His partner was RFC pilot Wally Wilkins. In their first few days at Holzmin-den, Thorn and Wilkins scoured the camp for weaknesses and found a major one while inspecting Block A.

Both of the barracks were constructed in the same way: each had a main block, fifty yards long, with wings at both ends that extended back and away from the Spielplatz. Each building had two entrances (one at either end) that faced the main grounds. Inside, stairs at both ends ran from the cellar up four floors to the low-ceilinged attic.

An entire third of Block A — including the wing closest to the main gate, outside all the barriers apart from the surrounding wall — was re-served for the Kommandantur, the offices and sleeping quarters of the German staff. Interior wooden walls separated this section from the quar-ters of the British officers, and it had its own entrance.

Thorn and Wilkins figured that if they could open up the wooden barricade on the attic level, they could enter the Kommandantur, proceed down the stairs, and exit Block A just beside the main gate. The gate was in the part of the camp occupied solely by Germans, so its lone guard was unlikely to be suspicious of individuals leaving through it, especially if they were dressed in German soldier's fatigues.

They began work immediately. Late that night, they snuck out of their rooms in Block A and made their way to the attic. In two hours, using a makeshift saw, Wilkins managed to cut a small panel out of the barricade wall, which was constructed from wooden planks, two inches thick and bound with wire. When they removed the panel, they found another wall of boards, thicker than the ones on their side and secured with six-inch nails bent at the ends. Wilkins was unfazed. He needed only to straighten the nails and sever their exposed ends. Then he could push the boards free. Their makeshift saw, however, would not do for the job.

Informed of the need for wire cutters, several of their friends searched the camp, and not half a day later a pair was nicked from a German soldier charged with fixing the fence. After lights-out, Thorn and Wilkins returned to the attic and finished their escape hatch. A quick inspection of the German side confirmed their theory that they could access the stairs to get to the door by the main gate. Then they replaced the two panels, hoping they would not be discovered before the planned getaway.

Next, they prepared to go. Another of the prisoners had smuggled a sewing kit into Holzminden. He proved to be an expert tailor. Within a couple of days he whipped up two pairs of gray trousers with red stripes down the sides and jackets dyed with ink and coffee bought at the canteen. Food for their border run was donated by their fellow prisoners. On September 28, the day they were set to go, Wilkins came down with a high fever. Knowing that the hatch could be discovered at any minute or that a new security measure might sink their plan, he gave up his place to Reginald Gaskell, a British Indian Army captain and fellow veteran of Fort Zorndorf.

After answering to their names at the final roll call of the day, Thorn and Gaskell returned to the barracks, donned their disguises, and placed their civilian clothes and knapsacks into plain sacks the guards often used during work detail. An hour later, they crawled through the barricade wall in the attic, replaced the panels behind them, and descended the stairs into the Kommandantur. Just before they reached the door they spotted Habrecht and several other Germans moving into the stairwell. They continued ahead, not saying a word, and nobody stopped them. Once outside, they made a beeline for the main gate and did not so much as slow their pace as they crossed past the guard. They were out, and easily away. The Dutch border was 150 miles to the west, and they planned to average 15 miles a day getting there.

Back at the camp, when lights-out was ordered, Rathborne rolled up some clothes and stuffed them underneath the blankets on his roommate Gaskell's bed, hoping that if a guard glanced into the room, he would mistake the shape for the missing officer. By the morning roll call, no alarm had been raised. When a guard called the names of Thorn and Gaskell, their fellow prisoners answered for them. Then Niemeyer took to the Spielplatz and called for Thorn — on account of some contraband found on him when he first arrived at Holzminden. Not wishing to risk further subterfuge, a British officer who had helped prepare the escape stepped forward. In a calm voice, he announced that Thorn "had left the evening before on a journey to Holland." A great cheer rose up among the prisoners, sending Niemeyer into a steam. He demanded the roll call again, and Thorn and Gaskell were found missing.

Commandant Habrecht, a man predisposed to inaction, left the matter for Niemeyer to handle. He ordered the prisoners to return to the barracks, and a search was initiated to determine how the two officers had escaped. A pair of bloodhounds was brought in. Freshly arrived from Clausthal and thinking quickly, Shorty Colquhoun, who shared a room with Thorn, sprinkled some cayenne pepper into his fellow Canadian's old shoes in an effort to put the dogs off the track. Then he took Thorn's socks and replaced them with his own. The same was done for Gaskell. Soon enough, the guards gathered up the escapees' remaining clothes and shoes and brought them out onto the Spielplatz. The bloodhounds, first taking the scent of the socks, began racing around the camp as if they were chasing ghosts. Watching from the windows, Colquhoun and the others could barely contain their laughter. Then the dogs buried their noses in the boots laden with pepper. After a good whiff, they went mad, leaping about, hurling themselves back and forth, their handlers barely able to keep a grip on their leashes. Shouts and hollers followed from the windows. Enraged by the scene, Niemeyer drew his revolver and brandished it at the barracks. He held himself sufficiently in check not to shoot.

After an intensive inspection, which failed to uncover the hatch, the Germans were at a loss as to how Thorn and Gaskell had got out undetected. A drain, sniffed out by the bloodhounds, was suspected as a possible route until its diameter was determined too small to fit a man. Still, it was cemented closed.

Wilkins, who was by now feeling better, decided to use the attic hatch for himself the following night. Others aimed to follow. For all its rings of defenses, Holzminden was not yet the unbreakable fortress that Niemeyer boasted.

Ströhen was its own busy warren of breakout artists. The commandant who replaced Karl Niemeyer when he was transferred to Holzminden cared more for maintaining military respect than preventing breakouts. At roll call, he made it his business to demand a proper salute from the senior British officers. He stood before them, one after the other, straightened his coat, snapped his heels together, and gave a sharp salute. The prisoners either ignored him or offered an exaggerated salute, a Japanese bow, or an Arabic salaam in return. Laughter usually crackled out afterward, but the commandant would always repeat the exercise the next day.

The prisoners showed the same obstinacy in their plots to get out of

Ströhen. Gerald Knight, who had built the false wall in the bathhouse outside the wire, was famous among the men. Days after his successful escape, his method undetected, six others had hid underneath the shower floorboards until after dark, then dashed away—only to be recaptured soon afterward.

Another gang tried an altogether more straightforward manner of exit. After the guards stepped away for a duty changeover, the prisoners grabbed an iron bar they had hidden in the yard and, using it as a battering ram, rushed the main gate. Its lock and chain failed to give way, and the men dropped the bar and scattered, followed by a shout advising them to stop and the crack of a revolver.

Another scheme, led by pilot Duncan Grinnell-Milne, relied on impersonation, namely of a German guard leading four orderlies out on work detail. The orderlies' outfits—a yellow stripe down the trousers and a yellow armband—were easily obtained from a cooperative orderly. Making a German uniform was not a simple task, but it was manageable. One prisoner provided his dark, calf-high boots and another his gray trousers. The red piping down the legs was sewn on with some cloth. A blue service coat was created from an old blanket, and a tall, black-peaked cap was shaped out of brown packing paper.

Finding a rifle, like those carried by guards when escorting prisoners, was another matter entirely. Such a weapon proved impossible to obtain, either by theft or bribery; left without a choice, they decided to make a fake: the stock was manufactured from scraps of wood, the barrel from an iron railing, the breech mechanism from bits of tin, and, finally, the sling from a worn leather belt. The assembly was sanded, polished, and painted to pass for a weapon in service.

Pink passes were carried by orderlies outside the wire, and these were forged from the linen endpapers of a book sent from England. To match the violet shade of the ink, they used a copying pencil, whose dye turned the proper color when steamed with an iron.

Once all was ready, Grinnell-Milne dressed in the German uniform and marched his "charges"—four of his fellow airmen—right through the gate. They were almost away when a guard recognized one of the men as a British officer and raised the alarm. Although their plot failed, the prisoners learned that just about any impersonation could be pulled off with some care and ingenuity.

Although his previous gambit at Clausthal had earned him a long stay in isolation, Caspar Kennard was as bold as ever in his bid for freedom. One late afternoon, he unlocked the gate with a forged key and struck off alone. He was on the lam for a week. Finding himself lost outside a village, he spotted a signal box beside a rail line with a location name stamped on its side. He could not quite read it and began climbing up the pole for a closer look. A railway man found him in this unusual position, and a chase ensued. Kennard was tracked down soon afterward.

After almost three weeks in solitary detention, Jim Bennett was in no fit state for an attempt of his own. His former accomplice Roy Fitzgerald had no such limitations, and he escaped Ströhen with another officer while Bennett served as lookout.

David Gray did not involve himself in any of these schemes, even the one with his former partner Kennard. He was resolved to have a foolproof plan in place before any future attempt. However, he would not have another opportunity at Ströhen. The decision had been made to send the most troublesome Allied prisoners, including Gray, Kennard, and Bennett, to Holzminden.

Ten

O n October 1, 1917, General Hänisch, head of the 10th Army Corps Division, visited Holzminden for the first time. Now numbering over five hundred, including British officers and enlisted ranks (the orderlies), the prisoners paraded into the Spielplatz and drew together in straight lines, under the close watch of Captain Niemeyer. The men showed proper form and answered their names promptly when called. They had only just started to receive food parcels to supplement their diet, and they intended to give the general no reason to stop deliveries or make their lives any more difficult.

From Commandant Habrecht down, the staff were all dressed in their finest uniforms, their boots polished to a shine. Niemeyer was first among them to bring his hand to his peaked cap in sharp salute whenever the general addressed a question to him about the camp or what additional security measures could be put in place. Another handful of prisoners had gotten away only the night before, their method unknown, and Niemeyer intended to use the escapes to get himself promoted over his superior.

The general was quiet throughout roll call, but as he toured the barracks and other facilities, he made no secret of his feelings toward the prisoners. They were "barbarians" and "*Schweinhunds,*" and, in his opinion, "they did not deserve to be allowed to live, let alone receive letters." Niemeyer agreed. No treatment was too harsh for the enemy. Near the end of his short visit, Hänisch allowed Major John Wyndham, who had replaced Rathborne as senior British officer at the camp, to address him. Rather than showing him the respect of a sit-down in the Kommandan- tur, the general held the meeting in front of the cookhouse. Forty-six years old, an army lifer and veteran of several campaigns, Wyndham was uncowed. In German, he first demanded better accommodations for his men. "There are no public rooms, no library, one solitary cookhouse, and no bathroom," he said.

Hänisch turned to Habrecht and Niemeyer. They spoke quietly, then the general responded that a proper bathroom and another cookhouse would be provided. The rest were luxuries. "Is it to be understood that this is a strafe [punishment] camp?" Wyndham asked.

"If it may please the English officers to understand that. It is deserved though." Hänisch looked at his watch. "Next please?"

Wyndham asked for the Spielplatz's security fences to be moved back to allow for more expansive exercise grounds.

"Later, perhaps, we will see, but now impossible."

Then Wyndham looked at Niemeyer directly and demanded that the camp officer be removed immediately as a result of his conduct at Ströhen — notably the bayoneting of prisoners. Hänisch looked from Wyndham to Niemeyer then back again. No. Niemeyer would remain. Wyndham maintained his calm, difficult though it was. He had one more demand. The prisoners deserved parole walks in the countryside but not under the pledges they had been required to sign at Holzminden. Specifically, two clauses on the parole cards printed by the Germans were unacceptable. First, the men should not have to accept that "the penalty for breach of parole is death." Second, the officers should not have to promise to "obey all orders of the non-commissioned officers conducting parties on walks." Both clauses were beyond the pale, Wyndham said. There was the men's honor to consider.

Hänisch chortled. Such was the men's honor that they had violated pa- role at Schwarmstedt by hiding tins of food to be used in escape while on their walks. Wyndham, who had been at the camp, denied this vehemently. The general responded that the recent breakouts at Holzminden might well have been perpetrated during parole walks; there could be no other explanation. Knowing better, Wyndham labeled this a slanderous lie.

"*Baralong!*" Hänisch shouted, referring to the British decoy ship that had sunk a U-boat and executed its survivors more than two years before.

"*Lusitania!*" Wyndham returned, losing his reserve.

"If every Englishman in this command got his deserts, he would be shot," the general said, and with that dismissed Wyndham and marched off to the Kommandantur. Niemeyer followed close on his heels, like a dog cleaving to its master.

In his office, Habrecht gently suggested to Hänisch that the British major, and the prisoners overall, deserved some modicum of respect. Niemeyer interjected that respect was something they were given too much of. Within forty-eight hours of the general's departure, Habrecht was ordered to pack up his office. Niemeyer was now in charge.

In some of his first acts as commandant, Niemeyer ordered a guard to fire at a group of prisoners in the barracks building who were mocking the Germans during their morning drill marches; he made the sick and invalid stand in the parade ground for hours in the cold; he shut all the prisoners in their barracks for a day; and he ordered any officer caught in the act of a breakout to be shot on sight.

Still, the escapes continued.

"Three more out last night, sir," an orderly told Harvey. "And the commandant is hopping mad!" Harvey was glad for the news—and for the meal the orderly had brought with him. But then the door to his cell closed, leaving him alone again but for a single skittish mouse that peeked out from behind the coke stove when all was quiet.

For almost two weeks, Harvey had been held in a sliver of space in the cellar of Block B, provided only with a straw mattress, a rickety table, a

stool, and a jug of water. He was allowed out at set times to use the toilet
— and then always on his own, aside from the guard charged to accompany him. Otherwise he had to use a foul pail in his cell. Unable to bathe
or shave, he grew a Rasputin-like beard. There was a narrow window high
on the eight-foot wall of his cell through which he could see the boots of
those passing in the yard. His underground quarters felt like a tomb. *I am
half sick of shadows,* he thought, reciting the words of Tennyson's "The
Lady of Shalott."

There were others in the adjoining cells, but the walls were thick, and
one could only shout so loud for so long before growing hoarse. Harvey
suffered from the chill — his stove lacked fuel, and the cement floor and
walls retained the cold of the surrounding earth. At night, the rats came
out in numbers that rivaled those in the trenches along the front. His fellow inmates ran competitions on who could kill the most vermin in a
night.

Many of the Pink Toes were at Holzminden, having all come on the
same train, and through the help of an orderly who served in the cells,
Mossy and friends sent books down to Harvey to occupy his time. He
devoured *War and Peace* and several other classics. However, Tolstoy did
little to inspire, and although Harvey tried to write poetry, nothing of any
value emerged.

His loneliness was finally broken by the arrival of an Irish roommate.
The cells were beginning to fill up with prisoners caught on the run after
the rash of breakout attempts utilizing the attic hatch, including the originators of the hatch, Thorn, Gaskell, and Wilkins. Happy for the company,
Harvey and his new companion debated history and shared books. Harvey even gave lessons on writing ballades and triolets in exchange for cigarettes. Even so, the "moldiness" he had first experienced at Schwarmstedt
set deeper within him. "It is not the physical hardship," he wrote of his
time in solitary. "It is the purposelessness of it, and the awful monotony,
that sickens the heart . . . Nothing could prevent the creeping paralysis of

prisondom from gradually overtaking me, and the time came to me as to other men when I was too hopeless even to fight against it."

In Cell 5 at Clausthal, Cecil Blain was also in solitary confinement. By October 12, barely over a fortnight since his capture and Heinrich Niemeyer's ultimately empty threats to have him shot, he was already set on his next attempt. Rather than cowing Blain, his past failures had made him even bolder and more impetuous.

His partner this time was John Parker, an RFC pilot and son of a civil magistrate in South Africa, who was also in solitary. A bribed guard, who despised the commandant almost as much as the prisoners did, had provided them with civilian suits, flashlights, maps, a train timetable, and instruction in the German phrases that would enable them to buy a one-way ticket to Düsseldorf. All they needed now was a metal saw and wire cutters, neither of which the guard dared risk smuggling in to them. Blain expected these items would be coming soon, though, thanks to a note he had secured to the lid of a teapot and smuggled out to an accomplice.

Outside in the snowbound yard Harold Medlicott rolled a cigarette as the morning roll call began. If Blain had a twin in terms of age, looks, and daredevil's joie de vivre, then Medlicott was it. An ace of the No. 2 Squadron, he had been known in the RFC for having never seen a German aircraft he did not attempt to attack. With five kills to his name, and the honors to match, he was finally shot down in late 1915. In the two years since, he had become legend in another way: as a real-life Harry Houdini with almost a dozen breakouts under his belt, several carried out in broad daylight. One time, he slid down a bell-shaped castle tower — his cell at its top was so high the Germans did not believe it needed bars. Another time he extended a rickety plank of wood straight out from a second-floor window to cross a deep moat surrounding an old prison fortress.

When Windy Dick came out to oversee the roll call, Medlicott lit his cigarette and took a long drag. Smoking was prohibited during roll call, and if this were not transgression enough, he sent a cloud of smoke straight into the path of Niemeyer, who halted abruptly in front of him. This prompted Medlicott to draw yet again on his cigarette, casually exhaling another cloud of smoke. "For this" — Niemeyer ripped away the cigarette — "I give you three days and no messing."

Medlicott was sent into the block of isolation cells beside the pigsty at the northern end of Clausthal — just as he had planned. On his person were hidden the metal saw and wire cutters requested by Blain. The bribed guard who worked the block delivered him into Cell 10, the one nearest the wire fence that surrounded the camp. Medlicott sawed almost completely through the iron bars on the window before being moved to another cell by the same guard. In this way, he would not be implicated in Blain and Parker's plot. He preferred to escape on his own.

At 8:00 p.m. that night, Blain pushed open his cell door. Earlier he had fixed a thin piece of wood from a cigar box into the latch so that it did not lock properly when closed. He crept in his socks to the cell where Medlicott was held, to obtain the wire cutters. He thanked his doppelgänger, and the two promised to meet again — in free Holland. Then Blain let Parker out, and they went into the now-empty Cell 10 to finish the cutting of the bars with a file.

Medlicott and the others in the block kept watch from their cell windows, tracking the movements of the patrolling guards. Once the path to the wire was clear, they shined their flashlights at their doors. On this signal, Blain and Parker pulled the severed bars away and climbed through the window. At the wire, they made quick work of cutting a hole; they buried the cutters in the yard to be retrieved later by Medlicott, then hurried out and away from Clausthal through the slushy snow.

They needed to be in Goslar, fifteen miles away, by 2:00 a.m. to catch the night train to Düsseldorf. From there, it was only a couple of nights' hike to the Dutch border — a far better solution, they figured, than making the whole two-hundred-mile journey on foot. Torrential rain and some mistakes in reading their map caused them to arrive in Goslar just as their train was leaving. They found the station crowded with a com-

pany of German soldiers, singing boisterous songs and playing harmon-
icas as they awaited their own train. Undaunted, in their now-drenched
civilian suits, Blain and Parker entered the station and looked up the next
train headed to Düsseldorf: it was not until 5:45 a.m. They took seats in
a quiet corner and acted like they were sleeping, no easy task when every movement and word from the soldiers had them thinking they were
about to pounce.

The night passed without incident. When the ticket booth opened at
5:00 a.m., they asked the clerk in German for two "third-class single tickets to Düsseldorf." She did not understand their much-rehearsed line, nor
did they understand her response. Frustrated, she waved them away, but
not without first drawing the attention of the railway official manning the
turnstiles. He approached Blain and Parker and asked for their passports.
"I think we had better bolt," Parker said to Blain in the Cape Dutch familiar to both men from their time in South Africa.

They ran from the station through the carriage yard, dodging their
pursuer, and took refuge in a stand of woods. With their supply of only
four days' food, there was no way they could tramp the distance to Holland. The town of Langelsheim, which had a railway station, was five miles
away. They decided to walk there. The timetable indicated that the train
to Giessen, where they could take another straight to Düsseldorf, would
soon be arriving. This time they had no trouble obtaining tickets.

At Giessen, they hid away from the station until the train to Düsseldorf
was about to depart. The railway officials barely gave them a second look,
and they hurried onto the train.

The third-class carriages were packed, and Blain had to stand in the
corridor, his knapsack in his hand. A conductor passed through checking tickets, and when he saw Blain in the corridor, he began shouting
in German. Unable to understand him, the young pilot cupped his ear
and feigned deafness. Feeling chastened, perhaps, the conductor led Blain
into a carriage and asked another passenger to give up his seat for him.
Blain found himself sitting next to Parker, who kept his cap drawn over

his face. A young German woman across the aisle kept staring at Blain, and he thought she might be suspicious of his boots, which were decidedly English by manufacture. Parker was sure she only had a crush on the handsome young man.

They arrived into Düsseldorf and took a tram to a bridge that spanned the Rhine. It was a cloudless Sunday morning, and they stopped for a short meal break in an adjacent park. A middle-aged German man in an ill-fitting suit approached them. By his long, studied gaze, they figured him to be a police detective, but rather than risk finding out for sure, they took off across the bridge, hailed a ride on another tram, then headed into some woods northwest of the city.

As they waited for nightfall, three hunters with double-barreled shotguns came upon them after their dog flushed a rabbit out of some nearby bushes. Blain and Parker sprinted away, then separated as the hunters gave chase. Other locals joined in pursuit. At one point, Blain was forced to duck into a backyard garden, hiding amid some pea sticks. Such was his fright that he mistook a stick for a trigger cocked at his ear when in fact there was no one in sight.

That night, he returned to the woods to try to find Parker, not least because his friend had their knapsack of food and their one decent map. But Parker was nowhere to be seen. Blain marched west, using as his guides a compass and a scrap of tissue paper on which he had made a rough sketch of the surrounding area from memory. He hoped to cross the Dutch border near Venlo, some thirty miles away.

He soon became lost in a forest and decided to stop for the night. He stayed hidden through Monday, then ventured off after dusk, first in search of water and food. He ended up eating some raw turnips and drinking stagnant water out of a wagon rut — then vomited. Pushing away the nausea, he made good progress across the countryside and spent the daylight hours of Tuesday in a swamp. From there, he found his way onto a railway that he followed until dawn on Wednesday. He was sure he was near the border. Crossing the rails, he slipped and pulled the hamstring muscle in his left leg, and hobbled into some woods again to take cover and rest. With every hour that passed, he was weakening from thirst and a lack of food. Risky as it was to travel during the daytime, he needed to keep moving.

After finishing his last cigarette, Blain sneaked through the woods. The bright afternoon sun dried his damp clothes, and the pain in his leg eased. He spotted a string of sentries spaced a hundred yards apart at the far end of a turnip field. The border — half a mile at most. He was so close now.

Creeping back into the cover of the trees, he decided to cross that night. Once the sky darkened, he moved forward again. When he reached the edge of the woods, he dropped to the ground and crawled. For two hours, he slithered through the turnip field, muddying his clothes black. He was close enough to hear the footfalls of the sentries and to see their moonlit shadows pacing back and forth across the beaten track of what he felt sure was the border.

He began to time their movements, growing accustomed to their patterns, and waited a long spell before he felt ready. Finally, he crept toward the track, ears keen for any sudden movement or signal of alarm. Hearing nothing, he scurried across. He was almost on the other side when he heard the approach of a border sentry. He moved his foot from the track a mere instant before the German stepped in the same spot. Face buried in the weeds, he kept motionless, breath caught in his chest, heart beating like a trapped animal.

When the sentry continued on his way, Blain rose and ran into a thicket to hide. He wanted nothing more than a decent meal, fresh water, a warm shave, and an even warmer bath. The thought of such creature comforts almost brought him to tears. Up ahead, he saw a town lit up. He had no map but was certain it must be Venlo. He wanted to cry out in joy at the sight of it.

He tried to clean his clothes of muck as best he could, but after three days of striking through woods and fields they were little more than rags.

He headed into the town, slightly dragging his injured leg behind him. Next, a bark in German came from behind. "Halt!" He turned to find a German soldier, rifle at his side. He asked the soldier what the hell he was doing in Holland. "This is not Holland, it is Germany."

Blain tried to talk his way out of detention, saying that he was a worker from Venlo who had got turned around in the woods, but the soldier would have none of it. He later learned that if he had only followed the beaten track a couple of hundred yards to the left, he would have reached Venlo. Instead, he had never left Germany. He was crestfallen at having come so close. Any dreams of beefsteak, a good drink, and a hot bath quickly evaporated. Only black bread and insults awaited him on his return to Clausthal.

Upon his arrival, a semicircle of guards with fixed bayonets surrounded him. Then Heinrich Niemeyer strode forward. The camp officer was in a fury, tearing at Blain's muddied suit until the airman was almost naked. Blain managed to palm his compass and twenty marks, and kept them hidden.

He was dispatched to a new cell, this one with a guard posted outside his door around the clock. Parker was returned to the camp soon after. While crossing a river, he had lost his rucksack (and his clothes, which were bundled inside). He hiked naked for a few miles, then hid out in a chicken coop only to be discovered by its owner. It was an ignominious end to a brave flight. Niemeyer promised Blain and Parker that, after a long stay in isolation, they would be out of his camp for good.

Throughout October, batches of prisoners continued to arrive at Holzminden, many among them with repeated escape attempts to their record. Over sixty men came from Ströhen, including Gray, Kennard, and Bennett. The new prisoners gathered in the Spielplatz, its grass now trampled into a muddy soup due to rainfall and the daily tread of hundreds of boots. Prisoners stood on one side, guards on the other, then Karl Niemeyer performed his typical routine for newcomers. Most of the newcomers were familiar with Milwaukee Bill (as he was commonly known from his tales of bartending in that city) from their stay in the moor.

He began by addressing his guards. "Look at these criminals and mark them down. If I see any German speaking to them he will be sent to the front." He pointed to the prisoners. "These are not officers and gentlemen, they are criminals, and I hope you will treat them such."

To which one officer stood forward and said wearily, "Oh shut up, Niemeyer."

Niemeyer flushed. "Did you tell me to shut up?"

"Yes, I did," the officer answered.

"Then I'll have you arrested immediately. In five minutes!" he blustered.

Some of the officers chuckled at his lack of certainty, some a little too loudly. Niemeyer's English often made him the butt of jokes among the men, who nevertheless knew they took real risks in angering him. Before having his guards clear the Spielplatz, Niemeyer delivered one more promise to the men, apropos of nothing. "You are very clever? Yes? Well, I make a special study of this escaping. You will not escape from here. You think I, the commandant, know nothing. You are wrong. I know damn all."

Stifled laughter followed his inadvertent acknowledgment of the men's disdain for his intelligence — or lack thereof — as the prisoners were hurried at the point of bayonets to their assigned barracks. Once they had settled in, they quickly learned of the prison's vulnerabilities — notably the removable panel in the attic. Despite intensive searches, additional sentry patrols, the widening of no-man's-land, and harsh interrogations of anyone who had escaped and been caught on the run, Niemeyer had yet to discover the attic-hatch method devised by Thorn and Wilkins. More than a dozen prisoners had used the hatch, and there was a veritable German uniform factory in one of the barracks rooms. However, not a single man had yet succeeded in making the long journey from the camp to the Dutch border. It was risk enough to escape the walls of Holzminden, but that was only the first step to freedom.

Eleven

G et up!" A guard pounded on the door at 8:00 a.m., rousing Gray and the three officers with whom he shared a small room in Block B. The pounding, and the call, were repeated down the corridor. The men knew that if they did not rise immediately, the guards would enter their cells and shove them out of bed with the butts of their rifles.

Since arriving at Holzminden, Gray quickly realized that Niemeyer had created an environment intended to dehumanize the officers by a thousand petty humiliations, starting with the barracks. Although the buildings were clean and waterproof—a vast improvement over the shabby huts in the Ströhen moors—prisoners were forbidden to put pictures on the walls or coverings on the windows, and they were allowed only the small lockers provided for all their belongings. This left the rooms devoid of any sense of personalization, even those chambers designated for senior officers like Gray. The overcrowding made it worse, as did the prohibition against opening windows.

Apart from the dining hall, which could seat only a hundred men at a time, there was an absence of common rooms in which the men could assemble. This meant that most prisoners ate where they slept. The officers conducted church services at the ends of corridors or in stairwells, where gatherings for lectures, card games, and the like were also held. Men constantly scrambled over and around one another, like ants in a nest. There was no privacy; one was almost never alone with one's own thoughts.

Roll call was at 9:00 a.m. sharp, and the prisoners spilled out of the barracks onto the snow-dusted Spielplatz to make it on time. Stragglers and those who failed to properly salute — or to stand at attention in uniform — were rewarded with a stay in solitary for a day, or three. "Cost price" the commandant called it in his idiosyncratic American jargon, as if his punishments were a matter of simple straight-dealing rather than petty whim. No matter how cold the day, the men were always forced to wait an interminable length of time as one of Niemeyer's lieutenants walked up and down the lines, calling out names and checking them off his list.

Gray found that waiting was one of the most subtle, but key, instruments of harassment used at Holzminden. Once morning roll call was over, he stood in line for a wash at the taps in the yard. Then he lined up again for a paltry breakfast of bitter coffee and biscuits hard as hammers. After that, he joined the crowd of men making their way to the notice-board on the Spielplatz to see if they had a new parcel. If they did, they joined another line and waited to receive it, then they waited again while the guards checked their items for contraband, hacking into packages or spilling out their contents. The queue for parcels started in the morning, and unless you were there early, you might still be waiting at the end of the day. There was another line to the "tin room" to access the contents of previously received parcels, chiefly foodstuffs not allowed to be kept in the rooms.

Gray waited to use a stove, of which there were too few, to cook his lunch. He waited for yet another round of inoculations. He waited to use the lavatory. He waited to buy firewood at the canteen. He waited to get his ration book for bread and wine. He waited for letters that did not come. He waited day after day for his name to be called at the 4:00 p.m. roll call. After that, he rushed to the barracks to wait in yet another line if he wanted more than the dregs of whatever watery stew they were serving for dinner — once, a whole cow's skull was found floating in the cauldron they dished it from. By 6:00 p.m., when he was locked into Block B for the night, he had been standing for hours, time stretched out to agonizing lengths he never could have imagined before his life as a POW. Lights-out was hard set at 10:00 p.m.

The small tyrannies imposed on Gray and the others at Holzminden were almost limitless. Despite — or perhaps because of — the inviting countryside outside the walls, Niemeyer refused to grant parole walks beyond the limited terms set by Hänisch, in protest over which the prisoners had ripped up their cards. As a result, they had only the half oval of grounds inside the wire for exercise and recreation. This was at best 410 yards around, and it was occupied by two cookhouses, horse troughs, a woodshed, a parcel office, a potato patch, and a dozen straggling trees.

They tried to create a cricket pitch and soccer field in this limited space, but Niemeyer prohibited most games. They were told that one of the arc lamps had been broken by an errant ball. Their offer to pay for its replacement was met with silence. A gymnasium had been built for the original barracks, but it was set between the inner wire and the surrounding walls — out of bounds. It would have been ideal as a recreation space for the men, particularly as the weather got worse. And so, when not in line or sitting in their packed rooms, prisoners wandered back and forth in the crowded Spielplatz like penned cattle.

Bathing facilities were a horse trough that had hot water only twice a week, and the men had to wash in full view of the rest of the camp. A shower house had been built on the senior officer's request, but Niemeyer decided to use it to shelter his Alsatian guard dogs instead. He even posted a sign outside that read, WHEN A MORE SUITABLE PLACE IN THE CAMP CAN BE FOUND FOR THE DOGS, OFFICERS MAY HAVE BATHS ON TUESDAYS AND FRIDAYS.

Theft was pervasive. The *Landsturms* (or "landworms" as the British called the typically older militiamen) oversaw the parcel room. It was bad enough that in "inspecting" items, they destroyed, with shameless glee, cakes, bread, meat, and other food sent to the prisoners, but they also stole what they pleased, especially cigarettes and soap. Letters from home, often describing what had been sent, were "misplaced."

At the canteen, Feldwebel Welman was equally criminal. Goods were supposed to be sold at cost, but Welman charged triple the prices of other camps on everything from coffee, wine, butter, firewood, eyeglasses, pencils, razors, notepads, watches, and toilet paper. The prisoners were certain that he shared most of the profit with Niemeyer, who by Camp Order no. 13 "fixed" all canteen prices. Their commandant also extorted charges on every prisoner for such necessities as food, hot water, and fuel for the kitchens. Some figured Niemeyer was clearing the kingly sum of thirty thousand marks a month in profit.

There was no outlet to appeal their legion of grievances. Niemeyer refused to meet with Wyndham or other senior officers, nor would they have had much luck with him if he had. As far as Niemeyer was concerned, his countrymen were the ones suffering because of the British and their allies. Across Germany, food prices had shot up, and people were hawking heirlooms, furniture, and clothing to feed their families. Soup kitchens operated in most cities. "Meatless" Tuesdays and ersatz products (wheat flour extended with powdered hay; "butter" made with curdled milk, sugar, and food coloring) were the order of the day. Soaps had vanished from shelves, and tobacco was a "luxury" most often mixed with beech leaves. People surrendered their savings for war loans and their copper chandeliers, bronze bells, steam pipes, and even brass doorknobs to be melted down for the war machine.

As well as turning a blind eye to outright theft, Niemeyer set the tone of abuse at the camp — and reveled in it. He paraded about the camp grounds and barracks throughout the day, hands stuffed in his greatcoat, chewing on the big black cigar that was a fixture at the corner of his mouth. His voice could change from a dolorous coo at one moment — "I guess, you know, my dear sir" — to a tyrannical roar in the next: "You must not speak to me. I am the commandant!" He spat on the barracks floors in front of the British officers. He ordered rooms emptied by bayonet point and conducted searches that left beds and lockers in shambles. For no reason other than a sour mood, he sent men to solitary or closed the parcel room.

After only a short time, Gray witnessed how Niemeyer's rule, and the nonstop pinpricks that came with it, left the men feeling rattled and helpless. The abuses were far less severe than those Gray had documented in the secret report he had managed to keep hidden since his escape from Crefeld, but they were abuses nonetheless.

One officer at Holzminden wrote to his mother, "Time drags slowly on here, much the same day after day; it is extraordinary how restless one gets after a while — you feel that you must be doing something, yet cannot settle down to anything." Some had lost a great deal of weight; others were listless; a few were spiraling into madness. With winter coming, and very little fuel to heat their rooms, their lives were certain to grow darker.

Internment in Holland seemed a fool's promise, and the war showed little sign of ending soon. Each would have to find a way to survive the place they now called Hellminden, or the Black Hole of Germany. Gray knew that he would survive by escaping. He did not yet know how, but he was confident that with the camp packed with a master's guild of breakout artists, many of whom he called his friends, an opportunity would surely arise.

In late October, Kennard and several other officers made their break from Holzminden, starting through the removable panel in Block A. Locals in the area surrounding the camp were on the alert for any strangers, and like others before him, Kennard ran into trouble attempting to cross the river Weser, whose width and fast current made for a perilous swim. He was soon caught, returned, and sentenced to solitary.

He was one of the last to use the Block A hatch. After yet another intensive search, the guards found it at last, and a whole new series of security measures was put in place. The barricades in Block A were reinforced with iron sheets. Permit passes were instituted for the main gate and elsewhere. Windows were nailed shut. Barbwire fences were raised. The censoring of letters and inspections of parcels intensified. The barracks were scoured for contraband, and the number of guards increased.

Niemeyer dedicated every effort to ensuring that the black mark on his record owing to earlier escapes would be erased by the prevention of future ones. The Holzminden inmates were clearly jailbreakers of the first order, and he intended not only to make the prison impervious to their schemes, but to crush their spirits in the process. "You see, gentlemen," he announced to the whole camp, "you cannot get out now. I should not try; it will be bad for your health."

PART III

The Tunnel

Twelve

S horty Colquhoun, all six and a half feet of him, wanted to dig a tunnel. He saw no other way out. Although the tunnels they had built at other camps had fallen shy of success, he remained confident that such a plan could be pulled off at Holzminden. Desperation steels the spine that way.

Scouting the camp for the best place to start a sap was a simple exercise in eliminating options.

Given the number of Germans inhabiting Block A, Colquhoun crossed this location off the list straightaway. The cookhouses and woodshed in the Spielplatz were easy to access but too public and too far away from the surrounding camp wall, so those were eliminated as well. That left Block B. But where? Most of the cellar space underneath the officer's section contained detention cells, and guards watched over the corridor night and day.

The cellars under the orderly quarters in Block B, which were used to store wood, tins, bread, potatoes, and other goods, emerged as a possibility. Although guards did patrol this area, they did so infrequently. Further in the cellars' favor was their location adjacent to Holzminden's eastern wall. A tunnel would need only stretch some fifteen yards to reach beyond the camp wall — out into an unguarded field.

Now Colquhoun needed to get inside the cellars to see whether a passage could be dug there. Access through the iron-reinforced barricades that separated the officers' quarters from those of the orderlies in Block B was impossible. He considered knocking a hole in one of the ground-floor rooms on the barracks's eastern side to reach the eastern stairs, but any thorough inspection would likely uncover that.

Officers and orderlies each had their own entrance to the barracks: the officers' was in the west wing; the orderlies', in the east. Officers were forbidden to use the orderlies' entrance, and a guard posted twelve yards opposite the door took note of all comers and goers. But there was no oversight of orderlies entering the officers' section to carry out their daily duties. And it was here that Colquhoun found his plan: Obtain an orderly's spare uniform. Don the uniform inside the officers' quarters. Walk out the door and onto the Spielplatz. Turn left and walk the fifty-yard length of Block B to the orderly entrance. Enter the building without arousing the suspicion of the posted guard.

Colquhoun recruited his friend William Baxter Ellis, a young RFC pilot, to join him on the reconnaissance. A pair of orderlies they trusted provided uniforms and also managed to craft a duplicate key for the cellar door. On November 1, 1917, when most of the German guards were inside the Kommandantur during lunch hour, the two officers made their bid. Even though Colquhoun, tall and gangly, could hardly be considered inconspicuous, nobody paid him — or Ellis — any mind as, disguised as orderlies, they crossed the yard and entered the eastern wing.

The door closed behind them. Inside, they found that the layout was a mirror image of their own wing. They could either take the short flight of concrete stairs to their left up to the ground floor, or the ten steps to their right down to the cellar. They went down. Before they arrived at the locked cellar door, something caught their attention. The Germans had completely walled off the space underneath the flight of steps that led up to the ground floor. A quick rap on the six-inch wood planks revealed the space behind the wall to be hollow. They guessed the wall had been erected to prevent anyone from hiding there, or lying in wait to jump an unsuspecting guard. The men agreed that the space might well present the perfect opportunity: it gave them access to the cellar floor and walls, it was out of sight, and it was out of the way of the normal foot traffic of the guards. Starting a tunnel in one of the open cellars would have risked discovery, whether by a guard coming into the storeroom or appearing in the corridor as they exited the cellar through the door. If they could construct a trapdoor in the planks, then, Colquhoun was sure, they had a very good chance of keeping their activities secret.

"Will you join our tunnel effort?" That was the question on Colquhoun and Ellis's lips. The answer was an easy yes for Mossy, Rogers, and the rest of the Pink Toes at Holzminden. They had attempted such an escape at every single camp in which they'd been held. Gray was not a sure thing. Despite his sapper education and British Indian Army experience, he had avoided tunnels in the past. Colquhoun must have thought this time might be different.

He was right. Gray was in. He had good reasons to join this scheme. First, the access point in the cellar was absolutely ingenious. Second, the ground under Holzminden was far more stable than at Schwarmstedt or Ströhen. Third, the tunnel had a much shorter distance to run than its predecessors. Fourth, if they emerged unseen from its exit at night, they would have sufficient time to gain distance from the camp before they were reported missing at morning roll call. They would need this kind of head start to cross the Weser before daylight. As Gray knew too well, breaking out was only part of the battle.

Before getting too far ahead of themselves, they needed to determine that a trapdoor could be made in the wooden panel. If such a hatch or the mechanism to open it was in the slightest way visible, the Germans were sure to find it. Holzminden's guards were on high alert for the next escape attempt.

At Gütersloh, Crefeld, and Schwarmstedt, Rogers and Mossy had made an art of building sliding steps and hinged walls. In comparison to some of those projects, this new tunnel entrance would be a breeze. First they would need wood-working tools, and for these they would need a carpenter. Since their imprisonment, the men involved in the scheme had become practiced thieves. They smashed in a door in Block B, where they were housed, making sure to knock it off its frame and mangle the lock —something only an experienced tradesman could fix. A carpenter arrived later that day, his box of tools at his side. A guard accompanied him to watch over his work repairing what the Holzminden staff thought amounted to a random act of destruction.

Next, the diversion. Colquhoun and his coconspirators, including Gray, started an argument with the guard—some minor disgruntlement. There was a lot of shouting, and a few of the officers staged a scuffle. While the carpenter stopped work to observe the fray, one of the officers slipped behind him and nicked several tools from his satchel, including a fine-toothed, thin-bladed saw, ideal for precisely cutting wood.

After the melee, the men waited to see if there would be a search for the missing tools. What they suspected, and hoped, was that the carpenter, and the guard responsible for him, would not admit to having been duped by the officers. Their suspicion proved well founded.

The next day, disguised in borrowed yellow-banded tunics, Mossy and Rogers ventured through the eastern entrance of Block B, accompanied by an orderly who had agreed to keep lookout. A quick examination of the walled partition showed that the best place to create a door was near the bottom of the steps. There the planks were longest. At the top of the last plank, there was a small opening from some badly fitting boards where a slide bolt could be hidden. Reaching it would be a tight fit for even the most slender of fingers, but possible.

Mossy and Rogers were quick to the task. To better see what they were doing, they unscrewed the whole V-shaped panel from its placement. An inspection of the chamber behind confirmed exactly what Colquhoun had hoped: it was a space with access to the floor as well as the main, load-bearing walls on the eastern and southern sides of the building, and it was almost tall enough for a man to stand up in. Measuring five yards long and four yards wide, it was also big enough to pack the excavated soil and rubble for a fifteen-yard tunnel. This eliminated the need to smuggle the material out for dumping.

They cut a three-plank door out of the partition wall and then reattached it with two hinges on the back. Such was their precision that there was almost no visible seam between the eighteen-inch-wide door and the wall. They also mounted a bolt on the door, its latch just within reach behind the wall. After sweeping the sawdust into their secret chamber, they replaced the whole panel and secured the bolt. So snug was the fit, they could barely spot the door themselves. Tools hidden under their tunics, they walked back up the steps and out into the Spielplatz.

With a secure entryway in place, the tunnelers wasted no time, launching immediately into the digging. Colquhoun and Ellis had the honor of going first. Hacking at the concrete cellar floor was fruitless — and they had no idea how deep the concrete had been laid. The main walls, though thick, were at least a known quantity. They started on the southern wall, just a few feet under the landing. First, they removed the bricks. Then they dug into the concrete with a chisel. After a few inches, they hit some reinforced iron rods. Even the sharpest of hacksaws would be challenged by the iron.

They took the obstacle in their stride. What they needed was sulfuric acid to burn through the iron like a flame into paper. However, they could not exactly buy a vial of sulfuric acid in the canteen, and obtaining some via a coded message to friends or family in England would take too long — even if they managed to avoid its interception. They knew they needed outside help.

They wanted to keep their cabal small, twelve officers at most, to ensure the tunnel stayed secret as well as to limit the number of individuals going in and out of the building — the better to avoid detection. The success of their plan relied on orderlies, who were able to move around the camp unrestricted and obtain any items the officers needed. Willing accomplices were found, among them Ernest Collinson, George McAlister,

G. E. Razey, F. E. Sidwell, E. G. Harrison, L. W. Saunders, and Dick Cash. Of not being part of the actual escape, an orderly joked, "It's a case of women and kids first, sir."

One of the orderlies just so happened to know a civilian workman at Holzminden who had access to sulfuric acid. A bribe of fifty marks was enough to secure the workman's assistance.

Like the other orderlies at Holzminden, roughly 130 in number, Private Dick Cash of the 19th Battalion, Australian Imperial Force, had no plans to escape. If he did make a run for it and was caught, the best he could hope for was to be sent to the hell of a POW labor camp. Holzminden was far from a pleasure palace, but his chances of starving or being worked to death there were slim compared with the salt mines or the like, where he'd surely end up, given his rank.

When an officer was caught in the act of escape, he was typically returned to camp and thrown into solitary. Both custom and international conventions governed the treatment of officers, who fared better as POWs than members of the rank-and-file.

The British-born Cash might have avoided service on the Western Front altogether. When war had broken out, he was thirty-seven years old, a father of three, and owner of a small grocery store and photography business in Thirlmere, Australia, a railway town southwest of Sydney, where his family had emigrated many years before. Just a bit over five feet, two inches tall, he was thickset, with startling blue eyes and light-brown hair. He had first tried to sign up to fight in September 1914, wanting to do his bit, but the Australian Imperial Force refused him because of his age and small stature. The war was far from being over that Christmas, as many had predicted it would be, and eighteen months after his first attempt, Cash put in another application. Standards for enlistment having been lowered by this time, he was accepted. After training and the long voyage to Europe, he arrived on the front in March 1917.

His battalion saw its share of heavy fighting. On May 3, the men made

an early-morning assault on the strategic German stronghold at Bulle-
court. The Australians faced withering heavy-machine-gun fire in their
approach to the enemy lines. During the attack, Cash was shot in the
chest. The bullet punctured his left lung, but he continued ahead. A series
of mortars threw him first skyward, then sideways. Shrapnel pierced his
back, and many of his teeth were knocked out before he landed in a shell
hole, boots first. The ongoing barrage then filled up the hole around him
until all but his head was underground. There he remained for almost
thirty hours, trying to squirm his way free, before he was taken prisoner.
Field surgery and a torturous three-hundred-mile ride into Germany had
followed.

Cash managed to survive the maggot-infested squalor and rough attention accorded many wounded Allied prisoners and spent the next few
months bedridden at a hospital in Hamelin, a town within the 10th Army
District. He wrote numerous letters to the Red Cross and his family, not
sure if any were reaching their addressee. "I have no money and no clothes
and nothing to smoke," he expressed in one note. "But — with a little help,
I should be able to get my strength back." By September, he had recovered
enough to be sent to Schwarmstedt to work as an orderly, then he was
moved to Holzminden.

Cash had begun to receive a steady stream of care parcels and letters
from home, but the news that came with them brought only heartache: his
baby daughter Myrtle had died, as had his mother and one of his brothers.
His wife, Cissy, struggled to care for the family and keep their businesses
afloat. Compared with the horrors he had faced on the front and in hospital, Cash knew that he could abide the lesser evil of Holzminden for as
long as he had to in order to get back to her.

He lived with the other orderlies, many of whom were also recovering
wounded, in a barricaded-off section of Block B, farthest from the main
gate. Twenty men sleeping in double-deck bunks inhabited the same size
room that fit twelve officers. They crawled out of their cold beds before
the officers awakened and dressed in gray-blue tunics, trousers, and caps

sewn with bands of yellow cloth down the sides. Their prison number was stamped in red on the front of their shirts and the large letters KG (*Kriegsgefangener* — prisoner of war) on the back.

At 7:00 a.m., Cash began his day serving as the "nanny" or "batman" for five officers. While most of them were still asleep in their beds, he steeped a pot of tea and set out their teacups. He collected their uniforms, caps, and boots, and polished and cleaned them before the wake-up call. Then he ate his own breakfast and showed up for morning roll call. After that, he returned to his officers' rooms to make their beds, empty their ashtrays, and tidy up their quarters. Then he and a band of other orderlies swept the corridors and staircases. Twice weekly, they changed the bedsheets and beat the dust out of rugs.

Once lunch was over, the Germans typically assigned the orderlies to some menial task around the camp, such as bundling up paper or hauling firewood. Then they went back to straighten their "orphan" officers' rooms, make afternoon tea, and help serve meals.

Most of the work was fairly light, albeit monotonous, and they rotated rooms so they did not have to suffer any particularly needy officer for long. As one orderly wrote, "Taking the officers by and large, they were a pleasant and easy going crowd, perhaps inclined to be a little thoughtless." For those "tartars," Cash and the others could always exact a trivial retribution — a broken teacup, undercooked food — to signal that they would only be pushed so far.

None of this service seemed odd to Cash, his fellow common-rank soldiers, or the officers they served. Although they were all prisoners, so traditional was the separation between them that not even Niemeyer, who abused them all at every opportunity, ventured to make the officers fend entirely for themselves. European society had a rigid class system in its own right, and the military was another beast altogether. As one historian noted, "There was a wide, indeed gaping distinction between officers and men, emphasized not merely by separate quarters and messes and different uniforms and weapons but by different accents and dictions and syntaxes and allusions. In London an officer was forbidden to carry a parcel or ride a bus, and even in mufti — dark suit, white collar, bowler, stock — he looked identifiably different from the men. When a ten minute signal was called on the march, officers invariably fell out to the left side of the road, Other Ranks to the right."

However, they knew that they were all in this war together. They all faced the cruelties and whims of the camp commandant, the dreary repetition of days, the interminable lines, the thefts, the meager amounts of food, and most important of all, the absence of freedom.

A number of orderlies who had been transferred to Holzminden had helped officers at other camps escape, providing them with uniforms or acting as lookouts. They would do the same now with the tunnel plan. Cash, with his toothless smile, made clear to the officers his willingness to help.

On November 5, Guy Fawkes Day, Jim Bennett came out into the frozen Spielplatz for evening roll call to find Douglas Lyall Grant, Holzminden's best-fed officer, practicing the goose step right in front of Commandant Niemeyer. Arms swinging, knees high, chin stuck out like he was awaiting a punch, Grant gave it his all. For his comic show of protest, he was led off for three days in solitary detention. Something was afoot at Holzminden, and clearly Grant did not like it. That morning, without explanation or forewarning, several of the most senior and outspoken prisoners had been sent away, including Major Wyndham, Lieutenant Colonel Rathborne, and Captain Gray.

Throughout the day, and into the next, Holzminden received what one prisoner labeled an "eye-wash." Officers and orderlies alike were instructed to straighten their rooms and barracks. Whitewash came out by the barrel. The bathhouse was opened for use, burned-out electrical bulbs were replaced, windows were opened, and fuel was supplied to heat their rooms. The next day, they discovered the reason: a "surprise" visit from Dr. Römer, the Dutch inspector. Some of the prisoners had met Römer before, at Ströhen and Schwarmstedt, and despite their complaints nothing had changed for the better. By the generous welcome Commandant Niemeyer offered Römer on his arrival, they guessed that he was on the take and would deliver only a glowing report on the camp to his superiors, which would be passed on to Berlin and London.

The men tried to air their grievances over the unjust treatment they'd received at the camp, even in the presence of the camp commandant, but Niemeyer was always ready with an explanation or justification. On the poor quality of the food: this was simply a matter of "taste"; the men had their "private supplies," anyway. On charging for boiling water: the men were not "compelled to pay this sum." On the exorbitant prices at the canteen: "Most of the articles were sold at a loss." On the excessive stays in solitary, including those suffered by Kennard and others who had escaped from the attic hatch: the accused needed to be secured before their court-martial, only after that did the new fourteen-day punishment limit come into effect. On the lack of recreation space: the men were free to use their sleeping quarters for this purpose. On the long lines to obtain parcels or food tins: the prisoners simply showed a "lack of enterprise." On the absence of parole walks: the prisoners had chosen to tear up their cards rather than adhere to the rules.

Römer's visit confirmed there was no recourse to compel Niemeyer to improve conditions. The whole inspection was a charade, and even though Bennett had put on a brave face for his mother on his arrival at Holzminden from Ströhen, writing that he was "not yet able to form an opinion of the change," he knew from the start that his only option was to break out as soon as he was ready. Every day, he rounded the perimeter of the Spielplatz fifty times, clocking up roughly twelve miles in distance, to prepare his legs for the journey to the border. As he jogged, ignoring the curious looks of some of his fellow prisoners, he studied the shifts of the guards, the movements in and out of the main gate, the places outside the barracks where he might hide. No matter how hard he searched for a weakness in the camp's security, he found none. He dismissed the possibility of a tunnel — unaware that there was already one in the works — because of limited access to the cellars.

Ever optimistic that an opportunity would arise, Bennett wanted to be ready. His fitness plan was only the first step. The next was gathering together everything he would need once outside the walls. The number of failed escapes through the hatch proved to him that preparation was key. There were lots of men at Holzminden who had made a run for the border, and Bennett gleaned what he could from them in conversation.

He made a mental checklist: "A considered plan of the route to be taken, type of country to be met, most suitable spots to hide, how to cross the rivers and canals, food and drink for the journey, best kind of disguise, and how to obtain it. Last, and most important, maps and compasses." He intended to obtain his kit through coded messages to his family. Since his imprisonment at Ströhen he had lost many of his supplies, except for his naval uniform, which could easily be converted into a civilian outfit by stripping it of its brass buttons, rings, and badges.

Bennett began by sending a letter to his half brother John in London. He asked him to call in on a photography shop owned by a man named Stanford near Covent Garden. He wanted a shot of the Rolls-Royce he had bought in 1915 — to decorate his room, he said. Bennett had never owned such a car, nor did he have the funds for one. Stanford's was actually a well-known London travel and map shop.

He sent his next letter to his mother, thanking her for the recent parcel of food and clothes, though, he joked, "I have now enough peas to run a shop." Rice and packets of Quaker Oats would be better, he wrote, before mentioning, in an almost off-hand manner, "By the way, I hear from Mrs. J. Fitzgerald they have moved and now live at 39 Royal Avenue, Chelsea. I should like for you to call and give her my kind regards." He concluded, "Keeping in very good health + spirits and looking forward to seeing you in the ensuing year . . . I am your loving son." Mrs. J. Fitzgerald was a thinly veiled code word for his former escape partner, Roy J. Fitzgerald, who had made the home run to England from Ströhen. Roy would know exactly what Bennett needed for his own attempt. Then he waited, continued his daily walks, and searched for a way out as the weather turned bitter cold.

In late November, after six weeks in isolation at Clausthal, suffering almost daily harangues from Heinrich Niemeyer, Cecil Blain received the news that he was to be transferred to another camp. At the gate, Niemeyer gave him a smug look and said, "Good luck! Give my love to Piccadilly, Hyde Park, South Kensington, and all the rest of those places. Goodbye, Mr. Blain, goodbye." Blain promised himself that the commandant would pay the consequences if he ever tread on English soil — or if he came across him anywhere else, for that matter.

Guards escorted Blain by train to Ströhen. There, he was reunited with David Gray for the first time since their separation at Osnabrück almost a year before. They had many stories to tell about their individual attempts to reach Holland, many bitter lessons to share. Blain inspected his new camp for a way out and discovered, as Gray had since his arrival from Holzminden several weeks before, that the place was a "rabbit warren" of tunnels and hiding places. However, any possible openings the Germans had not discovered and blocked had a long line of prisoners waiting to use them.

Neither Blain, nor Gray, would have the opportunity; Ströhen was being closed and its occupants scattered among several other camps in the 10th Army District. Blain was going to Neunkirchen, a mining and industrial town in the crosshairs of British bombers, and Gray quickly back to Hellminden.

Thirteen

The head of the Prisoner of War Department, Lord Newton, found himself at the cluttered nexus of foreign, domestic, and military affairs. Based at Downing Street, his job was to assist British POWs in Germany and oversee the treatment of enemy prisoners held in Britain. The fate of more than one hundred thousand men depended on his ability to maneuver his government as well as deal effectively with the impetuous decisions of Kaiser Wilhelm II.

Throughout late 1917 Newton's desk was littered with reports about the Holzminden camp.

To start, he had the latest inspection report from the Dutch representative. According to Römer, who had visited Holzminden in November, there was little cause for concern. The officers' complaints were minor in nature and "could be obviated with a little mutual goodwill." After chronicling the need for modest improvements in the exercise grounds and sleeping arrangements, Römer concluded, "The general impression that I was able to gather was of a favourable nature. All the officers looked well and appeared to be in good spirits. . . . The Commandant, although maintaining strict discipline, appeared desirous of doing everything possible to render the life of the prisoners as bearable as circumstances could permit."

Lord Newton doubted the official report. He had received troubling secret intelligence about Römer from contacts in the Foreign Office. Informants suspected that he had compromising connections with German high officials, and according to Römer's former colleagues, he was "professionally incapable," "amenable to bribery," and "a pathological liar." Further, he had issued similarly positive reports of other camps controlled by Hänisch that were contradicted by a binder full of interviews from escaped prisoners.

Similar testimonies were now coming in to London about Holzminden, one by an RFC captain who smuggled a coded letter out of the camp. He recounted a string of brutalities, including the time when four guards cleared his room to make way for newly arrived prisoners. "The first officer was seized by the throat and shaken; the second was struck with a rifle, and the third chased down the passage, his pursuer jabbing at him with his bayonet." Other prisoners, who had been sent away from Holzminden only to escape from their next camp to Holland, recounted much the same. One asserted that Hänisch ran his camps with "organized malevolence." Another that "Holzminden was an inferno." Something needed to be done, Lord Newton knew, but he had few good options on the table.

In the past, he had tried the diplomatic route, submitting letters of complaint. These had little effect. He had also sat down with the Germans and negotiated to improve conditions, most recently in the summer of 1917. Both parties had agreed to reduce punishment lengths and to begin exchanging some prisoners, but Newton's trust in this process had been eroded by reports indicating the Germans were continuing indefinite detentions and had only just begun returning POWs — and in limited numbers, at that. The other tool available to Lord Newton was instituting reprisals against German POWs until things got better for the British. But this only provoked countermeasures by the enemy, a tit-for-tat "special treatment" that worsened conditions for all.

When it came to Holzminden, Lord Newton and his staff decided that the best way forward was to push for another inspector to visit the camp and to demand that Hänisch be immediately removed from command. Before they could move forward, however, the British War Office and the Foreign Office needed to weigh in on the matter. Reports and handwritten memos were exchanged between the various departments, but any action, low though its chance of success may have been, proceeded at the glacial pace of bureaucracy. And so the men at Holzminden remained there — at the mercy of faithless agreements, without protection, notwithstanding the best intentions of those charged to provide it.

Like most veteran prisoners, Gray knew that help from the outside was not coming any time soon. Returned to Holzminden from Ströhen in mid-December, he immediately resumed the tunneling work started by Colquhoun and Ellis. On one of his first days back, Gray met with two officers at 11:00 a.m. in Room 24, on the ground floor of Block B's officers' quarters. From under a false bottom in a wooden box the men withdrew several sets of uniforms worn by prison orderlies. After donning this garb, they smudged their faces with dirt, the better to look like common-rank prisoners who had just finished a work detail. Then they waited to get the call from their team of lookouts.

One orderly stood watch at the entrance to his quarters, making sure there were no guards lingering in the stairwell or cellars. Once he counted the last guard to leave for his midday meal, he walked onto the Spielplatz and scratched the top of his head. Colquhoun, who was loitering outside the officer entrance, ostensibly reading a book, received the signal. Advancing to the door, he glanced toward the Kommandantur to ensure no guards were on their way to Block B, then hurried inside and straight to Room 24. "All clear," he said.

With that, Gray and the two other officers put on their black caps banded in yellow, stuffed some struts of wood under their shirts, and emerged from Block B.

Other officers in their cabal kept a keen eye on the guard stationed in no-man's-land twelve yards opposite the orderlies' door. If there was any indication the guard sensed something amiss, the men were to mount a distraction.

The tunnelers figured this was unlikely. Roughly two platoons of thirty guards each patrolled the camp grounds. They rotated beats and hourly shifts frequently to maintain sharpness. By circumstance, and to the benefit of the tunnelers, this routine resulted in the same guard occupying the same spot only once every other week. With 550 officers and over a hundred orderlies, the chances of a guard detecting an unfamiliar face entering the quarters were slim.

Gray and his digging partners arrived at the orderlies' door without trouble. On closing it behind them, they waited for another lookout to confirm that all was clear. Only then did the three move down the steps. At the panel wall, they were met by another orderly. He reached into the narrow hole at the top of the secret door and unlatched the bolt. The eighteen-inch-wide door swung open, and the three officers stepped sideways into the dark chamber behind. The orderly closed and bolted the door behind them. He would return in two and a half hours so the officers could get back to their quarters, change, and make the afternoon roll call.

Thin lines of light between the planks were all that illuminated the space until Gray struck his lighter and the shadows of the three men danced upon the low walls. After unburdening themselves of the wooden struts they had smuggled inside their shirts, they lit a few lamps. These were made from empty shaving-cream tins with holes punched through the top from which extended wicks made from twisted cloth soaked in alcohol. They could now see well enough to change out of the orderly uniforms into the plain work outfits they would wear while digging. For Gray, these damp, streaked clothes used by all the tunnelers were anathema, as even in captivity he strove to keep himself spotless and his shirt and pants pressed to within an inch of their lives. The work clothes smelled too, as did the whole chamber — a mix of mud, rot, sweat, dead mice, and stale air. Stifling his disgust, Gray put on the clothing.

In the time he'd been at Ströhen, Colquhoun and the Pink Toes had burned through the iron rods in the southern foundation wall — just up from the cellar floor — by pouring sulfuric acid on them from cups made from molded clay. From there, they had started the tunnel proper. Using spoons, kitchen knives, and the legs of their iron bedsteads, they created an oval sap, almost one and a half feet in diameter and supported by the wood struts. Initially, they extended the tunnel three yards straight out from underneath the orderlies' entrance. The depth was minimal, and the men could hear the voices of the guards and prisoners walking above. Then they veered the sap sharply to the left (eastward) toward the camp wall. To increase its depth, they dug at a forty-five-degree downward slope for roughly six yards before leveling out.

The ground, a compacted blend of yellow clay, dirt, and loose rock, was tough to burrow through, but they still managed to cut about a foot a day. By the time Gray returned to Holzminden, the tunnel was approaching the eastern wall. Their excavated debris nearly filled the entire space underneath the stairs. They had made remarkable progress, and now it was his turn to do his bit, no matter his reluctance to enter the dark hole.

Gray knelt down by the tunnel entrance, pushing into the chasm the shallow washbasin the men used to collect the dirt they tunneled through. Then he followed it, lamp in hand. The earth crowded around him like a tomb.

Since being released after a monthlong stay in solitary, Will Harvey had bunked with several of the Pink Toes in a small attic-floor room. The place was a funhouse of compartments hidden behind wall panels, sliding windowsills, and loose plank floors, all to hide the contraband Mossy, Rogers, and a few other Pink Toes had collected for their latest bid for freedom. Although he had been informed about their newest tunnel, Harvey did not push to be a part of it. His failed escape, then the long punishment that followed, had put him off further breakout attempts.

As winter deepened at Holzminden, his mood only darkened further. There was never enough food, what they did have was almost exclusively tinned, and some of the men were suffering from malnutrition. There was scarce fuel for the stoves, leaving the barracks frigid. Many had already stripped their rooms of any available wood to burn — bedboards, locker doors, even whole pieces of furniture.

Niemeyer continued to harass them at every turn. He shut down access to the bathhouse and the parcel room on a whim. He promised the new senior British officer that he would reopen negotiations with respect to parole walks only to rescind the promise soon afterward. He gave his consent to concerts and theatricals, then retracted it just before a scheduled performance. Then there were his rages, rising from out of nowhere. On the evening of December 14 Private Turner, an orderly, was running across the Spielplatz to the latrine when Niemeyer stopped him in the yard. He asked the young private where he was headed in such a hurry. "The latrine, sir," Turner said. "You may shit yourself," Niemeyer screamed, "or you may shit in your bloody hand. You may shit where you like, but you are not going to the latrine tonight."

In response to such treatment, some of the prisoners fought back. Some engaged in small acts of resistance. A Scottish officer marched out to the bathing trough in the Spielplatz every day, no matter the lack of hot water or how much snow was on the ground, and washed himself while bellowing, "The Scots are a hardy race!" Others crafted an effigy and dangled it from an attic-floor window, a noose around its neck. Niemeyer went berserk, firing at the dummy as the prisoners bobbed it up and down. The glass shattered in several windows before the prank ended. Another officer dumped a sack of potatoes from a window as Niemeyer passed underneath.

The greatest resistance of all would be to escape. Two prisoners tried to hide in the bottom of the trash cart that was emptied outside the camp each day, but were unable to endure the malodorous heap long enough to make their break. Another madcap plan was put together by RFC pilot Robert Capon and Royal Newfoundland Regiment lieutenant Andrew Clouston.

Using dining room shelves, the men constructed a chute, and Capon, formerly an astronomer at the Greenwich Observatory, engineered a seat running on tracks. Shortly after Niemeyer shamed Private Turner simply for trying to answer nature's call, the pair executed their plan. On a foggy night, they extended their cobbled-together chute out the first-floor window of Block B's officer wing. The chute stretched far enough to sit on the barbwire that topped the camp's northern wall. After settling onto the sliding seat with their kit bags secure in front of them, Clouston and Capon were off. They made it halfway down the chute before the seat jumped its track. They pitched off the side and landed almost at the feet of a guard. As well as sending the two officers to the jug (solitary), Niemeyer instituted a collective punishment for the entire camp: both barracks were shut for twenty-four hours and the dining rooms locked. The men could neither exercise nor cook their meals.

Every time Niemeyer foiled a plot, he would smugly gloat. "Gentlemen, you have taught me a lesson," he boasted after stopping a trio of prisoners attempting to escape, one of whom was shot in the wrist by a guard. "I shall not forget it. You need not trouble any more. Good morning."

Harvey weathered Niemeyer's punishments and buffoonery, but because he was uninterested in revenge or escape he had little to occupy his time. The "moldiness" of prison was settling over him again. He rarely took walks in the yard anymore. He did not have the will to shave. He did not write.

Then, one December evening, he lay down on his bed and discovered that his friend Mossy had sketched in chalk on his ceiling some ducks frolicking in a pond. They reminded Harvey of the ducks in the pond beside the Redlands, his Gloucestershire home. For a long time, by the flickering light of a lamp, he stared at the ducks.

And then, unable to contain himself, he started to laugh. Uproariously. His roommates hurled boots, sponges, and other sundries at him to be quiet, but Harvey kept laughing. "What the devil is the matter?" they asked.

"I was just thinking," he said. "What an extraordinarily funny thing is a duck." After the wake-up call the next morning, he sat down and began a new poem — the first in a long while. It was all thanks to Mossy's unexpected gift.

> *From troubles of the world I turn to ducks,*
> *Beautiful comical things*
> *Sleeping or curled*
> *Their heads beneath white wings*
> *By water cool,*
> *Or finding curious things*
> *To eat in various mucks*
> *Beneath the pool,*
> *Tails uppermost, or waddling*
> *Sailor-like on the shores*
> *Of ponds, or paddling*
> *— Left! Right! — with fanlike feet*
> *Which are for steady oars*
> *When they (white galleys) float*
> *Each bird a boat*
> *Rippling at will the sweet*
> *Wide waterway . . . !*

· · ·

At Christmas, Colquhoun announced that the tunnel now ran beyond the wall and would soon be finished. They should all finish preparing their escape kits and be ready in the new year.

There were great celebrations throughout camp for the holidays. The men sang carols, handed out homemade cards, raised money for the British Red Cross, staged a pantomime of "Sleeping Beauty," and ate whatever feasts they could muster. Despite Niemeyer's ban on the sale of wine, Douglas Lyall Grant threw a grand affair supplied with a cellar's-worth of bottles that he joked cost more than a night out at London's swanky

Carlton Hotel. Such was their revelry — clapping hands, stomping feet, howling to the heavens — that at one point they wondered if their party was causing a disturbance in town.

In another room, one of the tunnelers put together a lavish menu using most of his stores of food — signaling his optimism of their soon-to-be-found freedom. Using shaving mirrors for serving plates and blankets for tablecloths, the men had a fine time.

The following morning, Boxing Day, Niemeyer announced that twenty officers, most of them prisoners since 1914, were being sent off by train to Holland. After half a year of promises, internment transfers had come to the 10th Army District. A few slated to leave were part of the tunneling party. Since the sap was almost complete, they did not feel the need to recruit replacements and thereby risk revealing its existence. The men shared farewells at the gate, and many other old-timers hoped they would be next.

But into this cascade of goodwill and good news came a terrible surprise from Niemeyer in the form of a new security measure. Without explanation, the commandant ordered guards to take up permanent stations outside the stone walls of Holzminden. When the guards took their positions, the tunnelers' hearts sank. One guard was standing opposite the east postern gate, at almost the exact location Colquhoun had set for the tunnel exit. Had someone informed on their operation? Could they still manage to escape from that spot if they waited for a shift rotation? Would the guard stations be temporary? There was no intensive search, so it was likely their secret was safe. But the men decided that the shift rotation would not allow them enough time to break through to the surface and get away unseen.

They watched day after day to see if the guards abandoned their new posts; they remained. The consequence was profound. To extend the tunnel beyond this new guard's line of sight, they would have to proceed another forty-five yards past the barren flat field that bordered Holzminden until they reached some rows of rye, which would provide the necessary

cover only come July. It was January now. Without such cover, the tunnelers knew, they risked a bullet on emerging at the exit; they all remembered
what had happened to Morritt, at Schwarmstedt.

At a foot a day of digging, this distance calculated to almost twenty
weeks of work. Such an amount of time would make keeping the tunnel secret almost impossible. One errant word, one slip-up caught by a
vigilant guard — and all would be lost. Then there was the sap itself. A
fifteen-yard tunnel was a manageable affair, but at sixty yards, cave-ins
would be more likely, as would obstructions that demanded a change in
direction.

More important, the time spent underground would become even
more insufferable. The farther they dug, the longer it would take — and
the more exhausting it would be — to wriggle through to the end of the
hole. Such long periods in such a cramped space so far from a safe retreat would be both physical and mental torture. Finally, a sap of such
distance would run short of fresh air. Some in the team lost heart, but
not the once-reluctant Gray, one of its senior leaders. He was determined
to continue. The officers would need more men. Gray turned to Caspar
Kennard.

Fourteen

Caspar Kennard wriggled on his belly through the tunnel. Dragging a sack of tools and the circular basin behind him, he used his forearms and the toes of his boots to move himself through the tight, low burrow. Cascades of loosened dirt fell down into his collar. The dirt stung his eyes and grit lined his mouth. None of this discomfort compared to the rising swell of fear that seized him. He hated confined spaces, and even though every instinct told him to break loose from this burrow, to retreat, he continued ahead.

His life had shifted in such strange and unimaginable ways over the past two years: from ranching in the open ranges of the Argentinean Pampas, to flying in the wide blue skies over England and France, to trading one solitary-detention cell for another. Not one of those cells could compare to the dreary darkness of this sap.

But since recruitment to the secret effort early in the new year, Kennard had managed his claustrophobia. There was no better way out, especially given the chance to get a head start before a manhunt was launched, than through a tunnel like this. His own impetuous run from Holzminden had proved this fact.

On reaching the tunnel face, Kennard lodged his tin-can lamp into the dirt by his side and drew out the gauge created by the Pink Toes to maintain a consistently sized hole. Too small, they would not be able to crawl through without a collapse. Too big, they would waste time and excavate too much dirt that would have to be hauled out and stored away. The gauge was of basic construction: two thin boards — one 18 inches long, the other 14 inches — secured by a pivot at the center. Kennard swung the boards open until they formed a cross and placed them in front of him, the shorter board vertical and the longer horizontal. The ends marked the boundaries of their roughly oval tunnel.

Once the gauge was fixed, he began to dig, using a chisel and trowel to scrape, stab, and pry loose the earth ahead of him. Progress was almost imperceptible, akin to emptying a bucket of water with a thimble. Only the slowly rising mound of dirt and stone under his chin gave any sign of progress. When this mound impeded him, it was time for the basin at his feet. He stretched his arm under his body, rotating at the torso to lengthen his reach. As he moved, the roof and walls littered dirt all over him. He dragged the basin up his side until it lay flat on the base of the tunnel. Completing such a simple task in such a small space was exhausting. Kennard's fear of the walls closing in on him only heightened the strain.

After scooping the mound into the basin with his hands, he screwed his body sideways again to push the basin back down to his feet. Then he tugged at its attached rope so his mates knew to haul it out. A moment later, the shallow basin skittered and danced its way into the darkness behind him. He took a brief rest from the strain of maintaining a constant fixed position on his belly, arms out ahead of him, neck craned. He was sweating heavily, his nerves frayed.

After he had advanced a little farther, he stopped digging and made a brace for the ceiling and walls. These braces were placed every three feet to prevent a collapse. He had brought some planks down with him, nicked from the support boards of the beds in the barracks and cut to size. The tunnelers had taken so many of these boards that new arrivals to Holzminden often found their beds collapsing under them if they sat down too quickly.

First, he wedged a board into the roof. On the floor he set another of the same length. The third plank he angled between the two horizontals, then knocked with his fist until it stood on the left edge of the tunnel. He did the same on the right. An experienced sapper had found that the oval shape of the tunnel was sufficient to carry the weight of the earth above. Kennard could only pray that their reinforcements would hold.

On January 26, 1918, Jim Bennett stood on the icy parade ground, waiting for morning roll call, when a line of police officers followed by plainclothes detectives marched into the camp. They were from Berlin, Niemeyer informed the men, and they would be conducting a special inspection. All prisoners were to return to their barracks and wait in the corridors by their rooms until called. No one would be allowed back into the yard until the detectives had finished. Searches were common at Holzminden, but a quick rifling through their belongings rarely uncovered their hiding places: compasses secured in the handles of shaving brushes; maps folded inside book covers; civilian clothes and money concealed in false bottoms or sides of footlockers. This search, however, was something altogether different.

Bennett was worried. Although yet to determine a path of escape, he had collected a fairly complete kit. Six weeks after sending the coded letter to his family about obtaining a photograph of a Rolls-Royce, a parcel arrived containing a badminton bat. He noticed that the leather binding on the handle was slightly loose. On unwrapping it, he spotted a plug cut into the wood. Inside the hollow handle was a rolled map and a small compass, two items critical for any home run to Holland. If these were found by the detectives, he might not have another chance to replace them; and he would most certainly find himself back in solitary confinement.

Similar fears pervaded the barracks, especially among the tunnelers. The intensive inspection might uncover the secret door cut into the cellar stairs wall. A mad scramble ensued as prisoners tried to bribe guards with soap and wine to pocket their contraband — or at least to allow them to hide it away for the time being. There were also fake scuffles and a hullabaloo to distract the detectives from their job. One prisoner clapped his hand onto a guard's back, sticking a card to his tunic chalked with the message "You know my methods, Watson." As the guard stormed down the corridors, laughter followed him.

The detectives went from room to room, for hour after hour, and uncovered forbidden goods hidden behind beds, underneath floorboards, and on the prisoners themselves. Among the piles of contraband they collected were wire cutters, maps, German money, tinned food, and civilian clothes. While the inspection was under way, prisoners pickpocketed watches, cufflinks, and even a hat from the detectives. They also managed to steal back a few of the sacks of contraband while the Germans were occupied elsewhere.

In the evening, they finally came to Bennett's room. He waited out in the corridor, on edge that his cache would be found. Inspired by the false wall built by Gerald Knight to effect his escape from Ströhen, Bennett had installed a false beam in his ceiling, camouflaging its seams with the same mixture of cornstarch, dirt, and cobwebs Knight had used. The detectives looked high and low through his room but missed the unusual appearance of the beam.

After twelve hours, the search at Holzminden finally ended — the tunnel undetected. Crowded in their corridors all day, given nothing to eat, the prisoners were miserable and on the verge of rebellion. Niemeyer shut them in for the rest of the night. Although relieved his kit was safe, Bennett was beginning to lose hope that he would find a way to escape the camp. Since the recent death of his eldest brother, Robert, who had been an RFC pilot stationed in France, Jim wanted nothing more than to be home with his family.

Normal life, as far as that was possible, resumed at Holzminden the next day.

One prisoner likened the routine there to the diary entries Mark Twain quipped he kept as a boy: "'First Day — Got up, dressed, went to bed.' 2nd Day — 'Got up, washed, went to bed.' 3rd Day — 'Got up, dressed, went to bed.'" The rigid schedule of roll calls and meals, long lines, torments by Niemeyer, and early lockdown reinforced this slog, but not all was oppression for those who were open to the possibilities.

As January moved into February, Will Harvey found his way to that place of possibility. He realized that surrounding him at Holzminden were a multitude of characters from all over the British Empire. "A motley crew," a fellow captive described: "Australians — South Africans — Canadians — New Zealanders — Irish — Scotch — English and Welsh." Every branch of the armed services was there too: pilots, cavalrymen, infantry, engineers, sappers, and garrison gunners. All manner of conflicting personalities was represented. "The intellectuals regard with disdain the flighty scandalmongers. The foxtrot outfit squabbles with the churchgoers, both requiring the same room at the same time for their widely different purposes. Then there are the drunks and the blue ribald army — the studious and the do-noughts — the night birds and the gamesters."

Most of the prisoners had no intention of burrowing a tunnel or concocting an elaborate breakout scheme. They filled their hours in other ways, taking advantage of the small liberties that Niemeyer now allowed them. Some of the men checked books out from the bustling library — its diligent attendant had collected almost five thousand volumes. Others joined study circles to discuss architecture or the evolution of mankind. Some took classes taught by other prisoners practiced in farming, construction engineering, bookkeeping, horse management, and town planning as well as French, Russian, German, and even Portuguese. There were hockey teams knocking about on a half-sized oblong ice pond formed on the Spielplatz, and officers sought to best each other in jujitsu classes. Bridge and poker sessions ran around the clock, often fueled by too much wine, and there was even a knitting circle. Several prisoners became amateur painters and sketch artists.

They also formed an orchestra. Some prisoners were professional musicians who wrote and performed original pieces. "There was a man there who seemed to be able to play anything," one orchestra member later recalled. "He taught me the double-bass and trombone. The orchestra kept me going . . . It kept our spirits up; it would have been terrible if we'd just had to mooch about all day long."

Will Harvey loved music and composed a few pieces himself. He gave a lecture on the "Relations of Music and Poetry." Such was its popularity that he packed the dining hall with two hundred men on two consecutive nights. "Nothing has the power of music to lift one out of one's surroundings," he argued, "and to none more poignantly than to prisoners-of-war does Music bring her valiant reminder of things 'Outside,' the refreshing comfort of a world of realities transcending human chance."

The orchestra accompanied the upstart Gaiety Theater, which Niemeyer finally permitted, perhaps in part because it offered his guards free entertainment. A rotating cast of prisoners-turned-actors from the "British Amateur Dramatic Society" put on variety shows and plays in the dining hall of Block B, pushing together the tables to make a stage. The night after the big search they ran a sketch comedy called *The Touch of Truth*. Other productions included *Home John*, *The Just Impediment*, *The Crimson Streak*, and *The Pigeon*. Besides actors, the theater occupied a small army of prisoners who became practiced stage hands, set designers, costume makers, and directors. James Whale, who would later become famous for his early Hollywood films *Frankenstein* and *The Invisible Man*, got his start in drama at Holzminden. "Pots of paint, wigs, flats, and all the properties in true Bohemian confusion," he wrote. "And yet on show nights they jumped together like magic."

Harvey, too, began to savor this magic — and the antics that came from creating it. One of his roommates played some of the female roles in drag, and Harvey found his friend's unusual effect on the other prisoners hilarious. "They insisted on giving up their seat to me," he recounted to Harvey. "It was quite pathetic to see the efforts made to engage my female interests in subjects no sane POW would consider. How pretty the room looked! And the costumes, so picturesque, weren't they? . . . I had to pull them back to reality by swearing vigorously."

Only in fleeting moments since first being captured had Harvey managed some respite from the "green mold" of imprisonment. At Schwarmstedt he had even given a talk on the best way to lessen its terrible toll,
namely "the comradeship of men." But it took the worst of Holzminden,
and his dark time there, for him to completely embrace his own advice.
Mossy's ceiling sketch — and the humorous poem it inspired — had put
him on this path. In friendship and community, Harvey escaped the
prison at last, without ever reaching beyond its walls.

The arrival in December of Harold Medlicott had bolstered the mood
throughout the camp. The officers believed that if anybody could escape
Holzminden and humiliate Karl Niemeyer, it was Medlicott. A legend
even to the German guards, he had broken out of nine camps already,
never using the same method twice. In his usual bluster, Niemeyer assured Medlicott that Holzminden was escape-proof, a claim that guaranteed any success would be all the sweeter for the camp.

On Sunday, February 10, Medlicott and his partner, Captain Joseph
Walter, were ready to go. Their plan was timed to the second. The orderly
Dick Cash provided the needed wire cutters — he had traded food with
a German workman for the tool. Cash was more than willing to take the
risk: the week before, Niemeyer had cut off parcel deliveries to the orderlies after accusing them of shirking their duties.

At 3:30 p.m., wearing old Burberry jackets, rucksacks looped over
their shoulders, Medlicott and Walter emerged from Block B. It was an
ordinary afternoon in the camp. Officers warmed their hands around the
cookhouse stoves; some strolled about the Spielplatz. Patrolling guards
paced the grounds. Nobody paid the two any mind. In the bright light
of day, they made a hard right turn and crossed the gap between the two
barracks blocks. Without hesitation, they lifted the single strand of wire
that marked no-man's-land. At the barbwire fence, a few feet beyond, they
bent down and quickly cut a hole.

Prisoners spotted the brazen move from the windows of both barracks blocks. At first they could not quite comprehend what they were seeing. Two sentries were walking a beat in no-man's-land behind each block — surely they would notice them. But the officers had carefully timed their movements: at this point the sentries were walking away from each other, headed to the western and eastern ends of each barracks block, their backs to the two escapees. Once they reached the end of the blocks, however, they would turn around and come back. If they turned early, Medlicott and Walter would be lost. There was the guard who patrolled outside Holzminden's perimeter wall to contend with as well.

Still Medlicott and Walter continued. They were now at the northern wall. Medlicott hoisted his partner up on his shoulders, and Walter snipped a hole in the barbwire palisade. As soon as the hole was complete, he passed the wire cutters down to Medlicott, pushed through his rucksack, then crawled through after it. Still, no alarm was raised.

Medlicott threw the wire cutters back across no-man's-land for Cash to retrieve. Then, just as the two guards made their about-face, he scaled the wall like a spider and dove through the hole in the palisade. No alarm was raised from the sentry posted beyond the perimeter.

Outside the wall, Medlicott and Walter calmly stood by the wall, unfolded gentlemanly Homburg hats from inside their jackets, lit cigarettes, and started down the road like two villagers out for a Sunday stroll. What the men didn't know was that a sharp-eyed German guard watching over the isolation cells in Block B had, through a small, high window, caught sight of them mounting the wall. By the time the guard ran up the steps into the yard, the two breakout artists had turned off the road and were heading toward a span of woods half a mile away up an incline.

They were still within sight of the camp when the alarm was finally raised. At first they kept to a fast walk, hoping they might yet be mistaken for civilians. When guards poured out of the main gate and headed in their direction, they quickened into a jog. Soldiers from a nearby garrison, alerted by telephone by Niemeyer, cut them off before they reached the woods.

When he was brought back to Holzminden, to the sound of cheers from the officers, Medlicott looked like a caged animal ready for another break. Niemeyer met him in the yard, flushed with pride. He clapped his hand to the escapees' chests and declared, "All my boys come back to me." When the officers standing in the windows would not be quiet, Niemeyer ordered his guards to fire at the barracks. Nobody was hit, but the crashing glass forced the men to back away. Medlicott and Walter were brought down into the cellars and eventually sent away, not to be seen again at Holzminden.

At the next roll call, triumphant at the capture of the great Harold Medlicott, Niemeyer boasted about his "unblemished record" of no successful home runs to Holland by the prisoners in his charge. But if he thought that the foiled attempt had crushed the morale of any who would dare to be next, he was wrong. As one prisoner wrote to Medlicott's family, the staggeringly brave display only proved to them all that "it was impossible for the Germans to confine a determined man."

Fifteen

In late February 1918 the tunnel plot ran into trouble yet again. The sap was some twenty-five yards long when the men began to encounter roots and flat rocks embedded in hard clay. Progress slowed, and the tunnelers emerged after their shift with cuts to their hands and a brawl's worth of bruises from bumping their arms, legs, and heads against the stones. They suspected they had run into an ancient riverbed.

At the same time, their team was falling apart. Since the Boxing Day announcement about prisoners being transferred to internment in Holland, similar declarations came almost weekly. Often these were contradicted the very next day — names dropped, dates postponed.

Mossy, Rogers, Ellis, Colquhoun, and a handful of the original tunnelers received word to pack their bags. Rather than welcoming the news, they were devastated. They had spent their time in captivity risking death, suffering solitary confinement, and exhausting themselves — all with an eye on escape. They saw the transfer as failure, especially since, under the terms of the agreement between the Germans and the Allies, released soldiers were forbidden to return to the battlefield. Further, although they would be free from Niemeyer and the trials of Holzminden, they would be leaving their friends behind in Germany, among them Will Harvey, who was being moved to another camp, Bad Colberg, on account of his "bad character." As Colquhoun said, "I felt like a deserter, nothing more or less." Given the choice, he would gladly have traded places with someone to remain.

At the end of February, Gray said his goodbyes to Colquhoun and the Pink Toes. They left the sap in his hands, as the "Father of the Tunnel." Now only Kennard and RNAS observer Frederick Mardock remained from the original team. Gray would not only need to figure out how to burrow through the layers of rock the men had encountered, but also to recruit a new band of tunnelers to the effort.

Picking the right men was essential. They needed to be resilient, cool-headed, brave, and most of all discreet. Not even their roommates could know about the tunnel lest word slip to someone who might give them away, either deliberately or inadvertently. Thanks to Hänisch sending the most diehard escape artists to Holzminden, Gray had a long list from which to choose. He entrusted Mardock, whom he had known since Osnabrück, with the task of sitting down with potential candidates.

Quietly, usually at night, over a glass of wine or some treasured brandy, Mardock held his meetings. Walter Butler and William Langran were both infantry officers who had been captured during the first fighting on the Western Front. They were such troublemakers, they were considered ineligible for transfer to Holland. They were perfect for the team.

Next Mardock recruited Sublieutenant David Wainwright of the Royal Navy. Wainwright had been on board the HMS *Nomad,* a British destroyer, on May 31, 1916, when it was sunk during the Battle of Jutland, the largest sea battle of the war. Time and again he had rankled his captors with his escape schemes. Next was Oxford-educated Neil McLeod, Second Lieutenant of the King's Own Scottish Borderers. He had been shot and captured in early 1917, in advance of the Allied offensive at Arras. He'd escaped from other camps twice since then, until being delivered to Holzminden. Lieutenant Arthur Morris of the Royal Northumberland Fusiliers had also proven tough to keep locked up.

Gray then added Robert Paddison and Clifford Robertson. Like Colquhoun, they were officers of the Canadian infantry. They had been caught in April 1917 while trying to take German emplacements during the Battle of Arras. Fellow Canadian Andrew Clouston was also invited to join the team. His scheme to escape by chute over the Holzminden wall might have failed, but he had shown his fearlessness. Mardock also recruited his fellow RNAS pilot Colin Laurence. The two shared the same rare experience of having force-landed off the coast of Belgium before being taken ashore by U-boat. Since being captured with Bennett, Laurence had attempted to escape from several camps. He was one of those who had broken out through the secret panel in Block A but was captured again after becoming lost in a fog.

All told, that made a core group of twelve, to which Gray decided to add a supplemental work party of six to dig, serve as lookouts, and perform other tasks. The only distinction was who would have priority of escape on the night they decided to use the tunnel.

Two of his first selections were both observers: Peter Campbell-Martin and Jim Bennett. In early 1918, Campbell-Martin was shot down west of Brussels. He escaped from a German encampment in a small village the day he was captured, only to be nabbed nine days later while trying to make it to Holland. At his first prison camp, he escaped again. Campbell-Martin and Gray had much in common; both were born and raised in India, and military educated. Bennett was an obvious choice, not least because Laurence knew him to be brave and trustworthy. Although his first tunnel, at Ströhen, had been discovered, Bennett was inspired by the bold escape of Medlicott and Walter to try anything. He was known as a hard worker, and — from his ceaseless walks around camp — he was surely in shape for the job.

One day in March, Gray was in his barracks room when some of the new team came in, back early from their shift. They explained that they had run into a hunk of sandstone whose dimensions they could not measure, although it was assuredly too big to break apart and haul through the narrow tunnel. He needed to come take a look.

Gray hurried from his room, changed into an orderly outfit, and made his way down into the secret chamber. Lamp in hand, he crawled to the face of the tunnel. Poking at the sandstone confirmed it was too hard to chisel into pieces. He bored holes in the dirt around the rock to see how far it went, but he could not find its edge. There was only one solution. They would have to tunnel around the obstruction, no matter how long it took. The news depressed the men, particularly since they were already engaged in the difficult task of cutting through roots and the compacted riverbed. More work, more time, more risk: Gray asked all of this from them, in no uncertain terms. And they accepted. As one of the tunnelers succinctly said, "The turn had to be made, and it was so."

Soon after, a new prisoner arrived at Holzminden: Cecil Blain. Happily and at long last, he was back together with Kennard and Gray. Blain became a key part of the team. He had spent over two months digging a tunnel at Neunkirchen, experience he offered to Gray, who accepted straightaway. If they were ever to break free from Holzminden, they needed every practiced hand available. Reports from the *Continental Times* and smuggled-in newspapers portended that it was unlikely peace would come anytime soon.

Just before dawn on March 21, 1918, Operation Michael was launched. Named after the sword-wielding archangel and patron saint of Germany, the offensive involved 6,608 guns and 3,534 trench mortars from German positions southwest of Saint-Quentin in France. Allied lines were hit with such continuous tumult and fury that the whole world seemed to be exploding around them.

Five hours after the barrage of artillery came the call "Out of the trenches!" Seventy-six elite German divisions hurled themselves on their enemy through dense fog, smoke, and clouds of chlorine and phosgene gas. More than a thousand planes provided air support. General Erich Ludendorff, the operation's mastermind, mustered 1,386,177 soldiers for the attack. "We will punch a hole [in their line]," he told his staff. "For the rest, we shall see." With Russia out of the war, he intended to deliver a knockout blow against Britain and France in advance of the Americans joining the fight in great numbers. Put simply, Ludendorff's aim with the crushing offensive was to win the war.

Within days, the British 5th Army was in tatters, and a fifty-mile gap had been cleaved into the Allied lines. Two hundred thousand men were dead or wounded, ninety thousand had been taken prisoner, and thirteen hundred guns were lost. There was little but "open field" ahead of Ludendorff: the heart of France. Wilhelm II sang the praises of his soldiers, showered medals on his generals, and, over toasts of champagne, promised, "If an English delegation came to sue for peace, it must kneel before the German standard for it was a question here of a victory of the monarchy over democracy."

In the town of Holzminden, bells pealed and children were let out of school to celebrate. At roll call, guards boasted that "England ist kaput." Gathering the prisoners for a speech, Niemeyer was no less boastful. "Well, gentlemen, for you the war will soon be over. Germany will rule the world, and you will return to your homes. Our Kaiser has given an order that the flags shall be hoisted and that we should cheer the German victories." With that, he ordered a lieutenant to raise the flag atop the pole. In conclusion, he said, "Thousands of Germans are going west every day." To his surprise, the prisoners cheered — "going west" was a euphemism for a soldier dying.

Although the news in the *Continental Times* was always suspect, on March 25 its headlines were particularly sobering: "German Offensive Sweeping Success." According to the "Latest News" on the front page, "A considerable portion of the English army has been defeated." Long-range German artillery was bombarding Paris every quarter of an hour. The British were burning French towns as they retreated. "In the Grand Offensive," the paper's editor wrote with faux equivocation, "the victorious verdict is going to be won by the most brilliant leadership and the individual military intelligence of the men. On which side those

qualities stand superior, why, we leave it to our readers to judge for themselves."

Niemeyer claimed that Germany would win the war in three months.
But it was a fool's wish to believe he would show some magnanimity to
the prisoners until then. He seemed impervious to rebuke. Another inspector came in the spring, this time reporting accurately to the Dutch
legation on some of the abuses, but nothing changed. Dozens of former
Holzminden prisoners now interned in Holland chronicled these abuses
in even more scathing terms to Downing Street, but still nothing changed.
Public shaming of the Germans in the *Times* had no effect. Nor did diplomatic calls from Lord Newton to remove Niemeyer and Hänisch from
their posts. Reprisals against German POWs in Britain in the form of limited parole and privileges also did nothing to alter conditions at German
camps. Victory — and its guarantee of not being held accountable for his
crimes — only emboldened Niemeyer further, as it did with other camp
commandants. Escape fever ran high everywhere, particularly as the influx of Allied prisoners captured during Operation Michael overcrowded
the camps.

At Schweidnitz, a camp on the eastern edge of Germany, Lieutenant Colonel Charles Rathborne prepared for his breakout. He fashioned a suit out
of a Merchant Marine uniform. He forged a passport and travel papers,
stamping them with a Prussian spread eagle carved into the rubber sole
of a tennis shoe. He tracked the movement of the guards and found a
moment when only one was watching the wall. A little nighttime boxing
match might distract the guard from his duty, Rathborne decided.

He had briefly returned to Holzminden after being shipped out in advance of the November 1917 inspection visit. Then he was moved again —
to Schweidnitz. There, he declined to join two competing tunnel projects
because he was sure that one or the other would be discovered. Instead,
he aimed to hop the wall, and then, using his fluent German, buy a train
ticket to Holland. An army major was in on the plan.

One night in late March, while a group of prisoners were boxing in the yard under the arc lamps, Rathborne and his partner climbed over the wall. They walked into town and bought their train tickets. Rathborne even won a smile from the girl in the booking office.

They were in a crowded fourth-class carriage, awaiting departure and confident they were in the clear, when a station guard appeared and began moving through the carriage, checking documents. Rathborne handed over his passport. When asked why he was in Schweidnitz, seeing as his hometown was Leipzig, he rattled off, in German, that he was a "commercial traveler trying to sell some musical instruments." This seemed to satisfy the station guard, who moved on to the major.

When the second man stumbled on some responses, the two were asked to leave the train. In a guard room, they learned the reason. The stamps in their passports were wrong. Unlike Schweidnitz, which used the Prussian spread eagle for its stamp, the Leipzig stamp symbol was a lion. On such simple mistakes were the best-laid plans foiled. After a stay in solitary at Schweidnitz, Rathborne was returned to Holzminden. Niemeyer confronted him at the door of his cell in the cellars of Block B and told him that he was back at Holzminden because it was "impossible to escape."

A short distance from Rathborne's cell, three officers were cutting a path through the earth, aiming to prove Niemeyer wrong.

Cecil Blain was breaking his own promise never to tunnel again. As he clawed the dirt to drag himself forward, the flickering candle cast a devilish dance of shadows about him. Too often as he dug, rats scurried across his back or stared him straight in the eye. Worms and a host of unseen insects crawled through his hair and squirmed underneath his work outfit, which stuck to him like a mildewed second skin. And the air . . . there was never enough to fill his lungs as he forged his way around the sandstone wall that had slowed the tunnelers progress for weeks. As he advanced, he made sure to limit the swing of his elbows, the kick of his feet, the rise of his back. One indiscreet move in an unlucky spot, and the walls or roof might give in under the weight of the earth above. There would be no warning, no thunder boom to announce the cave-in. The dirt would simply cover him like a heavy shroud, immobilizing his body with its terrible weight, snuffing out his breath before he could cry for help.

At Neunkirchen he had known well the vagaries of tunneling into the earth. That prison, formerly a community center, was unlike any other in which he had been held. They slept in what had been the theater hall — eighty prisoners in double-bunk beds where the venue's seats had once been. The boarded-up stage provided an ideal location to start a sap unseen. After creating a secret entrance underneath the stage, Blain and several others burrowed through the ground toward the outside wall.

They rigged up a Morse code buzzer in the tunnel that would warn the men to lie silent whenever a guard was present in the theater, and built an electrostatic generator called a Wimshurst machine — for "entertainment," they said — to drown out the sound of their digging. Such was the racket its counterrotating disks made to generate static electricity that an elephant could have stomped on the stage and nobody would have heard it.

With these measures, Blain and his fellow tunnelers dug for two months undetected. It was an awful business. Their sap was always welling with water, and they suffered frequent wall collapses. Fortunately none was lethal, but the scares left the men on edge. They had almost made it twenty-five yards when an inspection rooted them out, and Blain was sent away with nothing to show for his work.

Now at Holzminden, he was back to the muck and the risk. And the farther they bored their hole, the more muck and the more risk the tunnelers had to endure. By early April, the tunnel was almost ten yards longer than the one at Neunkirchen had been, and it felt even longer, given the bends and pitches on the twenty-minute crawl to its end.

Finally, Blain arrived at the tunnel face. Today, he was the number 1 man in the shift — the digger. Slowly, but with a certain rhythm, he hacked with a makeshift chisel at the wall ahead, scraped away the loose chunks with a trowel, then filled the bowl with the excavated earth using a small hand rake. Even though he had vowed never to sap again, there was a part of him that enjoyed it. The danger, the toil, the teamwork — it was an adventure and a better way to spend his days than sitting in the barracks . . . as long as the candle wedged into the wall by his side continued to flicker and dance. If the flame dulled into a faint red, he was in trouble.

Back by the tunnel entrance, Gray was keeping the candle — and Blain — alive. The number 2 man, the pumper, he crouched in a small cave carved into an early left turn in the sap. There he operated what might best be described as a bellows. As the tunnel lengthened past the sandstone wall, the diggers found that they began to grow faint from lack of oxygen. A few grew delirious and had to be dragged out by their feet. Some method to supply fresh air was needed.

Gray and the others crafted a makeshift bellows out of wooden planks and a leather RFC jacket, set on a vertical stand. To pipe the air to the tunnel face, they collected round shaving tins, knocked out the ends, strung them together, and covered them with canvas. Links were added to its end when needed.

Being the pumper was monotonous, arduous work. As Gray heaved in and out on the arms of the bellows, the sound the machine produced matched the pace of his own breath. Kennard stood just a few feet away, inside the chamber underneath the staircase. He held a rope in his hand and waited to feel its tug. The number 3 man in the shift, the packer, he was responsible for hauling the bowl of dirt and stone when Blain was ready to send it back. He emptied its contents into cloth sacks and stacked them in the steadily shrinking space in the chamber. On a good, well-run shift, the digger would have another pile to put in the bowl by the time the packer was ready to have him pull it back.

During each four-hour shift, Blain, Gray, and Kennard rotated through the jobs. Being the digger for too long was simply not sustainable, particularly for the claustrophobic Kennard, who had to summon every shred of will to maintain his calm. The exertion, the foul air, the press of earth in every direction, the threat of collapse, all took their toll. To exit the tunnel, the digger had to snake backward, feet first, inch by inch to reach the opening. There was simply no space in which to turn around.

At 3:45 p.m., the shift was over. The three men shed their grungy work outfits, wiped their skin clear of dirt, and redonned their orderly uniforms. Now they had to sneak back to their quarters. First they had to wait for the all-clear. At this late-afternoon hour, guards often used the stairs, either to bring up supplies from the cellars or to deposit them there. Through the thin breaks in the plank wall, the tunnelers could see them pass. Finally, an orderly rapped on the secret door to the chamber, then announced, "Come out now." The three men unlatched the slide bolt and stepped out through the plank door. At first the light stung their eyes. Then they hurried up the steps as the orderly returned the bolt into place.

At the exit, they waited for one of their lookouts to give them another all-clear. With the single word, "Right," the three moved out, forcing themselves not to so much as glance at the guard opposite the door. If he got a look at their faces, he might recognize one of them as an officer. Onward they continued, to the right, trying not to walk too fast or too slow. They were famished, exhausted, and suffering stabbing headaches from the terrible air and the slowing of adrenaline. They relied on others from their team to intercept and distract any Germans who might be crossing their path from the cookhouse or elsewhere. At last, they were back in Room 24, where they quickly changed back into their officer uniforms.

Sixteen

Whether they were walking the yard, sitting in their rooms, or working their shifts, the tunnelers continually hashed out how, once through the sap, they would make it 150 miles to the border. The distance they would have to travel as fugitives would be far greater given the detours and circuitous route needed to avoid towns, major roads, and other areas. Gray was particularly aware that most escapes fell apart in this phase. Day and night, he considered different plans, searching for something foolproof.

Most of the tunnelers were banding up in teams for the flight to Holland, and Gray was committed to going with Blain and Kennard. He would not do a solitary run again; his own had proved how important it was to have partners who would look out for each other. There were few braver, tougher, and more coolheaded when it mattered than Blain and Kennard.

Travel by train Gray discounted, chiefly because a mass breakout would surely result in Niemeyer dispatching police or soldiers to every nearby station and alerting conductors to confront any suspicious passengers. This left a journey by foot. Moving at night and hiding out during the day limited their chances of discovery, but Gray also knew that there was almost no way to cover such a distance without being spotted and forced into some kind of interaction. They would need disguises and cover stories.

In previous attempts, he and his fellow breakout artists had pretended to be civilians or soldiers. But disguises and forged papers only went so far in an escape effort. If questioned while in enemy territory, they would need to respond in flawless German and have a legitimate reason for being in the area.

Gray spoke German fluently, but Blain and Kennard lacked proficiency. Blain knew Cape Dutch from his time in South Africa and could make a decent attempt at answering simple questions in German, but Kennard was unable to manage more than a few prepared phrases. Knowing this, Gray considered a plan where he would be in the position of speaking for both men: he would act as an officer escorting a pair of privates. However, that plan did not eliminate the possibility that Blain and Kennard would be required to speak if addressed directly by a German officer. Further, the uniforms the escapees would be wearing in disguise would never remain sufficiently clean to pass for military inspection after they had tramped through woods and slept out of doors. No, Gray decided, the three needed a plan that was sure to convince any doubters. Something fail-safe.

There was a lot the tunnelers needed to do in preparation. They needed good maps and compasses as well as food for fifteen days of travel and Tommy cookers to heat meals. They needed warm clothes and durable boots. They needed waterproof sacks to get their belongings across the river Weser. There were documents to forge, clothes to tailor, photographs to take. In the unoccupied Room 83, the tunnelers assembled a veritable escape factory — or, as they called it, "a temple to the Goddess of Flight." They hid items under the floorboards and behind sliding paneled walls, along with all manner of equipment used in their preparations, including locksmithing and woodworking tools, a sewing machine, and dyes, inks, and paper for passes. They had built their tunnel bellows in this room.

By mid-April they were hard at work making passes and creating backpacks from old jackets smeared with lard. In all these efforts, they had help. Since first arriving at Holzminden, Gray and the others had bribed and inveigled some of the guards and other Holzminden staff, turning them into willing accomplices who provided information or special items. Their poor treatment by Niemeyer made them easy turncoats. As one British officer described, when the commandant tired of abusing his prisoners, he vented his "black gusts of bilious passion" at his staff, often leaving them "literally trembling as he flayed them with his tongue." The war's harsh economic rationing was added motivation.

"Letter Boy," the commandant's clerk, was easily charmed with coffee and cookies. His work delivering mail gave him free rein to move about the barracks, and he met almost daily with the conspirators to pass along the latest intelligence or material he purchased on their behalf. What was more, he always knew when searches were coming and where they would occur. The "Sanitary Man" was the only civilian at Holzminden who could go about without a guard accompanying him. In exchange for some cash and something from Fortnum & Mason — the upmarket London grocery store — he would shop in town for any goods the prisoners requested. "The Typist," a young secretary in the Kommandantur, helped them for less mercenary reasons. She had fallen in love with Peter Lyon, a six-foot-three-inch Australian infantry officer who was a member of the back-up working party. Since his capture in spring 1917, Lyon had lost over sixty pounds due to an insufficient diet, but he had retained his good looks. While exchanging love notes with Lyon, the Typist provided sample passes and the paper stock on which they were printed.

Finally, there was Kurt Grau, a well-meaning camp interpreter. He had been stationed in India and once proclaimed, "I do not care for Germany. I do not care for England. My heart is in India." As Gray had served a number of years in the army there, not to mention it being his birthplace, he was able to convince Grau that he could help set him up in India once the war was over. Grau became a friend to their cause.

The tunnelers benefited as well from their continued alliance with several orderlies. Beyond providing access to their quarters, these men were also helping with the escape factory. With his photography experience, Dick Cash was foremost among them. Not only did the officers need photographs for their passes, each needed a copy of a map for his journey. It was one thing to chart a general westward course and quite another to have a map on hand to identify every village, road, waterway, and town they came across. The ability to do so might mean the difference between success and recapture. They had managed to smuggle into Holzminden a large military map that covered the expanse of territory they would cross from which copies were to be made.

Cash made a shopping list: camera, plates, chemicals, printer paper, and a carbide bike lamp to develop the film. With the officers, he started collecting what he needed. Each week, Gray asked for additional copies of the map, because as the sap lengthened the number of officers brought into the fold increased. Two of them, John Tullis and Stanley Purves, were Gray's roommates and provided cover for him during his frequent disappearances into the tunnel. Edward Leggatt, Blain's former escape partner from Clausthal, who had recently arrived at the camp, was also included.

On his emergence from solitary, Charles Rathborne became the senior British officer at Holzminden. Protocol required he be informed of the plan, and Gray also knew the lieutenant colonel was keen to mount his own escape and could stall other attempts that might result in their tunnel's discovery. When notified, Rathborne not only gave his blessing but volunteered to join the scheme and help in any way he could.

Thanks in part to his relationship with the Typist, Lyon had been welcomed into the group, along with RFC observer John Bousfield. Others were brought in to stand lookout as well as to obtain boards to brace the tunnel walls, sacks to pack dirt into, and tins to extend the ventilation pipe. With each additional member, the chance of exposure grew, but Gray accepted the risk. There was no other way to build a tunnel of such length and to orchestrate a well-prepared, properly supplied home run to Holland.

One afternoon, Gray finally struck on an idea of how to execute his own escape run with Blain and Kennard. He was in the tunnel chamber with the two of them, preparing to start their shift. Kennard lit a candle and kneeled down by the sap entrance. Looking into the dark hole, he muttered, "We must be bloody mad." In that moment, Gray had his inspiration. "That's it!" he exclaimed. Blain and Kennard looked at their usually taciturn friend as if he had suddenly lost himself. "Mad!" Gray chuckled. "Mad! That's the answer. It simply couldn't miss!" The two tried to get him to explain, but he said he wanted to think on it some more to investigate its faults and merits. "Come on, let's get on with it," he said, taking the candle from Kennard. "I think I've come up with the answer to our prayers, that's all." With that, he crawled into the tunnel, the first digger of the day.

In early May Jim Bennett was hacking away at a section of earth. He lifted up slightly on his knees and elbows to bring a pillow case filled with his shift's diggings up alongside his body. Every additional foot of tunnel seemed to bring another obstacle. In an earlier shift, he had misread the compass they used to keep on a straight line, and the sap took an unnecessary twist that had to be course-corrected. Water was beginning to seep into the tunnel — not enough to require channeling it out, but the walls were collapsing in parts, and a half-buried tunneler had to be dragged loose by his feet. Then there was the difficulty of hauling out the excavated dirt and stone. The relay system with the basin and rope became impossible. The rope got abraded on rocks and kept snapping, and the basin upended on the sap's many twists and turns. Now the digger filled a sack at the tunnel face and dragged it out with him.

Already exhausted, and anxious for some fresh air, Bennett began his long journey back in the half darkness. He squirmed a few inches backward, set his candle down by his chin, then pulled the cumbersome pillowcase of dirt and stone after him. Squirm. Set candle. Pull. Squirm. Set candle. Pull. He had to make sure not to knock down any of the braces, nor to disturb the tin-can snake that provided precious oxygen to the tunnel, nor to snuff out the light that kept any grip on sanity possible. A half hour — more — passed before he finally reached the chamber under the stairs.

Despite all the challenges, the tunnel now measured roughly forty yards. They were almost underneath the farmland adjacent to the prison. Twenty more yards of digging and they would reach the rye field where they intended to exit. The tall rye would provide cover from the guard stationed outside the fence on the night of the escape.

Bennett's kit was almost ready. Every week more parcels came from his mother — and his erstwhile partner Roy Fitzgerald. He was as fit as could be expected. The tunnel was hard work, but it kept him active. So too did the soccer matches Niemeyer now allowed on the Spielplatz. Finally, Niemeyer had relented on the onerous demands Hänisch had placed on allowing parole walks outside the walls. These strolls gave them some insight into the hillsides — and the breadth of the river Weser, which they would have to cross on their first night out.

Although Holzminden was becoming overcrowded with the deluge of prisoners from the now-stalled March offense, life there had reached a kind of equilibrium. Niemeyer still ranted and raved, charged outrageous prices at the canteen, and sentenced men to solitary confinement for the slightest offense. The prisoners struck back in their own ways. They charmed Niemeyer's precious dog with treats, sending the commandant into paroxysms of rage when his hound would not go to him when called. They refused to frequent the canteen until prices were lowered. They held parties, concerts, and theater productions in the barracks as if they had not a care in the world. As Bennett wrote his mother, "I am in very good health and quite fit to put up with any bad times the Germans take it up in their heads to give us." Despite this conviction, he was eager as ever to be free — and certain that he soon would be, thanks to the tunnel.

Then a run of bad luck and imprudence put everything in jeopardy. First, rumors of the scheme began to filter throughout the camp. With roughly two dozen individuals in the know, and the strange movements of officers in and out of their quarters, keeping their activities secret was unlikely. But it was one thing to hear a rumor and another thing altogether to receive useful intelligence on the tunnel plot. Then an orderly known to spy for Niemeyer in exchange for gifts of wine began asking around camp about where the tunnel's entrance was hidden. Betrayal was too great a risk for the tunnelers, and one night, while drunk, the orderly "accidentally" tumbled down the steps in Block B and cracked his skull. He never made another inquiry.

This risk averted, a greater one followed. In mid-May, on orders from Hänisch, Niemeyer instituted campwide reprisal measures in response to those put in place against German officers in Britain. Parole walks were suspended. All theater productions, concerts, and outdoor games were canceled. Worst of all for the tunnelers, a new schedule of roll calls began. Instead of twice a day at 9:00 a.m. and 4:00 p.m., the prisoners were now forced to gather on the Spielplatz at 9:00 a.m., 11:30 a.m., 3:30 p.m., and 6:00 p.m. These frequent assemblies cut straight into the middle of the four-hour tunnel shifts.

The tunnelers tried standing in for those on shift. When the names of the working crew were called, their mates answered for them, then moved down the line to respond to their own names. They pulled it off for a few days but were sure that continuing the charade day after day would surely see them caught. Instead, they began to rush to and from their digging sessions between the 11:30 and 3:30 roll calls, the only time of the day when most guards were away from Block B due to lunch. Roll calls took at least a half hour and, even hurrying, the teams of three had less than two hours underground.

Their recklessness quickly cost them. One day, after finishing a shift, a working party was rushing out of the east door of Block B without taking the usual precautions, and one of the officers was recognized by a passing guard. The guard tried to stop him, but the officer fled into the barracks through his own entrance. Niemeyer was informed of the incident, and a search of Block B followed, but the guard could not identify the specific officer.

Niemeyer ordered all prisoners onto the Spielplatz. An exhaustive inspection of the orderlies' barracks began. The tunnelers waited for the fateful moment when their secret door would be found. They imagined Niemeyer parading out of the barracks, a victorious grin on his face showing his delight at foiling another escape. Interrogations and punishments were sure to follow. After a long time, the prisoners were ordered back into their barracks. Once again, the secret door had eluded discovery. The tunnelers breathed easy at last.

Incensed that nothing had been found, Niemeyer vented his spleen on the guard who had failed to identify the officer in the orderly uniform by sending him to solitary for eight days. He also closed off the attic floor in Block B's officer section and posted a permanent guard on the steps outside the orderlies' door to check anyone who went in or came out. With this, the tunnelers lost their access point. It was a devastating blow.

The POW camp at Bad Colberg was almost two hundred miles due south of Holzminden. It was housed in a former sanatorium famous for its thermal springs. Will Harvey could not have asked for better surroundings. A villa. A nice room. Open windows. Tennis courts. Pine-covered hillsides with wildflowers and butterflies to enjoy on walks. Freshly shaven and looking years younger than he had the previous dark winter, he could almost forgive the camp commandant, a stubborn, dim-witted fool called Kröner, and his adjutant, Captain Beetz, to whom he gave a free hand, for spoiling the whole atmosphere.

Harvey had suffered from some ill-tempered jailers over the course of his long captivity, and he considered Beetz "the worst man in Germany." In the past, under such a hard regime Harvey would have retreated into himself, but Holzminden had changed him. He labored over his poetry, and he gave lectures, including one on the causes and effects of, and remedies to, war, in which he argued, "What, when all is said and done, is war but that same old savage, stupid mode of settling differences which was abolished and replaced by law in the case of the individual."

Harvey also made it his duty to resist oppression at every turn. One day in early May, guards stopped an attempt to cut through the wire fence.

In their subsequent search of the prison, they found escape contraband in three rooms. Harvey was an occupant of one of the rooms, which he shared with Harold Medlicott and Joseph Walter. The two incurable "jug-breakers" had been sent to the camp by Niemeyer after their failed run from Holzminden. On their arrival at Bad Colberg, the commandant had warned them that if they managed to break out again, "They would never get back alive."

Beetz ordered that the officers in those three rooms report to his office for questioning all day, every day, until the owners of the contraband confessed. Given that the Hague Conventions forbade collective punishment, Harvey and the others decided not to show up. The following morning, Kröner lined them up, demanding an admittance of disobedience that would result in their court-martial. When Kröner demanded to know why the officers had refused to report, Harvey answered for them.

"Herr Commandant," he said. "I am a lawyer. I have read much law, but never yet have I discovered any civilized people punishing prisoners without telling them what they were being punished for. I have not been told." If the order to report daily was not rescinded, Harvey said, he would send a complaint about the collective punishment to the Dutch ambassador in Berlin. Harvey won a reprieve for himself, but the others were court-martialed. Despite his defense of his fellow officers and submission of evidence of collective punishment, the judges ruled against them and ordered a sentence of months of solitary at another prison fortress.

No threat from Kröner would stop Medlicott and Walter. Prior to their removal, on May 18, they escaped. They were caught on the run, and on the morning of May 21, Beetz ordered eight of his most fearsome guards to retrieve them at the local train station. Before leaving, one of them was overheard saying, "Yes, they are two very brave men, but they will be shot."

Later that afternoon, the guards returned to the camp with two stretchers covered in dark sheets—clearly the bodies of Medlicott and Walter. According to Kröner, they had been shot in the Pfaffenholz forest after a "sudden dash for freedom" from the station. The senior British officer at Bad Colberg demanded to see the bodies. If they had been killed in the manner reported, the nature of their wounds would match the story. Kröner refused any such examination. While the guards watching over the bodies were distracted by several British officers, another officer rushed up and threw aside the sheets. Medlicott's and Walter's bodies were riddled with over a dozen bullets and several bayonet wounds. It was evident they had been murdered; Kröner's story was a patent lie.

The bodies were buried, and Kröner refused an investigation. The Germans reported that Medlicott had proven himself "one of the most dangerous characters in the country," and he and his partner were simply shot while trying to escape. Heartbroken over their deaths, Harvey vowed to never forget what the Germans had done and to fight as best he could for all his comrades in captivity.

Seventeen

At the eastern end of Block B's ground floor, Cecil Blain sat in the doorway of Room 34 in a deck chair, book in hand. He was not really reading; his job was to watch out for approaching guards. After a guard was positioned in front of the orderlies' entrance, the tunnelers had halted their activities for a week. The Germans were on alert, and anything out of the ordinary was sure to raise suspicion. During that time, news of the deaths of Medlicott and Walter reached Holzminden via the Poldhu. There was little doubt the tunnelers might face the same end if they too were caught escaping. Niemeyer had proved himself time and again to be willing to use force — either by bayonet or firearm — to make a statement. But the prisoners were undaunted.

Eager to return to their work, they decided on a path that Colquhoun and the Pink Toes had originally discounted when searching for access to the stairwell. At the time, given how long the tunnel might take to dig, the Pink Toes had decided that even the most carefully disguised access point in an officer's room posed too great a detection risk. But now, with only a month's digging left before they reached the terminus at the rye field, the team was willing to gamble. They could not afford to take the time to find a more secure path to the chamber: reports that the harvest was coming early that year, in mid-July, compelled them to accept the risk.

By knocking a hole through Room 34's eastern wall, they would be able to reach their chamber under the stairwell. Although working in Room 34 required them to expand the number of officers who knew about the tunnel, they accepted that risk as necessary. While Blain sat lookout, two officers chipped away at the eastern wall. First they broke through the plaster, then they started into the concrete behind. Over a number of shifts, over a number of days, their work continued. At the end of each session, they cleaned up, then covered the hole with a panel painted the same color as the wall. Bennett was a master at creating these illusions.

After a week, they had made little advance through the thick concrete. Had they been equipped with a sledgehammer, with the freedom to make as much noise as necessary, they could have made quick progress. But using a chisel and hammer, and doing so without alerting the guards to their scheme, was gaining them no ground. The team voted to abandon this avenue.

At the start of June, a storm hit Holzminden with gusting winds and rains. The tunnelers surveyed the barracks and grounds again, looking for a way down to their sap. Proposals were raised and dashed as the men brainstormed their options. More investigations were made. The focus turned to the attic floor of Block B. One idea piggybacked upon another, or was bettered, until an ingenious plan fell into place.

Niemeyer had maintained his ban on officers occupying the attic floor in Block B, closing off any approach from the western stairwell by securing the double swing doors with a metal chain looped between the steel handles and a heavy padlock. Picking the padlock would be too time-consuming, the tunnelers decided, but the handles themselves were fastened to the door by only six screws. Remove the screws, take off one handle, and voilà, they were inside. Replace the screws and handle behind them and nobody would be the wiser.

In the attic, they found a way to bypass the barricade wall that separated their quarters from those of the orderlies: the eaves. These ran the length of the barracks like a corridor under the steeply sloped roof. If they cut a panel in one of the rooms, the eaves were theirs to use to reach the eastern side. As nobody lived in the officer section of the attic, the Germans were unlikely to inspect any of those rooms too closely. To be safe, the team planned on making the opening behind a bed appear seamless with the wall using some mortar and distemper paint.

They also discovered a small door at the eastern end of the eaves that opened into an attic room where some of the orderlies slept. No doubt the original builders put the door there to access the space. The team could — after an orderly scouted the area for Germans — descend the stairs and reach their underground chamber. Not only did this solution give them access to the tunnel, it was a far superior approach. They would no longer need to risk masquerading as orderlies to get past the guards. More important, apart from showing up for roll calls, they could dig day and night. And so they began, quickly making up for lost time.

A lunatic who had escaped from an insane asylum. This was the role Gray wanted Kennard to play on their journey to the border. He could rant and blubber as he pleased, tear his hair out, convulse on the ground, speak in tongues or stay mute and wild-eyed — never would he need to utter a word of intelligible German, nor would he be expected to answer questions. Gray and Blain would pose as the attendants escorting him back to the asylum.

Finally, Gray had revealed his plan, and from his answers to Blain's and Kennard's questions, it was clear he had carefully thought out every detail.

What insane asylum? There was an institution in the town of Vechta, roughly forty-five miles east of the Dutch border. It was north of the most direct route to the Netherlands, but the extra miles were worth it if the route lent credence to their ruse.

What if they were stopped by the police or other officials? Gray would act as the senior attendant, making any explanations in German. If the questioning got dicey, or if Blain was asked to respond to any inquiries, Kennard, the "patient," would provide the perfect distraction. He could stage a psychotic episode, wrestling against their restraints, shaking, foaming at the mouth. They would need to constrain him, perhaps even force a tranquilizer into his mouth. Anyone attempting to detain the men would want to be rid of them quickly.

What kind of tranquilizer? Simple aspirin. Nobody would know the difference.

How would they explain traveling by foot and not train? Kennard was too dangerous to be trusted around civilians. This would also explain the rumpled, dirty state of their clothes. After all, the lunatic had been on the run, Gray and Blain had tracked him down, and they were now in the process of returning him to the asylum.

What would they wear, exactly? According to what Gray had learned from his inquiries, patients at Vechta wore simple gray shirts and pants with peaked caps. As attendants, he and Blain would wear plain civilian suits. All could be easily crafted at Holzminden. And their passes? The Vechta chief of police was named Günther. For added authenticity, they would forge the appropriate papers under his name.

It was clear to Blain and Kennard that Gray had covered all bases. Of all the disguises they had known their fellow escape artists to use, it was by far the most original. Gray would be Franz Vogel, senior attendant at Vechta Asylum. Blain: Carl Holzmann, junior attendant. Kennard: Kurt Grau, the lunatic. Kennard took the name of the German interpreter who had assisted Gray in gathering the information he needed to pull off the ruse. Satisfied with the plan, the three set out to prepare the clothes and passes they would need.

The others in the breakout team were also almost set with their border-run plans. Jim Bennett would go with Peter Campbell-Martin, the twenty-two-year-old fellow observer he had befriended since coming to Holzminden. Their kits were almost ready; Bennett was only in need of some good boots. Through a friend who had been transferred to Holland, he had sent his mother a letter asking if she could send them soon. "I hope you quite understand that it's impossible to do anything here without a decent pair of Boots when we are 150 miles from the frontier."

Rathborne intended to go by train again, this time alone. Needing only to look like a respectable businessman on a cross-country journey, he had little to prepare. He obtained two civilian suits and a leather satchel that held some food, a razor, soap, a towel, a hairbrush, and a hand mirror. To top off his look, he purchased a felt hat accented by a feather (in "true German style," he explained) and borrowed some spectacles from a room-mate.

The other tunnelers banded up in twos and threes and gathered what they could in supplies. None came up with an intricate scheme like Gray's; most spent their efforts on which route they would take to get to the border.

To help with that, Dick Cash was spending his nights in a darkroom he had set up in the attic, making maps for each of the escapees. He followed a slow but systematic process. The military map they had given him was too large to be duplicated in its entirety. The general route they would travel needed to be divided into sections, and each of these numbered, photographed, and printed — dozens of times.

Cash's monk-like shifts alone in the darkroom were laboriously routine. He took a photograph of a section with the camera, then developed the negative on the camera's glass plate in a chemical bath. After it dried, he started making copies of the section by placing a piece of photo paper on top of the plate, then exposing light through the negative onto it. Then he developed and fixed the print with more chemicals and set it to dry. The carbide bike lamp produced a steady, bright, but heatless light that was ideal both for developing and printing photos, particularly with all the inflammable liquids Cash used. There might well have been moments, surrounded in the half-light by photos hanging from clips on string, nox-ious chemicals permeating the air, when he thought he was back in Australia, working in his business, Cissy waiting for him to come home for dinner. But then a creak of the floor or the bellow of a voice outside in the yard wrenched him back to reality — and the very real danger he would face if caught. Of one thing he was sure: Niemeyer would have him shot.

All the same, he continued.

Just as the weather turned warm, escape fever hit Holzminden. On June 6, three prisoners attempted to abscond inside a rubbish bin. They were caught before the cart reached the gate. Days later, two diehard breakout fiends, Timothy Brean and Cuthbert Sutcliffe, made their own attempt, but in a more flamboyant fashion. Sutcliffe, whose nickname was Fluffy, often took the female roles in the camp's plays. Over the past months, he had grown out his hair past his shoulders, seemingly to better play the parts. But he had an ulterior motive: hair curled, cheeks rouged, and dressed like a "girl typist," Sutcliffe broke through the reinforced barricade in Block A and entered the Kommandantur. Brean was at his side, wearing a pristine German officer's uniform and dictating notes to his "assistant" as they headed out the barracks entrance. Sutcliffe sashayed out the gate, attracting nothing more than the admiring gazes of the guards. But Brean was recognized as a British officer, and the would-be escapees were seized.

None of these prisoners had informed Rathborne about their plans, and their attempts made the tunnelers anxious that another search or punishment order would stall — or, worse, uncover — their own efforts, particularly since rumors about a sap at the prison persisted. The men kept constant watch for any signs a search was imminent.

One day, a civilian worker entered the Spielplatz, walking around the perimeter of the wall with some kind of electrical contraption in his hand. The officers were sure he was using the equipment to detect the presence of a tunnel, but later learned that he was simply testing out the conductors on the arc lights. Another day, Niemeyer and his guards stopped by the eastern postern gate, directly above the tunnel, and tested the wire mesh on the fence. When one of the prisoners dared ask why, Niemeyer responded with a smile: "To prevent the escapes, you know."

Compounding this anxiety, Niemeyer had the whole camp riled up over his treatment of Captain William Leefe Robinson — the "English Richthofen" and the pilot who had shot down the first German Zeppelin. Since Robinson came to Holzminden in mid-May 1918, Niemeyer had made it his mission to break the Zeppelin killer. Robinson had rarely seen the outside of a solitary cell, and when he did, Niemeyer forced him daily from his bed at bayonet point, inflicted additional roll calls on him, restricted his movements, demeaned him in front of camp visitors, and whipped him in private. His treatment left every British officer spoiling for a fight.

Given these incidents, and the burden of leading the tunnel project at its most critical hour, Gray was uncharacteristically on edge when one day he found himself confronted by an irksome German attendant in the parcel room. Something about the man's tone, or look, or the way he mishandled packages from home set Gray off.

The two exchanged words, and the attendant grabbed Gray. The level-headed reaction would have been to submit, particularly at such a crucial time as this, but Gray had had enough. He rooted himself to the floor and refused to budge. Shouts of alarm brought a host of German guards. Perhaps to shield his embarrassment at being unable to manage the situation, the attendant accused Gray of brandishing a large knife that had in actuality remained on the table throughout the short scuffle. Gray was hauled down to a solitary cell, and Niemeyer sent him to Hanover for a court-martial.

For once, the scales of justice tipped in favor of a British prisoner, and Gray received only two weeks' solitary imprisonment for "simple disobedience." Through Captain Hugh Durnford, a fellow Anglo-Indian officer who spoke Hindi and who occupied a room in Block B right above his cell window, Gray was kept apprised on the tunnel's progress and was able to relay messages to the team. Gray urged Blain and Kennard to launch the escape once the sap reached the rows of rye, even if he was not yet free himself. The men could not risk a delay.

On one of the walls in Gray's cell, a previous prisoner had scribbled the line "Stone walls do not a prison make. Nor iron bars a cage." As Gray languished in the cellar, looking at those words, work on the tunnel approached its most critical hour.

One night near the end of June, Jim Bennett and his two shift mates crept from their rooms and climbed the stairs to the attic floor. Another officer unscrewed the door-handle plate, let them through, then refastened the plate so the padlock and chain were in place if a guard came by. The three men removed the panel that gave access to the eaves, hurried down the sloped space, and exited into the orderly quarters. At the bottom of the stairs, they slipped through the narrow door hidden in the panel. Swollen sacks of dirt and stone filled almost the entire chamber.

A half hour later, Bennett reached the face of the sap. Although their new entry method provided round-the-clock access, the tunnelers really did need every minute. The "last lap" of their dig had proven to be the most difficult, not only because of the distance from the entrance but also because they hit another layer of stones as they began to gradually angle the tunnel up toward the surface. After a long stint prying these stones loose from the hard clay, then filling his sack with dirt and rocks, Bennett shimmied his way back to the entrance to change places with one of his shift mates.

Several hours later, the three heaved their sacks over their shoulders. With the tunnel chamber packed from floor to ceiling with bags, they now had to carry out their excavated debris. When they climbed back up to the attic floor, they scattered the contents of the sacks about the eaves, then returned to their rooms. The finish seemed close enough to taste.

On June 30, a few days later, the team figured that their tunnel extended into the rye field. By a length of parcel string stretched from opening to end, it measured almost sixty yards. Infantry lieutenant Walter "Basil"

Butler, who had taken to the digging enterprise like a born sapper, volunteered for the mission of pinpointing the exact position of the tunnel's terminus.

Butler scrabbled through the hole while Bennett and several others stood watch at a fourth-floor window in Block B. For most of its distance, the tunnel ran nine feet underground, but the incline at the end brought Butler to within five feet of the surface. He had brought with him a long, stiff wire with a white cloth attached to its end.

Once at the far reaches of the passage, he slowly, carefully, pushed the wire up through the earth, keeping a close measure of how much was needed to reach the surface.

Their hearts beating expectantly, the tunnelers searched the field for any sign of the emerging wire. If the guard outside the wall were to spot a white flag suddenly issuing from the ground, they — and the tunnel — would be done for. After what seemed like a lifetime, the wire finally broke through. As Bennett described it, it "nosed its way up through the earth like some strange new plant." Then it disappeared just as quickly underground. The men witnessing it were crushed. The flag had emerged eight yards shy of the rye.

Eighteen

The tunnelers had no other choice than to keep digging. The rye field was farther than they had predicted, and the rises and falls, twists and turns of their tunnel had thrown off their measurements as well. Now they were fighting time and distance. Any day, the tall stalks of rye might be harvested and their cover lost. Desperate, they burrowed for shift after shift, with a frenzy that left them exhausted and rattled. Not only did they have to excavate another twenty-four feet of earth but they also needed to cut an offshoot chamber to house the dirt that would be brought down on the night they cut to the surface. One July day followed the next, the layer of compacted stones continuing to dog their efforts, and they had only advanced a few yards. They were simply not making the progress they needed.

After two weeks of suffering the heat and small confines of solitary complete, Gray emerged from the cellar more resolved than ever to escape. The tunnelers held a late-night meeting in the barracks to bring him fully up to date. They still had six yards to go to reach the rye field, and it was doubtful they would complete that distance before the harvest. The end of the sap was now almost within reach of the six rows of green beans that had been planted in front of the rye. Although the beans were only two feet high and were in range of the camp's arc lights, their dense bushy leaves would go some way toward concealing the emergence of the escapees from the tunnel. If the men stayed low enough to ground — and by

this time all the officers were experts at that — they could get to the cover
of rye and scramble away undetected. After some debate, the men voted
to revise their exit point and concentrate on getting to the finish.

When not on shift, the men finalized their escape preparations. Cash
had completed his stack of maps, and the tunnelers pored over every line
and marker, scouting the route they would take to avoid the manhunt that
was sure to follow their breakout. Some focused on the straightest path
west; others considered heading north for several miles; others planned
to loop southward first. They picked out bridges to cross, towns to avoid,
and forests in which they could bunker down at night. They all figured
they could travel, on average, ten miles a day. The debate was intense on
where best to cross the border into free Holland.

One officer's escape kit, stored in a host of hiding places around the
barracks, was typical: one compass, one map, one Tommy cooker, one
Dixie cup, nine hard-boiled eggs, five pounds of chocolate, eight sausages
in skins, two tins of Oxo cubes, one tin of chocolate powder, one tin of tea
tablets, one tin of saccharin, one and a half pounds of dried fruit, sixteen
ration biscuits, shaving tackle, soap, mending material, two pairs of spare
socks, one bottle of water, one piece of biltong (dried meat), one steel saw.
Some also had cigarettes, flashlights, German marks, rope, brandied cher-
ries, oats, and other items for what promised to be a long, hard trail. The
men tested their homemade waterproof rucksacks by floating them in a
large tin bath. "Bone dry," one tunneler declared after the test.

No one had prepared as elaborately as Gray, Kennard, and Blain. Disguised as an escaped lunatic, Kennard would not need papers, but Gray
and Blain created identity cards for themselves giving their aliases, the
papers stamped and signed with the name of Vechta's chief of police,
Günther. They had an official document, also with the forged signature
of Günther, explaining the nature of their business. "We hereby certify
that the two guards Carl Holzmann and Franz Vogel (Chief Guard) have
the job of transporting the lunatic Kurt Grau to the asylum at Vechta.
The above lunatic is forbidden to travel by rail or other public transport

and may not meet other people. All policemen and officials are earnestly requested to give all possible help in transporting this lunatic to his destination." They took the same care with their outfits, and even rehearsed scenarios in which they were stopped by police or soldiers.

In mid-July, as the tunnel's terminus neared the bean rows, Niemeyer unwittingly aided them in their preparations by lifting the ban on parole walks. It was an odd sensation for the men to walk casually out of Holzminden when they had been laboring so long underground to be free. Wearing his new boots that his mother had sent, Bennett took advantage of the opportunity. When it came to building stamina, it was one thing to circle the Spielplatz fifty times in an afternoon but quite another to hike across the open ground and into the hills.

On one walk, the guard accompanying them even allowed them to wade into the cool Weser to get relief from the hot summer sun. Some of the tunnelers pushed deep into the water, searching for the easiest crossing point. After all, as one of them noted, "In our parole cards there was nothing down to tell us not to notice things."

Other restrictions were also lifted. After a month of not being allowed any theater, the prisoners were permitted to stage a revue, *Home John*, in the Block B dining hall. The actors were costumed in tuxes and evening dresses, and one, playing a statue of William Shakespeare, dressed in white robes and stood atop a box engraved with the great dramatist's name. Gray played a small role, giving not the slightest hint that he had plans to escape the camp in a few days' time. Officers crowded into every available space in the dining room to watch the revue, and Niemeyer sent interpreters to make sure that no criticisms were made of the German Reich.

During a brief intermission, a newly arrived prisoner turned to the fellow next to him and asked indiscreetly, within earshot of the interpreters, "Are you in the tunnel?" The very utterance of the word sent a shockwave through the surrounding prisoners, some of whom were indeed in on the scheme. The interpreters gave no sign of having heard, nor did anyone dare respond, but it was further proof that the existence of the tunnel was common knowledge. There were whispers about it all through the camp. Even prisoners who were unaware of the nature of the plan knew there was an escape in the offing. Another recent arrival, who suspected Bennett was involved in the cabal and was pushing to be a part of whatever it might be, wrote in his diary, "Expect something big to come off any night now . . . The whole camp is getting kind of anxious." Such talk kept the tunnelers on constant alert for a search, but one had yet to be launched.

There were other risks too, chiefly from prisoners who aimed to make a run for it ahead of the tunnel break. In the wake of the latter attempt, they knew their own plans would likely suffer from a crackdown by Niemeyer. Rathborne made it his mission to quash any such escapes, the reprisals brought by the attempts the previous June weighing heavy on his mind.

Soon after the revue, he got wind of a scheme hatched in Block A. Several officers intended to short-circuit the camp lights at night. In the confusion that followed, a decoy crafted to look like a man climbing down to the yard would be hung from the windows on one side of the barracks, while the escapees cut the wire fences on the opposite side and dashed away. It was a clever idea, but Rathborne instructed its ringleader (call him Livewire) to put a stop to it. Livewire resisted. Rathborne made it clear that the tunnel had been in the works for almost nine months, and that, as senior British officer, he was forbidding all other attempts until it had gone ahead.

Livewire reluctantly agreed but asked to be part of the tunnel breakout. "Impossible," Rathborne said. Over the past several months, any tunnelers occupying rooms in Block A had gradually won transfers to Block B. At this late stage, any requests to be moved might raise suspicions in the Kommandantur.

Rathborne won the argument again — or so he thought.

Far from Holzminden, near the border the tunnelers hoped to soon reach, Will Harvey was planning an escape of his own. In mid-June, he had found out that his name was on the list of prisoners to be transported to Holland. He was sent to Aachen, a mere six miles from the border, to await his transfer. Captain Beetz had been glad to see him go, especially given his role advising his fellow officers during their court-martials. "These lies have been carefully made up for you by Lieutenant Harvey, I suppose," Beetz had growled to one officer whose clever defense had won him a reduced sentence.

At the camp in Aachen, housed in a former technical school, Harvey endured one delay after another. "Morgen früh," the officers promised, but tomorrow never seemed to come because of some argument that the Dutch were taking more British than German internees. Harvey and his fellow prisoners ran out of food from their store of parcels, leaving them to survive on German rations. On parole walks in the countryside, it was torture to see the steeple of a Dutch church so tantalizingly close. Letters from Rogers, regaling him with stories of "oysters and stout" available at all hours at the Dutch hotel where he and his fellow Pink Toes were interned, did not help.

Harvey concocted a plan to rappel down from a window in the camp's second-floor infirmary. He acquired a thick wire cable with which to make the descent. His tattered boots should hold together for the short journey to the border. There was no need for a compass or a map. By the third week in July, he was almost set to go when a decorated British Army captain, Henry Cartwright, who had been in captivity for roughly four years, most of the time spent concocting innumerable escapes, arrived at Aachen. Cartwright was to be transferred to Holland in a couple of days but did not want to give the Germans the satisfaction — nor to be relegated to a noncombatant. Harvey advised him of his own plan and offered Cartwright his cable to use first.

The next night, amid a downpour, Cartwright broke out and made his home run. During the rappel, the cable sheared off a piece of the infirmary window sill. After discovering the damage and linking it to Cartwright's escape, the Germans took measures to shut down any further rappeling attempts. Harvey might not get another chance to escape, but in aiding Cartwright, as in countless other efforts to help his fellow prisoners, he found freedom within. In his own way, he was a breakout artist.

On July 21 the tunnelers scraped away their last horizontal length of dirt and stone. By their measurements, their sap now reached beyond the first two rows of beans. The rectangular offshoot chamber that would store the diggings from their final push to the surface was also complete. At a meeting in the barracks that afternoon, the tunnelers decided on the following night, after lockup, as zero hour. Gray led the meeting. He wanted an orderly breakout. Nothing could be left to chance. Any unusual activity in the corridors of Block B, whether on the officer side or on that of the orderlies, might be noticed by a guard. He wanted no logjams within the eaves, the stairwell chamber, or, worst of all, the tunnel itself. The men would be on edge already, and he did not want a stampede or scuffle to erupt, nor any panic within the sap. Every man must know his place in the line and when he was to move. There was also to be a buffer of time to allow for any delays or hiccups along the way.

The first party to escape would be the thirteen officers (with Blain as the only late arrival) who were part of the original team assembled after Colquhoun and the Pink Toes left. Given Butler's prowess as a sapper, he would go first, to dig to the surface. Since he had teamed up with Langran and Clouston for the journey to Holland, those two men would follow him. The four remaining groups in the first party drew lots to determine the order in which would they leave. The final order thus emerged: (1) Butler, Langran, and Clouston; (2) Morris and Paddison; (3) Blain, Kennard, and Gray; (4) Mardock and Laurence; and (5) McLeod, Wainwright, and Robertson.

Once they were in the clear, the rest of the team would start to move. First off would be Rathborne. Then Bennett and Campbell-Martin, followed by Bousfield and Lyon, and finally Tullis, Purves, and Leggatt.

There were also others to consider: "the ruck." The team drew up a list of other officers who had contributed in some way to the escape. The more important their contribution, the higher on the list their name appeared. Outside of these individuals, each tunneler was allowed to nominate an officer they trusted to be included in the attempt. In total, there were sixty men on the list, almost 10 percent of the total camp population. To maintain secrecy, the men in the ruck would only be informed that the escape was in progress after lockup. Those willing to join would be instructed to ready what kits they could and await the signal to go. Allowing the tunnelers a head start, the ruck would begin to move an hour after the last of the core team was out of the sap.

None of the orderlies involved in the plot, including Dick Cash, were willing to trade Holzminden for a coal or salt mine, which would surely be their punishment if they were caught participating in the actual escape. They would not attempt a tunnel breakout. It would be reward enough for them to know that they had helped the officers successfully flee Holzminden. Humiliating Niemeyer was icing on the cake.

To oversee the escape operation in the barracks, the tunnelers nominated two officers who had volunteered to help. Captain Durnford, Rathborne's adjutant and a friend of David Gray, was selected to manage the list. He would be responsible for alerting each officer when it was time to go. Lieutenant Louis "Swaggy" Grieve would serve as doorman on the attic floor. Nobody would get past the short, barrel-chested Australian without his permission, not least because he was well loved by the whole camp for his Sydney cheer.

On the opposite side, four orderlies would take control: one to oversee passage out of the eaves, one to lead each officer down the stairwell, and two in the chamber itself sending men into the tunnel. All decided, the men went outside to the Spielplatz for what they hoped would be one of their last roll calls at Holzminden.

Commandant Niemeyer paraded through the rows of officers, decidedly less cocksure about the imminent victory of Germany over the Allies than he had been during the March offensive. Instead of boasting that the war would soon be over, he now spoke of how the conflict would never end.

He had good reason. The latest issues of the *Continental Times* chronicled U-boats sinking ship after ship in the Channel, and a British prime minister who proffered only "impossible peace ideas" that Germany would never tolerate. More accurate military reports from the Western Front brought far darker news. Three days before, on a fog-ridden morning, nineteen French divisions reinforced by four divisions of American troops mounted an offensive against the Germans in what would be called the Second Battle of the Marne. Allied forces were spearheaded by a barrage of artillery and a line of tanks. The French and Americans quickly tore through Ludendorff's front. Hounded by the RFC, the generals of the retreating German Army informed Berlin, "The situation is terrible."

Meanwhile, the Spanish flu was ravaging men in both sides of the trenches. By July, hundreds of thousands of soldiers were infected. Initial treatments of bloodletting and cold compresses did nothing to prevent its spread and little to abate the men's suffering from fevers and chills, rapid heart rates, lethargy, coughs, aching joints, and, in many cases, death.

Ludendorff was unfazed, saying only that his armies needed to grow accustomed to being outnumbered by the enemy. As for the influenza, he denied its very existence. With the flu beginning to advance across the German prison-camp system, commandants like Niemeyer would not have that option. But if the flu was Niemeyer's concern, he did not mention it at the last roll call of the day on July 21. Instead, as if sensing something afoot, warned his charges that they would never find a way out of Holzminden before peace was declared. "Well, gentlemen," he joked, "I guess, you know, if you want to escape, you must give me a couple days' notice!"

The next night, without giving Niemeyer the requested two days of notice, Gray gave the go-ahead. The tunnelers ate the heartiest meals they could assemble, donned their clothes for the journey, and inspected their rucksacks one last time before cinching them closed. At 9:00 p.m., the doors to Block B were locked. The men waited for the guard to complete his last check of the corridors and rooms and leave the barracks for the night.

And then the men found themselves facing an unexpected obstacle. Livewire, the ringleader of the proposed Block A escape plot, was discovered to have secreted himself in B. He had heard that the breakout was scheduled to come off that night and was determined to be a part of it. The officers were not about to accommodate him. First, Livewire was not on the list. Second, if it was discovered that he was missing from his own barracks during the final check of the night, an alarm would be raised. Rathborne quickly took control of the situation, ordering Livewire to present himself to the guard on duty and state that he had mistakenly found himself in Block B after lockup. Maybe he had lost track of time, maybe he had fallen asleep—whatever the stated reason, he had to go. Defeated, Livewire heeded the order.

To be on the safe side, the tunnelers postponed zero hour for the following night.

PART IV

Breakout

Nineteen

Tonight!" All through Tuesday, July 23, the tunnelers whispered the same promise to one another. Roused from their beds and herded onto the Spielplatz for morning roll call. "Tonight!" Drinking tea, eating stale biscuits for breakfast, waiting in line for one last parcel or letter. "Tonight!" Another roll call, shuffling about the yard, watching an impromptu game of soccer, spying for any change in the guard, a tasteless lunch. "Tonight!" Reading in their rooms, checking their kits again, debating the merits of the U.S. Army, playing poker, sitting, another roll call. "Tonight!" A gusting wind surged across the camp . . . a storm coming. Another circle of the yard, a stretch of the legs, a pot of coffee. "Tonight!" Talk of crossing the Weser, of the dogs the Germans used for manhunts, of soldiers on night watch in the town. The evening roll call, a final harangue from Niemeyer. Murky brown soup for dinner, since they needed to save their own food supplies for their run. "Tonight."

At 6:00 p.m., Gray assembled the team in the barracks. Their long captivity was almost over, and they were anxious, knowing well the perils that lay ahead. The men needed to be ready after lockup, he said. The halls and rooms were to be swept of any officers who did not belong in Block B. He needed lookouts at the entrance to deter Livewire or any other interlopers. There could not be another postponement.

The tunnelers left to prepare, and Gray met quickly with Durnford. The two were of similar age and experience and shared a particular style:

well-trimmed mustaches and a military bearing. A decorated officer of the Royal Field Artillery, Durnford was captured in the Ypres Salient after getting lost amid the ruined, featureless landscape in August 1917. He had known about the tunnel for months but considered it nothing but a fool's errand, sure to be discovered. Now that it was finished, he regretted not being on the list to escape, but he swore to do everything he could to see it come off smoothly. "If B house harbored no aliens that night," Gray told him, "the escape would take place." Durnford left to inform Swaggy Grieve, the hulking Australian guarding access to the eaves.

As the sky darkened and clouds swept across the rising moon, Gray waited with Blain and Kennard in his room. The three passed the time until lockup, examining their maps again, going over their plan for the first few hours of their run to Holland. Blain turned over and over in his hand his silver cigarette lighter, on which he had prematurely inscribed "Holzminden — Escaped July 22." Kennard wandered about the small room, practicing for his role as the madman. He rolled his eyes, jabbered incoherently, blew spit bubbles, and whimpered like a wounded animal. "Oh, shut up and listen for a minute!" Gray interrupted at one point, drawing his attention back to the maps. The tunnel's leader was feeling the tension just like all the other men.

Throughout Block B, officers were nervously waiting. They ate what food they could stomach and smoked cigarettes. Some drank a glass of wine to bolster their courage. Others refused, believing a drink might dull their senses when they most needed their wits about them. Bennett remained sober. In his mind, he played out the journey through the tunnel, then the swim across the Weser. Once on the opposite bank, he hoped to navigate quickly — and quietly — through the surrounding fields of corn and rye, eluding any pursuers. Rathborne strode the barracks hallways and checked with the watch at the entrance to ensure there were no more surprise visits from Livewire. He stopped in to say goodbye to Durnford. When he put on his feathered cap and glasses to show his disguise, Durnford praised his look as "wonderfully Teutonic." Then he wished him good luck.

Blain and Kennard returned to their own bunks shortly before 9:00 p.m. At the turn of the hour, the door to Block B was shut and locked on the inside by the lone guard. No matter how long the officers had been prisoners, that resonating clang never lost its impact. Rathborne confirmed that there were no interlopers inside the barracks. One hour more to wait. They put on their escape outfits, layering their pajamas over them. These would keep their clothes clean on the crawl through the tunnel.

All the while, they kept an ear out for the passing footsteps of the guard making one last round of the barracks. If they heard him entering any of their rooms, the tunnelers knew to jump into bed and throw their blankets up over their clothes.

The minutes ticked away. The wind continued to gust, and the occasional flash of lightning illuminated the sky in the distance. Rain had yet to fall, but surely it would soon start. If they did manage to break out from the tunnel, the storm would leave them soaked to the bone before they even reached the Weser. Finally, at 10:00 p.m., as was his routine, the guard finished his last check and exited the building. The door locked shut again.

Fifteen minutes later, Gray informed Durnford that all was clear. Time to go. Durnford made his way through the corridors, alerting those in the ruck that the escape was moving ahead and that each man should be ready when his time came. Some tried to cajole and bribe him into revealing their place on the list, but Durnford was incorruptible.

Boots in hand, the better to keep quiet, and kit bags looped over their shoulders, the core group of tunnelers crept out of their rooms. Together, they climbed the stairwell to the attic. The handle of the swing doors was removed, and they entered into the attic of Block B. In the room fitted with the hidden panel, the team assembled one last time. There was no need for speeches, nor last-minute instructions. They wished one another well—Good luck, Godspeed—then Butler disappeared into the eaves. Outside, the storm howled. As one officer described, thunder cracked and boomed like the "finale of a gigantic orchestra." The tunnelers could not have asked for better weather to mask their movements on breakout night.

A religious man, Butler muttered a short prayer before pushing his kit bag into the tunnel and following it in. The only other officers in the chamber, Andrew Clouston and William Langran, would join him in thirty minutes, giving him time to cut through to the surface. The first stretch, with its downward slope, was easy going. Scores of times he had crawled his way through the sap, but this time was different: the others were depending on him like never before. He needed to move quickly, and his burrow to the surface must escape detection from the guards. Otherwise, nine months of heartache and labor would amount to nothing. Worse still, it might get them all shot. Kit in one hand, candle in the other, he managed to squirm through the tunnel with efficiency. He knew every turn, dip, hollow, and rise by heart. He knew when to duck his head or worm sideways to avoid a protruding stone. He continued to pray as he went.

At the tunnel's end, he put his kit to the side. Sweat soaked his hair and collar. Without pause, he started digging a path straight upward. The trowel made easy work of the soft dirt and clay, which poured down on top of him—coating his hair, covering his eyes and ears, trickling down his neck—yet he paid no mind to the discomfort. The quicker he bored to the surface, the more time they would all have to get away from Holzminden. Any delay would mean fewer officers in the ruck would be able to make the escape.

Finally reaching the surface, Butler took his first breath of fresh, free air. At best, his hole was only six inches in diameter, but it was a start. Rain pelted down, and the light from the camp arc lamps shone brightly.

He dug faster now that he could kneel up in the tunnel and lengthen his arm, energized by the fact that freedom was within reach.

Langran and Clouston joined him as planned, and the two of them packed the earth piling up around Butler into the offshoot chamber. Clean air poured into the tunnel from the expanding exit. By 11:40, the hole was wide enough to climb through to the surface. First, Butler pushed his kit out of the tunnel into the field. Then, using his arms and feet to brace the side of the six-foot-deep hole, he slowly rose. His hair was sopping, and rain mixed with dirt poured down his grimy face. As he eased his head out of the tunnel, he was pleased to discover that the exit was just past the first two rows of beans. He emerged into the field. There was no time to rest before his partners joined him.

He crawled forward on his belly to the first row of beans. Hiding amid the dense leaves, he searched for the guard stationed outside the wall. The arc lamps and the shadows their light cast made it hard to see. As far as Butler knew, the German might be standing still, looking directly toward the tunnel exit, having detected movement of some kind. Then the guard coughed, and Butler saw him against the darkness of the wall. He was pacing to and fro, obviously unalarmed. In that second, the rain halted, the clouds overhead gave way, and moonlight shone down on the field.

Minutes before, Private Ernest Collinson, an Army Service Corp driver, had been staring toward the bean rows from the first-floor window of Block B's orderly quarters. For over half an hour he had searched through the darkness for any sign of Butler. By now he should have cut through to the field. Perhaps, Collinson thought, he had missed him because of the lights and the sheeting rain. Butler might already be in the rye field or moving toward the Weser, but he had no way of knowing for sure. And Gray and his team needed to know definitively that Butler had made it out before they proceeded into the tunnel themselves. They were depending on Collinson.

Gradually, the moon broke through the clouds. There, amid the bean rows, he spotted a hunched shape. Butler. In the next moment, the figure crawled toward the stalks of rye, followed soon after by two others.

Collinson hurried from his observation post toward the stairwell. In his socks, he barely made a sound. On the attic floor, he clambered through the small door, quickly crossed the eaves, and knocked on the two-foot-square panel leading into the officers' quarters. Grieve pulled aside the panel. Butler made it, Collinson reported. Little else needed to be said.

The next batch of tunnelers began filing into the eaves. "Mr. Blain," Collinson said, impressed by the sight of the Blain's civilian suit underneath his pajamas. "You're all togged up like a proper toff." Blain widened his arms, as if offering an embrace. "Dance?" The officers laughed quietly, then continued down the eaves. Collinson followed them through into the orderly quarters. When he offered to lead them down to the entrance chamber, Kennard said, "Don't bother, Collinson, we'll see ourselves out."

They shook hands, and Gray thanked Collinson for his efforts on the men's behalf. No doubt Dick Cash was also there to see them go, now with a new set of teeth thanks to a collection the officers had taken up to pay a local dentist. "Go on with you," Collinson said. As the tunnelers moved toward the stairwell, Collinson called out, "The best of luck to all of you —and don't forget to drop my missus a line when you get home."

"Chocks away," Blain said, tossing his kit ahead of him into the hole, but the bravado he had maintained throughout the evening quickly dissipated as he crawled in after it. He was the sixth man into the tunnel. Kennard followed, then Gray. Those who had gone before them had left a few tin-can lamps burning along the path, but given the passage's many kinks and turns, the three crawled mostly in the pitch-black. They did not want to waste time by holding candles of their own.

In the lead, Blain kept to a good pace. He pushed his rucksack ahead of him. Wriggled a few inches on his elbows. Pushed. Wriggled. When his jacket caught on a rock or when he slowed to take a breath, he felt Kennard brush up against his feet with a push of his own bag. During one stretch, which was illuminated by candlelight, Blain suddenly found himself staring straight into the face of a rat. Its eyes looked like black beads. He had encountered his share of rodents in the tunnel, but they still sent shivers down his spine. Before he could brush the rat away with his arm, it disappeared into the darkness ahead of him, no doubt its senses alive to an exit into the field.

As he continued, he found himself panting for breath, and his arms grew heavy from pushing his kit ahead of him. In all his shifts underground, the tunnel had never felt so long nor looked so ominous. The shadows cast about the narrow, misshapen bore resembled monsters waiting to attack. He wanted nothing more than to be free of it. Then he saw, up ahead, a light shining down into the tunnel. The Germans must have found the sap exit, he thought. They were lost. He would have scrambled away had there been anywhere to go. Instead, he lay flat and motionless as a stone.

"What's up?" Kennard asked, his voice little more than a muffled mutter. His claustrophobia was making him more anxious than ever. Blain angled his head to the side, his eyes adjusting enough to the light to see that it was simply the glare of the arc lamps through the hole. But he found himself immobilized all the same. Thoughts of the Pink Toes at Schwarmstedt overcame him, thoughts of Bill Morritt, shot as he emerged from underground.

Behind him, Gray added his muffled voice to the demand to know what was the problem. Kennard thumped the back of Blain's boots. Finally, the young pilot wrenched free and moved ahead again, his heart beating like a drum in his chest. After several more feet of crawling, Blain reached the tunnel exit and breathed a cool draft of fresh air. He rose to his knees, then to his feet, in what he figured might well become his vertical grave. Only the encouragement from Kennard and Gray kept him moving.

Blain eased his kit out into the field, then squirmed himself upward. As his head rose out of the tunnel, he expected to hear the crack of a gunshot. When he was met only by the patter of raindrops, he finally caught his breath again and calmed. It was almost 1:00 a.m. Sixty yards away, Holzminden was cast in a ghostly pallor of white by the arc lamps swinging in the wind. The guard paced back and forth by the wall, his rifle tucked under his arm, his coat collar tight around his neck. The wind blew from the southwest, providing them audible cover for movement. Taking care anyway, he eased himself slowly up into the field. He kept his body low as he scrambled through the rows of beans.

Then he stopped and looked back toward the tunnel exit. Kennard, then Gray, then the others behind them emerged in close succession. It was like their heads and feet were almost connected. They resembled to Blain a huge, mud-splattered crocodile, and he almost laughed at the curious but exhilarating spectacle.

As he reached the stand of rye, some fallen stalks rustled beneath him. Even with the steady beat of rain, the sound met Blain's ears like a series of small detonations. He waited at the edge of the field for Gray and Kennard to reach him. In whispers, they debated advancing into the rye versus crawling along its edge until they were far enough away from the camp. Taking charge, Gray made the decision to proceed directly through the stalks. It was the quickest way, and he was sure that the rainfall and wind would sufficiently drown out the noise of the stalks underfoot.

The three threaded their way into the rye field, with Blain convinced the guard would soon hear their movements and set the dogs on their trail. When no cry of alarm was raised, he relaxed enough to straighten up from his crouched walk and hasten his pace.

After traversing the rye field they came to the main road that ran between Holzminden and Arholzen, the nearest town to the northwest. They knew, from the reports of their German accomplices, that during the night the police patrolled the stretch of road on bicycles, and they waited at the side of the road until they were sure the coast was clear.

Then Gray led them northward through more fields of rye and corn, to the top of a low hill. They dropped their rucksacks to the ground and took a brief rest. They had been on the run for a half hour. In the distance, the town of Holzminden looked to be floating in a sea of surrounding darkness. They could not distinguish the two barracks blocks, which seemed to blur together as one. The three officers savored their freedom at last.

They were masters of their own fate again. The air they breathed never tasted fresher; the hunk of Caley's Marching Chocolate never sweeter.

"Bet Niemeyer wouldn't be sleeping so well if he knew where we were," Blain said.

"Let's hope nothing disturbs his slumbers until morning," Kennard replied.

"Just let's make sure," Gray said, "we never see that bastard again."

They let the thought linger, then tramped down the hill to the Weser. The river served as a natural barrier to any escape westward. Bridges over it were routinely patrolled, and its fast, deep waters had delayed — or altogether foiled — earlier runs from Holzminden. They needed to cross to its opposite bank before first light of dawn, at roughly 4:30 a.m. Otherwise, they were sure to be recaptured.

Twenty

Charles Rathborne thrust his body into the tunnel, the fit almost as tight as a cork pushed back into a bottle. The already stout officer had been made stouter by the pair of suits he wore: one was to be thrown away after the trip through the tunnel; the other was his disguise — a German civilian on a cross-country train journey.

He had only once before been down into the sap and had never made the passage through its full length. He was quite unaccustomed to the claustrophobic environment and the effort it took to crawl through. The fact that his face was almost level with the dirt floor only deepened the horror. Nonetheless, he kept pushing himself forward, grunting and sweating as he went. Behind him, Jim Bennett was like a racehorse stalled behind a mule, but there was no way around the senior officer, nor could Bennett do anything about the walls and roof of the tunnel being abraded by Rathborne's movement.

Alerted to the "all-clear" at midnight, Bennett and Campbell-Martin had hurried down through the orderly quarters and into the chamber. They were the fifteenth and sixteenth men into the tunnel. Despite Rathborne's troubles, he was not the first to disturb the already marginal structural integrity of their burrow. With their kits and their eagerness to reach the exit, some of the officers who had gone before had knocked out struts, loosened rocks that had been dug around long before, and left chunks of dirt (as well as tins of food fallen from their rucksacks) along the path.

Once the ruck arrived, the state of the tunnel would surely deteriorate further.

After over an hour in the tunnel, Rathborne finally squirmed free. Stretched out in the bean rows, he was certain he could hear the sentry breathing. Bennett rose from the sap after him, followed by Campbell-Martin. They wished each other well, then Rathborne wriggled on his belly into the rye stalks. Once deep inside the field, he lifted up to his hands and knees and continued on. Such was the denseness of the cornfield beyond that he found himself almost trapped in the midst of its narrow rows. Finally he broke free, crossed a cabbage field, and brazenly hiked alongside the road that led south from Holzminden. If stopped, he believed he had a good chance of talking his way out of the situation. The others were headed west, the direction in which Niemeyer, when alerted to the escape, would immediately begin the search. Rathborne had decided to go the opposite way. He planned to catch the first of several trains toward Holland in Göttingen, thirty-five miles to the southeast.

Bennett and Campbell-Martin made their way through the same rye and corn fields as Rathborne had traversed, but traveling much more quickly and in the opposite direction. Their route might be the first to attract a search party's attention, but they intended to move at such a pace that no one had a chance of catching up with them.

In Block B, Durnford made his rounds, alerting members of the ruck about when they could take their turn at escape now that the core team of tunnelers were out. At 12:45 a.m., he knocked at the door of thirty-four-year-old Jack Morrogh of the Royal Irish Regiment, number 22 on the list. "Your turn, Major, and God bless you," Durnford said. Morrogh thanked him and rushed up the two flights of stairs to the attic.

In the attic room, Grieve told the major he would have to wait a bit longer. Someone was stuck in the tunnel. Morrogh hunkered down beside the dormer window, listening to the gale outside and the intermittent rain. Now and again, he looked out the window to watch the German guards on their rounds. Little did the one stationed outside the wall know that at that very moment there were men tunneling through the earth directly under his feet.

"All clear," an orderly announced from the eaves. Grieve allowed Morrogh and several other officers to pass. They crept along the length of the barracks, down the stairs, and into the chamber. After shaking hands with a fellow Irishman, Corporal Mackay, Morrogh entered the tunnel for the first time. Following a quick descent of the initial slope, he found himself in the pitch-black. The tightness of the space did not surprise him as much as the noise. The long snake of men ahead of him — their heavy breathing, wriggling bodies, clanging kit bags, and curses — made for an awful din. He wondered how the guard above could fail to hear them.

Morrogh inched forward. The passage was in sorrowful shape. He wrestled past broken struts and piles of dirt and stone. Just as he began to gather some kind of rhythm, using his grip on his rucksack to pull himself forward, he felt like he hit a wall. Then the wall started to move. The man in front of him was clearly trying to worm his way backward. Morrogh tried to shout at him, but, with his face inches from the damp earth, his voice was muffled. Stuck and panicking, the man ahead thrashed about, kicking his legs and twisting back and forth. Meanwhile, the officer behind pushed at Morrogh's heels. Caught between the two, Morrogh was terrified.

Finally, the individual ahead jerked his way free, and Morrogh began crawling again. He was tired, desperate for some fresh air, and harried by the continuous noise of men. He managed only a few feet before he encountered a large stone blocking his path. The officer in front must have dislodged it in his panic. Using his rucksack, he shoved the stone a few inches forward, hoping he might find the place on the tunnel's wall where it had broken loose. If it had fallen from above, there was no hope.

Bracing his legs, he thrust against the stone again. Then again. Then again. He was damaging the sides of the tunnel, but he had no choice. Feeling with his hands, he discovered the slot where the stone had separated from the wall. With one last shove, he returned it to its place. The tunnel was disintegrating with the ruck's every movement. Morrogh feared he might never find his way out.

David Gray scanned the banks of the Weser for the narrowest point to cross. The storm had tossed and roiled the black waters, which looked like an ocean between them and the opposite shore. As he scouted ahead, Kennard spotted a dilapidated fence bordering a nearby field and had an idea. He started breaking off slats. Blain joined him. Roped together, the wood could serve as a makeshift raft for their clothes and rucksacks. By the time they had gathered enough pieces, Gray had found a point to begin their swim. It would still be at least 140 yards across to the other bank.

The three stripped down to their underwear, bound their clothes up, and placed everything on the roped-together fence slats. Their watches, before they, too, went into their rucksacks, read 2:15 a.m. The men were already soaked through by the rain when they slipped into the tepid water. The shifting clouds overhead cast the river alternately in darkness and moonlight. Fearing a patrol, they waited for cloud cover before pushing away from the bank.

They swam furiously for the other side, each holding onto a side of the raft to keep it steady. Waves swept over their heads, and by the movement of the trees on the opposite shore, they could tell that the currents were dragging them swiftly downstream. On they went, kicking their legs and swinging their arms. Halfway across, they were already breathing heavily, their limbs weary.

A whitecap almost pitched over their raft, but they managed to keep it afloat. Desperation and nothing else drove them to reach the western shore. Finally they climbed onto the banks and collapsed with relief.

After taking a moment to recover from their exertions, they emptied the raft. The wind and rain chilled them to the bone as they dressed again in their damp clothes. Kennard dragged the raft up the bank a few hundred yards to throw off the German bloodhounds that were sure to follow on their trail. Gray suggested they march as far north as possible that night, believing that the search area would concentrate on the forests west of the Weser. Blain and Kennard agreed. At first, they followed the road bordering the river. Although it ran a sharp, serpentine course, Gray figured the extra distance on the road could be covered far faster than tramping a direct line northward through forests and muck-mired fields. Gray and Blain both carried heavy rucksacks with their food stores (biscuits, black bread, Oxo cubes, and tins of ham and tongue) and other key supplies. Kennard carried their reserve kit, containing extra clothing, tobacco, and chocolate. If they happened on anyone along the way, he would have to ditch it quickly. A madman on the run would not be expected to have provisions.

By 3:30 a.m. they had circumvented Heinsen. Outside the town, they shed their pajamas and stashed them in some reeds. They had managed to keep their outfits underneath clean. The small village of Polle was empty as they walked down its main street. A dog barked at their presence, but otherwise they passed through unnoticed.

A half hour later, they reached another riverside hamlet, Brevörde. Its scattering of old cottages, their walls bulging from settlement over time, looked dark and abandoned.

With dawn approaching, they marched a little farther north before veering off the road into some thick woods to hide out during the daylight hours. They were roughly nine miles from Holzminden, a distance they hoped gave them a sufficient head start after the alarm was raised. The men ate a light meal—a tin of ham and some black bread—and smoked cigarettes. Blain got a good chuckle when he shared with them his observation of how the men streaming out of the tunnel had looked like a crocodile emerging from the earth. He volunteered to take the first watch.

Exhausted, Gray and Kennard assented and went quickly to sleep. Blain stared out into the surrounding darkness of the woods.

When Bennett and Campbell-Martin arrived at the Weser, they came upon John Bousfield. In the scramble outside the tunnel, Bousfield had lost his traveling companion, Peter Lyon, and reluctantly decided to go on ahead alone. The three officers undressed and bundled their clothes into their rucksacks, which they tied to their waists with ropes. Then they began across the rough waters.

An unsteady swimmer at best, Campbell-Martin soon found himself overwhelmed by the fast current. Together, Bennett and Bousfield dragged him to shore. After dressing, they struggled through a cornfield, following the same route to Heinsen that Gray had chosen. Once past the town, they abandoned the road and headed into the forested hills to the west.

Although Bousfield had been a champion three-mile runner at Cambridge, he was hard pressed to maintain the pace set by Bennett, whose long, loping stride seemed to eat up the ground underneath him. After a few miles, as daylight crept over the eastern horizon, he finally slowed. Bousfield argued that they would have a better chance at evading discovery if they bedded down in some farmland. A field of rye would provide superior cover, he argued, and they would be alerted to the presence of any pursuers by the crackling of their footsteps through the stalks. Convinced, the three hiked onward until they found a stretch of rye.

Six miles south of Holzminden, Charles Rathborne bedded down alone in a fir plantation, next to a spring of water. He watched the sun break into the sky before resting his head on his small bag and falling into a fitful sleep.

There was trouble in the tunnel. Lieutenant Edgar Garland, a New Zealand–born pilot, was halfway through when the man in front of him stopped moving. Garland rattled his boot, but the officer did not react.

Perhaps he had fainted, Garland thought. He had a flashlight, but its narrow beam did not penetrate far in the twisting burrow. "What's the idea?" he shouted. "Having a rest?"

"The tunnel has fallen in, and they are trying to clear it," the man in front finally called back. "It will only take a few minutes."

Garland rested his head down in the dirt and tried to calm his breathing. The air was already bad from all the men crowded down in the hole. If there was a blockage, it was sure to get worse. Moments later, he felt someone jamming up against his feet. The chain of officers behind had caught up. "What's wrong?" a voice at his feet gasped weakly. Garland explained, confident that the obstruction would soon be cleared and he would begin his home run to Holland. But the obstruction would not be cleared.

Several feet shy of the exit, the sap had caved in completely. A number of officers had made it through, including Jack Morrogh, but now dirt and stone had cascaded down the slope and rendered it impassable. Major Marcus Hartigan, a thirty-eight-year-old veteran of the Boer War and next in line to break out, only just managed to scramble backward before being buried alive. His desperate attempts to reopen the face of the hole with his hands in the inky darkness were fruitless. There was too much earth blocking his path. If he was to survive, then the men behind him needed to abandon their escape and push themselves back out of the tunnel before oxygen ran out. There were more than a dozen of them in the hole.

Back at the sap's midway point, Garland waited. Fifteen minutes. Then half an hour. Nobody was moving, and from the gurgling sound echoing through the sap, the men were starving for oxygen. With his own arms weakening, he was sure he was suffering the same. Now and again he flicked on his flashlight for some relief from the impenetrable darkness. Thoughts of death pervaded.

He had almost lost hope when he sensed the officer behind him finally retreating. Garland followed, hauling his rucksack behind him. Time and again, the line halted. The men's strength was depleted, and their coats and kits kept snagging on rocks. After much strain, Garland reached the long slope that ran up toward the tunnel entrance. He might as well have tried to climb a cliff backward. Then someone grabbed his legs and pulled him out.

Alerted to the cave-in, Durnford and Grieve had organized a chain of men to haul bodies from the tunnel as they neared the chamber. The first concern was to get everybody out alive. The second was to do so before 6:00 a.m., an hour fast approaching, when a guard would unlock the doors and send the orderlies out on their duties. If they failed to clear the sap, and if men were still moving about the orderly quarters, they risked the breakout being discovered long before the morning roll call at 9:00 a.m. Three hours could prove the difference between escape or recapture for those officers who had safely made it out.

Some in the ruck had fainted or were too weak to evacuate the tunnel on their own. Garland volunteered to drag them out. With great effort and risk of falling victim to another collapse, he crawled deep into the tunnel again. He managed to muscle one officer after another back through the hole.

Shortly before 6:00 a.m., he had helped out all but Hartigan and the officer behind him. He and a few others remained in the chamber to retrieve them while the orderlies and officers snuck back to their rooms and removed any signs of their nighttime activity. From the windows, Durnford watched for any hint that the breakout had been discovered, but the guards walked their normal rounds. The men might yet make it to the first roll call without any alarm being raised.

A half hour later, they succeeded in extracting Hartigan and the other officer. Neither was in great shape, but they were breathing. While they recovered, Garland and the others crept back up the stairwell, across the eaves, and into their own quarters.

Soon after, Hartigan and the other officer came straight out of the eastern orderly door of Block B. They should have returned to their rooms through the attic, like the others had done, but after their experience in the tunnel, they were not thinking straight. As they crossed to the cookhouse, guards seized them. Officers were not allowed onto the parade ground before 7:00 a.m., and certainly not officers exiting the orderly quarters in muddy clothes. Minutes later, Niemeyer stormed up to them, demanding to know what they were about. Neither answered.

The standoff was interrupted by the arrival at the eastern postern gate of a red-faced and clearly incensed farmer, complaining that a parade of men had stamped about his fields in the night, ruining his crops. Niemeyer and his guards followed the farmer out of the gate and found the hole dug in the earth between the rows of beans.

"So, a tunnel!" Niemeyer exclaimed. He turned to one of his lieutenants, a man called Mandelbrot, and ordered him to lock down the camp to determine how many prisoners had escaped. While the guard headed for the barracks, Niemeyer ordered another guard to climb down into the tunnel to find its starting point. The guard eyed the gaping hole, then his commandant, and shook his head. There might be officers still in the sap, he said. Next Niemeyer tried to send his dog into the opening, but the animal balked at the order as well.

Niemeyer strode off to the Kommandantur. He rang the local police, the town's garrison commander, and, finally, General Hänisch in Hanover. A manhunt needed to be launched. No effort could be spared. Mandelbrat had locked both barracks and restricted all the prisoners to their rooms. He had never much cared for Commandant Niemeyer and his constant derision, and as he went about the corridors counting the men, he could barely suppress a thin smile as silence met his calling out the name of officer after officer. Murmurs of excitement from the prisoners followed him through the barracks. "The tunnel has gone, boys," one British officer crowed to his roommates.

A grand escape had indeed come off—the only question was how many had managed to get away. Mandelbrat finished his count and went to meet Niemeyer in the Spielplatz. "Neun und zwanzig, Herr Captain."

From a barracks window, Durnford watched the scene unfold. Later, he vividly described the moment: "Niemeyer's jaw dropped, his moustachios for a brief instant lost their twirl, his solid stomach swelled less impressively against his overcoat. Just for a moment he became grey and looked very old. But only for a moment." Then Niemeyer went beet-red. He cursed and kicked the ground and shook his fists at the officers watching him from the windows. When they started to jeer at him, he ordered his guards to shoot at anyone appearing at the glass. Several shots were fired but, accustomed to Niemeyer's tactics, officers in the crosshairs were able to evade the gunfire.

Niemeyer ordered guards to be posted at the tunnel exit and beside the locked doors of the barracks. Nobody was allowed out for any reason, and any officers gathering near the windows were to be shot. He charged his lieutenants with locating the tunnel entrance by any means necessary — even if they had to dig up its entire length.

Throughout the barracks, the officers reverently repeated the number of men who had made it out of the camp: "Twenty-nine! Twenty-nine!" It was the greatest breakout of the war — the greatest, perhaps, in the history of war.

Twenty-one

Hunkered in a stand of corn stalks on Wednesday, July 24, Bennett listened to the distant voices of the search parties and their barking dogs as they scoured the woods a quarter mile away. Now and again, some ventured closer to the field where he hid with Campbell-Martin and Bousfield, but they dared not move during daylight hours. A couple of horse-drawn carts carrying soldiers also passed on the nearby road.

The hunt was intensifying, and from previous experience they knew that the German Army would have informed the surrounding villages about the escape, asking civilians to be on the alert. Unless they put many miles between them and Holzminden, and soon, the net would continue to tighten. Still they remained in the fields, anxious and unable to sleep.

Only when it was well after dark did they continue, moving as quietly as possible through the forest. It was a starless night, and they had trouble maintaining their compass course. They soon found themselves lost in a gully and were forced to backtrack through the dark woods until they again found the right path. At one point they spotted someone they feared was a German soldier carrying a large backpack. They tried to evade him only to hear him call out in English. It was Philip "Murphy" Smith, a twenty-two-year-old Irish cavalry officer and member of the ruck.

The small group started out for Hummersen, down a road bordered by thick forests, when two men emerged from the trees in front of them. It was Mardock and Laurence, who had recently come to a crossroads and were confused as to which direction to take. They informed the others that Major Morrogh was a short distance away. When Morrogh caught up with them, they numbered seven. The area was seemingly crawling with escaped prisoners.

The men huddled together in the woods, sharing stories of the breakout. Morrogh regaled them with his adventures of the past few hours, including accidentally setting his entire tin of matches on fire, almost being stumbled upon by a woman and her two children foraging in the woods where he lay naked while his clothes dried, and awakening in midafternoon, standing in a clearing in "full view of anyone who might be there." For the first time in his life, at the most inopportune moment, he'd found himself sleepwalking.

His fellow officers chortled at these stories, and their voices and laughter grew louder as they engaged in welcome camaraderie, billows of cigarette smoke rising from their midst. Finally, the men put an end to the careless banter; they needed to put as much distance between themselves and Holzminden as possible. It was too dangerous to travel in such a large pack, they decided, so they split apart. Bennett said goodbye once again to his former pilot, Laurence, and the others, before he and Campbell-Martin started off on their own. They had fallen far short of their anticipated pace of ten miles a night.

Heavy rucksacks digging into their shoulders, Gray, Kennard, and Blain threaded through a forest in the dark. They kept to single file, keen for any sound other than the call of night birds or the skitter of a squirrel through the underbrush. The three had started that day's march before dusk, balancing the risk of being seen against the benefits of getting beyond the ten-mile radius in which they expected Niemeyer to concentrate his manhunt during its first twenty-four hours.

Where they could, they followed the roads, but these tended not to be straight — and often directed them toward some hamlet or town they needed to avoid. They also found themselves hiking through fields and patches of forest. In his many years in the military, Gray had become a skilled orienteer, and his steady compass bearings saved them from the many misdirections and lost time suffered by their fellow fugitives.

Shortly after midnight, they reached the hamlet of Gellersen, a distance of roughly fifteen miles from Holzminden. On the outskirts, a farmer spotted the trio, too late for them to turn back, hurry into a field, or otherwise find cover. They continued, hoping that Gellersen's main street would be abandoned at that hour, much like the other villages they had passed that night.

To their surprise, they found the opposite was true: oil lamps flickered in many of the windows, and huddles of Germans stood outside their cottages, clearly on edge. The three pilots were sure that news of the Holzminden escape had reached Gellersen and that the villagers were alarmed by the possibility of an enemy fugitive in their midst. It was time for the men to put their aliases to the test.

Before reaching the first house, Kennard had slipped his rucksack to Blain. Blain and Gray then bookended Kennard, each with a firm hand on his arms. Kennard made the occasional effort to pull away from their grasp, whereupon his two minders would wrench him back in line. Gray never hesitated as they advanced through Gellersen. Unless they were stopped, he did not intend to explain their presence. He was on official business, with the papers to back him up.

Conversations halted as the three passed, and they felt the eyes of every villager on them. Whispers and murmurs followed in their wake, and soon a number of townspeople were trailing after them. A confrontation was inevitable, Gray knew, but the closer they were to the far side of town when it occurred, the better opportunity they would have to run off if — or when — it came to that point. Throughout, Kennard struggled against his escorts and occasionally rolled his eyes wildly.

When they reached the last cottage, a few villagers finally crossed their path, forcing them to stop. Gray drew out his papers: his identity card in

the name of Franz Vogel and the letter stating his duties as chief guard at
the Vechta insane asylum. With a glance toward his increasingly agitated
charge, Gray recounted in perfect German how the man he was escorting, Kurt Grau, had recently absconded from the asylum and should be
given a wide berth. This had the intended effect on some of the villagers,
but Gray was concerned about any doubters in the crowd. He asked to be
provided some water. His charge was prone to convulsions, he said, and
the low growl rising from Grau's throat was an indication that one was
coming on quickly. "A quietening drug" should calm him.

On cue, Kennard tried to break loose. Blain grabbed his arm and
knocked him roughly on the side of the head. Gasps of shock rose from a
few of the villagers, while one ran off to fetch some water. Playing to his
audience now, Kennard whimpered and shook as if he had no control
over his limbs. Gray explained to the onlookers that they could only travel
by night, since encounters such as this one only set the lunatic off.

When the villager returned with a glass of water, Blain put his hand
out to bar him, leaning over to Gray and briefly whispering in his ear.
Gray nodded. No glass, he explained to the man. Grau might break it and
use the shards as a weapon. With that, they had the villagers completely
fooled. A pewter mug of water was found while Kennard thrashed about
like his tunic was on fire. He managed to give Blain a blow in revenge
before being wrestled to the street. Blain and Gray pinned him down by
his arms and legs. He only fought harder until a pill (aspirin) was forced
between his lips and washed down with the water. Sparing no drama,
Kennard continued to writhe underneath Blain and Gray as it took effect.
With every moment, he seemed to grow weaker, his twitches more spas-
modic, like a condemned man dangling from the end of a rope. Finally,
he was still.

The villagers looked on in shock, but Gray promised that the patient
would awaken in a short while, no worse off than he was before. During
the wait, Gray and Blain enjoyed some wine, bread, and cheese from an

elderly farmer, who clearly had taken seriously the request from Vechta's chief of police, as stated in the men's papers, to give the guards Vogel and Holzmann "all possible help" in bringing Grau back to the asylum.

They also gained some useful intelligence from the villagers: a manhunt was under way for some Allied POWs, and a company of soldiers was in the area. They were searching the countryside and guarding the road and railway line due north of Gellersen. The two guards could not have been more grateful for the insight. Finally Kennard fluttered his eyes awake, and Gray and Blain assisted him off the street. Together, they led their groggy patient away. Once clear of the village, they celebrated their success, although Kennard bemoaned the ill treatment his role had demanded of him. He was especially disappointed that his minders had not saved him so much as a crumb of the bread and cheese they'd been given.

By the morning of July 25, none of the fugitives had been caught, and Niemeyer vented his rage on those who remained behind. He instituted new "emergency orders," stating that they were for the safety of the prisoners. However, the list posted on the cookhouse wall and on the doors of the barracks reflected campwide punishment:

1. No officer of Block A was allowed to enter Block B for any purpose — and vice versa. Penalty for violation: 3 days in isolation.
2. No officer was permitted to enter any room but his own for any purpose. Penalty: 3 days.
3. No officer was allowed to stop/loiter in the passages. Penalty: 3 days.
4. Parole walks stopped.
5. Theatrical performances forbidden.
6. Baths closed.
7. Parcel and tin room shuttered.
8. Activities in the Spielplatz stopped.

Lieutenant Colonel Arthur Stokes-Roberts, now the senior British officer at the camp, asked Niemeyer to lift the restrictions, which allowed the
prisoners to do nothing more than "eat, sleep, and breathe."

"Go away!" Niemeyer barked. "I do not like you. I forbid you to speak
to me or any of my lieutenants."

The new rules were almost impossible to follow to the letter, and a
dozen officers were sent to the jug by the end of the first day. Niemeyer
made the rat-infested cells even more uncomfortable by covering the windows with boards, keeping the electric light burning day and night, and
sending a guard into every cell once an hour to "see that the prisoner was
present."

Then there were the arbitrary abuses. A guard shoved an officer down
the stairs for not moving fast enough. Lights in both barracks would suddenly be turned on in the middle of the night, and any officer who tried
to switch them off was sent to solitary. An Australian private questioned
a guard about a new order and was hauled off to the cellar for two days
without bedding, food, or drink. Upset over this treatment, one officer
dropped a plank of wood out his window, narrowly missing Niemeyer. In
typical response, guards randomly fired into the block.

Most resistance, however, was passive. Officers showed up to roll call in
unbuttoned uniforms or without boots or tunics. They refused to salute or
respond to German commands. This incensed Niemeyer, and he had his
guards charge a line of officers, one of whom was stabbed with a bayonet.

He grew even more furious when it was revealed that the tunnel entrance, whose location was only determined by digging up the entire
length of the sap, had been right under the noses of his guards for months.
His rage festered when the residents of Holzminden began coming to the
camp to see the great tunnel and to wonder aloud how it could have gone
unnoticed. A photographer even came to take pictures of the scar of up-
turned earth that led from the field to the eastern entrance of Block B.

No amount of punishment seemed capable of satisfying Niemeyer. He was obsessed with recapturing all twenty-nine of the escapees. Such a mass breakout would not only be an embarrassment to Germany, it would prove ruinous to Niemeyer's career. As part of his campaign to find them, he posted notices in local and national newspapers to ask for cooperation: "We urgently and under all circumstances request help to get hold of all escaped officers in the interest of the defense of our country. We particularly call on the country populations, berry pickers, hay collectors, youth military groups, hikers, and hunters to look out for anything suspicious. We know from experience that fugitives tend to hide in forests. At night one should watch out for any noise and especially the barking of dogs in villages. A high reward is promised for assistance." The reward offered was five thousand marks, a considerable sum in wartorn Germany, for any information that led to the capture of a Holzminden prisoner, dead or alive.

On Thursday afternoon, Rathborne attempted to bed down in a stand of woods for some desperately needed rest. But he found little reprieve from the biting ants that crawled down his collar and up his pant legs. Bouts of rain dampened his clothes, but there was never enough to collect. He was not yet so desperate to drink from puddles, but he soon would be. Finally the sun set, and he started off again on his hike south to Göttingen.

The woods were empty but for a soldier and his girlfriend, who were in the middle of undressing as Rathborne passed. The young woman caught his eye, but a simple *gute nacht* kept the two lovers to their embraces. Rathborne continued on.

By dawn on the twenty-sixth, he was within a dozen miles of Göttingen. His boots and pants were soaked from walking through the rugged countryside, damp with morning dew. Discretion should have kept him in hiding during daylight hours, but the thought of another ant assault and a hot afternoon without fresh water drove him to take only a short rest before continuing. With any luck, he could catch a train that evening.

After brushing off his suit, straightening his hair, and doing whatever else he could do to make himself look presentable, he hiked along the road.

By 3:00 p.m. he was headed into the outskirts of Göttingen. Set on the river Leine, Göttingen was a university town, surrounded by ramparts. On his way into its town center, Rathborne came across a tavern. He wanted to test out his ability to pass as a German civilian, but more than that, he needed something for his parched throat. He figured that as long as he kept any talk brief, nobody would be any the wiser that German was not his mother tongue.

The tavern's owner, an old woman who looked as much a part of the place as the scuffed bar, slid him a beer. Rathborne had drunk fine-quality drafts in the past, in Berlin and Munich, but none tasted better in his lifetime than that beer that afternoon. Furthermore, his short conversation with the barkeep boosted his confidence that he could pass himself off as German.

After leaving the tavern, Rathborne walked on, but without a map of the town he soon found himself lost in its tangle of streets. Half-timbered houses and steepled churches abounded in every direction. It would not do to ask for directions, even if he figured it unlikely that the manhunt would extend to Göttingen. Finally, he came to a sign pointing to the station. Along the way, he dropped into a stationery store that was sure to have a train timetable. There would be too many authorities, police and soldiers alike, to risk wandering about the train station. When he arrived, he wanted to buy his ticket and board straightaway.

There was a five o'clock train south to Bebra. From there, he should be able to find a connection farther south to Fulda, then one due west to Cologne. If he had any luck, he could be out of German territory within thirty-six hours at most. Shortly before his train was due to depart, he headed through the rounded stone entrance of Göttingen's main station. At the ticket window, valise in hand, he bought a ticket to Bebra. The clerk did not pay him a second glance.

But when he showed his ticket to the gate attendant, he was informed that there was no five o'clock train to Bebra. His confusion seemed to pique the attendant's suspicions. Rathborne quickly apologized for his mistake, then exited the station as calmly as he could. A glance behind him reassured him he wasn't being followed. A few blocks away, he checked the timetable again. The train he had thought left in the evening had departed at 5:00 a.m. that morning, but there was a train at 8:00 p.m.

Not wanting to be seen loitering, he bought a ticket to the cinema. The film was unmemorable, but the newsreel showing the macabre scene of the kaiser's soldiers standing over Rathborne's fallen countrymen during the spring German offensive, struck him to the core. The war had seemed at a remove during his time in prison.

Minutes before eight o'clock, he returned to the station and boarded his train. From his comfortable seat, he watched the fields and hills he had marched through that morning pass by in a blur.

Jim Bennett and Peter Campbell-Martin earned every mile it took to get to the border. They could take no unnecessary risks. There would be no train rides, no beers in pubs, no gifts of food. Neither of them spoke more than a few words of German, and if they ran into a patrol or a villager out for a stroll they would have to run or hide.

Although they traveled only at night, they took special care nonetheless. They scouted every road and railway line, never crossing until they were sure it was clear. Bridges were forbidden territory, and any towns had to be circumvented, regardless of the distance required. When they spotted even the most harmless-looking civilian, they took cover and waited them out. As a further caution, they always walked twenty yards apart from one another. This kept their talking to a safe minimum, and, if confronted from the front or behind, one of them would have the opportunity to escape.

They often came across huts or barns that would have made for better, warmer lodgings than another hideout in the woods or in a field, but they resisted the temptation, fearing a farmer might discover them. They also kept a strict schedule of alternating watches during the day while one of them slept.

Despite all these measures, they were spotted by a policeman on a bicycle early in their flight to Holland. He shouted at them to stop, but even after he drew his pistol Bennett and Campbell-Martin ran, bolting in separate directions. In the moment of hesitation it took the policeman to decide who to shoot, they both managed to get out of range. The policeman took off after Bennett on his bike. Bennett eluded him, but then an attachment of German Army cavalry chased after him. Running faster than he ever had in his life, Bennett finally shook them loose. It took a while to reconnect with Campbell-Martin, and by then he was too exhausted to go much farther.

With incidents like this and all their precautions, they were making slow progress on their 150-mile journey. Every hour they spent on the run heightened the risk of being captured. Equally troublesome, they had only limited food stores, and attempts to forage something to eat at the farms they passed proved fruitless. Their one hot meal a day was usually a fistful of oats mixed with Oxo cubes, but they quickly understood that only stricter rationing would see them to the border without starving.

Twenty-two

After their antics in Gellersen, Gray, Blain, and Kennard slept in a copse of trees instead of attempting to cross the road to Arzen. They had barely left the woods after sundown on July 25 when they spotted a company of soldiers. Scrambling into the forest, they hid in the underbrush. They were close enough to the soldiers to see their bootlaces. Gray deciphered from their conversation that another patrol had nabbed an escaped prisoner down the road. There was nothing they could do to help him.

After the soldiers had trailed away, Blain struck his lighter, and Gray examined the map. Every alteration of their route was laden with compromise. A longer distance weighed against a smaller risk of encountering another patrol; moving quickly down a roadside balanced against the safer but more taxing option of a hike through the countryside.

They struck through some fields to circle around the soldiers before crossing at a well-hidden stretch of road. Then they marched on a northwestern course, at times cutting through farms and forested hillsides, at others keeping to the winding roads. Every couple of hours, they took a break and smoked cigarettes, hands cupped over the ends so the orange glow was not seen in the dark. By sunrise the next day, as they headed toward Hohenhorn, they took advantage of some dense woods to hike on through the daylight and make up for lost time.

Over the next two nights, much of the hours spent in a steady downpour, there were no main roads to follow. They took a yeoman's journey, down country lanes and muddy paths, halting often at the sight of soldiers and civilians who were clearly part of the Holzminden manhunt. They never stopped for any length of time, knowing well that a tracker or a bloodhound might be closing in on their trail. The patter of the rain was their only cover.

As the bright red dawn of Sunday, July 28, was breaking, they reached the outskirts of Exter — only thirty-six miles from Holzminden as the crow flies. With the many twists and turns of their journey, they had trekked much farther in their five nights on the run. And they still had a long way to go.

Twenty-four hours earlier, Rathborne had arrived into Berba. After resting outside town, hiding himself in a stack of corn, he had a late breakfast of beer at a local tavern, listening to his waitress's bitter complaints about the shortage of potatoes. He then returned to the station and headed on to Fulda. His train came in too late for him to go straight to Cologne, so he bought a ticket to Frankfurt. He rode in a third-class carriage on a slow local train, as had been his plan. From experience, he knew that conductors and the police were much more rigorous in their inspections of express trains and better-class carriages than the ones he was on.

The train stopped in almost every town along the route. A downside of third class, beyond the relative discomfort, was that it was full of chatty passengers with too much idle time on their hands. A German soldier on leave from the front railed against the nefarious Brits and even thrust a propaganda leaflet, dropped by the RFC, into his hand. A young girl across from Rathborne chattered away as well.

On his arrival at Frankfurt, he cleared out of the station as quickly as he could to avoid any chance encounters with the authorities. His gray suit was dirty, but that was nothing compared to his white shirt, which was so soiled he might well have spent the night in a coal mine. He stopped into a tailor's shop to replace it, but when asked what size he needed, he could offer only a blank stare, then made a fast exit. He had no knowledge whatsoever of German sizes.

There was more trouble when he went to eat dinner at a restaurant. The garrulous owner said that he could not quite place his accent. Rathborne replied that he was Polish by birth, but he did not stay for dessert in case he had to explain any more about his background. The next couple of hours he spent in the cinema before it was time for his overnight train to Cologne. He slept fitfully on the one-hundred-mile journey, arriving at the station on Sunday morning at 9:00 a.m.

Although the skyline of Cologne was still dominated by the twin Gothic spires of its main cathedral, the city was in a sorrowful state. Most of the shops were shuttered, and those that were open — butcher, bakers, and grocers — had long lines snaking out the door. People on the streets had a forlorn gaze, and men, both young and old, hobbled past with war injuries.

Concerned about his appearance, Rathborne visited a barber for a shave and a haircut. His next train — to Aachen, the spa town a mere five miles from the Dutch frontier — departed that evening. He spent the afternoon in parks, beer halls, and the cinema. He was becoming an expert in whittling away the hours, seen but unseen, and had become accustomed to presenting himself at the ticket booth: a travel-weary businessman who just wanted to get home.

At 9:00 p.m., two hours after his train rumbled out of Cologne, Rathborne arrived into Aachen. He hopped on a tram that terminated at the Ponttor, the medieval gateway northwest of the old city center. From there, he walked to the town's outskirts. He had a meal and a glass of gin at a small bar, fortifying himself for the last leg of his escape. Then he hid out behind a railway embankment. With map and compass in hand, he charted a route to the border that kept clear of any roads or villages.

At 11:30 p.m., the sky completely dark, he stashed his valise by the embankment and started west. He had gone only a short distance and was walking through fields when a steady rain started to fall. The pitter-patter masked the sound of the crackling stalks underfoot. For an hour he pushed his way through the crops. Then all of a sudden a pack of dogs started barking. He dropped down and laid flat, sure that the dogs were close enough to chase him out. When the dogs quieted, he heard the voices of soldiers. For a long while, he remained absolutely still as the rain soaked through his clothes, leaving his skin cold. Neither the barking nor the voices came any closer. Finally, Rathborne decided to move ahead.

He crawled on his hands and knees, fallen corn stalks cutting his hands as he went. He heard soldiers now and again but decided that his best chance was to continue. He was uncertain as to how far he had gone — with the dense stalks it was slow going. On he crawled, hoping the border would come sooner than the pounce of its sentries. He must be so close now.

On their own, or in bands of twos and threes, many of the tunnelers and the ruck were recaptured and returned to Holzminden. Captain Frank Sharpe and Lieutenant Bernard Luscombe, numbers 28 and 29 out of the tunnel, were the first to come back through the gates. Niemeyer glowered at them as they passed. The two had made little preparation and had only a slim head start before the tunnel was discovered. Soldiers nabbed them fifteen miles downriver, on the banks of the Weser. With the return of each tunneler, the mood among the Holzminden prisoners darkened. Would any of the escapees manage the home run to Holland?

Although filthy and stinking, Sharpe and Luscombe were sent immediately to the cellars. No bath and no change of clothes were offered, and they were put on a bread and water diet.

When Niemeyer finally appeared down in solitary, he was in a venomous mood. He removed Sharpe's gold watch from his wrist and put it on the table. Then, using a knife, he stabbed and crushed the family heirloom into bits. He ordered the guard to tear the civilian outfits Sharpe and Luscombe were wearing into "ribbons." The two were left half-naked with strict orders that nobody was to communicate with them nor provide them with any additional food. As far as Niemeyer cared, they could rot in the cells. He promised to make that official with a court-martial.

Others soon joined them. The police, soldiers, and bloodhounds sent out on the manhunt had less impact than the countless German citizens marshaled to look out for the escaped prisoners. Whether it was out of patriotism or greed for the reward, they were incredibly effective. Butler, the first out of the tunnel, was nabbed after he stole a bicycle in a village. Others were flushed out of fields or seized at crossroads. When guards brought in Mardock and Laurence, morale among the prisoners deflated. It looked like none of the fugitives would make it to Holland.

By Monday, July 29, ten of the twenty-nine escapees had been returned to the camp. The men's sorry states — grubby outfits, sallow faces, bodies narrowed from loss of weight — only further darkened the mood in the camp.

Niemeyer swelled pridefully in his blue greatcoat with each recapture. Never one to let good fortune pass by without boasting about his own hand in it, he shepherded in reporters to chronicle each return. They wrote down what Niemeyer dictated, with embellishments for color. Without exception, Niemeyer insisted that the prisoners had only succeeded in their escapes because of British accomplices outside the camp. There was an army of spies in the vicinity, he claimed, with no end to their abilities when it came to providing clothing, food, intelligence, and even a spare sapper or two.

Although Niemeyer tried to wring a confession from the captured escapees, none of them admitted to even using the tunnel, let alone having dug it. All of his attempts to bribe the orderlies, Cash included, into informing on the conspiracy and its members also failed.

These efforts, and Niemeyer's abuse of the returned prisoners, stirred the pot of rebellion throughout Holzminden. Stokes-Roberts believed that the mass escape would surely see Niemeyer removed from his position. But when General Hänisch sent an officer to investigate the events, he made clear that Niemeyer would stay. No war crime or level of incompetence seemed capable of dislodging him from power.

Silent resistance continued nonetheless. One day, the officers lit cigarettes and pipes at roll call. Such was the amount of smoke that the parade ground looked like a bustling factory. Another day, they refused to answer their names when called. Another day, they came out bare-chested. Each time, Niemeyer sent in his guards to herd them back into the barracks, each time with a little more violence. So many prisoners had been arrested for violations that they eventually had to be housed in the town jail.

Niemeyer focused most of his attention on seeing the fugitives returned. By July's end, fifteen prisoners remained out. But Holland was a long way away. By looking at where the other escapees had been caught, Niemeyer drew a bead on the remaining men's westward line of flight: Holzminden, Bodenwerder, Hamelin, Lohne, Bielefeld, Ahaus, Gronau, and on to the Dutch border. He called for local assistance along that path. Even if the prisoners did find their way to the border, Niemeyer knew well that in their bedraggled and half-starved state, they would be easy pickings for the German sentries. He was confident that he would win out in the end.

Then one day while in the Kommandantur, he received a telegram sent from Holland. It was written by Lieutenant Colonel Charles Rathborne. It said: "Having a lovely time [STOP] If I ever find you in London will break your neck [STOP]."

The first of the breakout artists had made it.

Always careful, but as fast as they could manage. That was the maxim of Bennett and Campbell-Martin. By dawn on July 31, they had made up for their earlier slow pace, and the Dutch border was now only some fifty miles away. Another few nights of trekking, avoiding trouble or misdirection, and they should be within reach of a crossing.

They had become skilled interlopers. Rye fields could not be trusted for a daytime hideout because the harvest was beginning. Corn and wheat fields were better. Whenever they reached one, they made sure to enter it without leaving a trace of a broken stalk or a heavy footprint. After they were inside the rows, they could march more swiftly: nobody but a search plane would see the damage, and the Germans had yet to bring these to bear in their hunt. Villagers were trouble enough, and the whole countryside seemed to be pocked with hamlets that time had clearly forgot.

A few times, they crossed paths with bands of their fellow tunnelers —evidence of like minds and a shared map. There was little time for a "cheerio," let alone swapping stories, but they all had plenty to tell. Tullis and Purves had linked up with Edward Leggatt by the railway line between Hövelhof and Bielefeld, a large industrial town. Together they had accidentally knocked a German off his bicycle, been chased by three middle-aged women, avoided a patrol of teenage Boy Scouts by climbing a tree, and watched a lover's quarrel while hidden under a bridge. In between these episodes, Leggatt sketched scenes of their escape in his notebook while Tullis and Purves took turns reading a book on polar expeditions they had brought with them. The diversions kept the miseries of their daily marches—including Leggatt's feet, blistered raw from ill-fitting boots—temporarily at bay.

After Bennett and Campbell-Martin split off from Bousfield, he traveled with the two Irishmen, Morrogh and Smith. They had run into their share of Germans, but their closest shave came while hiding in the only place they could find one morning—a strip of wheat bordered on either side by stacks of cut rye. They had their boots off and were making tea when some farmhands and a small dog came out to the field. While the three fugitives lay still on the ground, the farmers hauled out some of the harvest from either side of them. All was well until Bousfield sneezed. The farmers surely heard the sound. The three fugitives readied to sprint away, boots in hand, but luckily the Germans continued with their work, probably thinking the sound had come from one of their fellow farmers on the opposite side of the wheat patch.

Bennett and Campbell-Martin would need ample supplies of luck, endurance, and skill as they marched on toward the border. They were almost out of food, their bodies were weary, their nerves frayed. And the riskiest leg of their journey was about to begin.

The dogs were barking in Twiehausen. Rain poured from the sky, and the surrounding land was too thick with mud to allow them to circumvent the hamlet easily. Gray, Kennard, and Blain thought they wouldn't have any trouble passing unnoticed through the single lane of cottages in the middle of the night. But with every cottage they passed, it seemed, another dog began to howl. They would have had a better chance tiptoeing stealthily through a kennel with cuts of steak around their necks. The only cover was provided by the cottages' front gardens, so they stuck to the lane, despite the din of dogs barking and scratching at windows. A few doors opened, with villagers peering out to see what was causing the ruckus. Earlier in their journey, they might have sped through the hamlet or avoided it altogether. But more than a week without proper rest, hiking miles every day, sleeping outdoors, eating half rations, and wearing damp clothes had left them cavalier in the face of risk.

Finally, they cleared Twiehausen, the cacophony of barking dogs fading into the distance. They hadn't been stopped that time, but the three knew well that it would take only a single mistake — the misreading of a sign, a careless hiding spot, an inquisitive passerby — for all to be lost. They had already passed the longest time any of them had been out on the run before.

The next night, the sky was bright with stars. Navigation would have been easy except they spent hours trudging through the swamp that encircled much of Dümmer Lake. Mosquitoes bedeviled them. By the time they reached dry land, they were covered in bites. It was almost dawn, on August 1, but they continued until they had gone around the town of Damme. Every one of the eleven miles they traversed had been a painful slog. Finally spent, they hid in some woods to rest. All three men had lost weight during their almost two years of captivity, and after the past several days of strain, little nutrition, and limited water, they were like skeletons. Their clothes hung loosely on their frames, their eyes stared listlessly, and they were all suffering from colds. When the afternoon sun blazed directly over their resting spot, they barely grunted in conversation. Blain's eyes were creased and his cheeks sunken; he looked twice his age. Gray tried to lighten the mood, pointing out that they were now only fourteen miles south of Vechta. They might as well simply head up to the insane asylum, he joked; they looked like they belonged there. Blain and Kennard managed a grin — laughter took too much effort.

After dusk, they pushed through their exhaustion and marched at a swift pace down the road to Vehs. Due south of their route was Osnabrück, where they had first banded together to escape. It felt like a lifetime ago. They covered sixteen miles that night, but in their ambition stopped too late to find anywhere other than a narrow thicket of trees in which to hide. By their map, Gray determined that they were roughly forty-five miles from Sellingen, the Dutch border town, and that they should make their cross to freedom in four nights. They had rations enough for only two. Determination would need to cover the rest.

Twenty-three

As the sky brightened on Friday, August 2, Bennett and Campbell-Martin came to a road at the edge of a moor, roughly fifteen miles from the border. The only places where they could hide for the day were an open ditch leading into the wetlands or a hedgerow near a farmhouse a short distance away. They chose the hedge and crept inside its twist of branches.

In the late morning, Bennett was on watch while Campbell-Martin slept. He heard the chatter of young children approaching. They must have seen their footprints or a break in the hedge. The voices came closer and closer. As they drew near enough to peek inside the tangle of brush, Bennett shut his eyes and pretended to be asleep, not wanting to scare them. The children grew excited, but Bennett had no idea what they were saying. A moment later, the kids fled toward the farmhouse, calling out to their parents in alarm.

Bennett shook Campbell-Martin awake. They grabbed their rucksacks and scrambled from the hedge. Shouts rose from the farm as they dashed across the road and into the moor. They slogged through the shallow channels that extended like laneways through the soggy bracken and moss. It was an exhausting effort, but they gained some distance from the farmhouse. After an hour, although they were still stuck in the open moor, they thought they were clear from any pursuers. Then they spotted a pair of cavalry officers leading their horses into the bog. Bennett and Campbell-Martin knew there was no chance they could outpace the horses.

Panic soon gave way to a plan, as devised by Bennett. From the horses' movement up and down the ditches, it was clear that the Germans had a systematic search plan. He decided to use the soldiers' rigid pattern against them. As the horses labored down the channel next to the one in which they were hidden, Bennett readied to give Campbell-Martin the sign to go. The cavalry reached the end and directed their horses up and out of that channel and into the one occupied by the two fugitives.

In the narrow window of time while the horses heaved themselves through the soup of peat, thick grasses, and low shrubs, Bennett and Campbell-Martin doubled back into the channel the cavalry had just vacated. They hid themselves, bodies pressed flat against the walls of the ditch. Their timing was flawless, and the cavalry unwittingly moved over the exact spot in which they had been hidden seconds before.

They remained hidden on the edge of the channel until the early afternoon, when their pursuers were but specks in the distance. After reaching the outskirts of the moor, they spent the rest of the day inside a drainage pipe that ran underneath a country lane.

Later that day, after dark, they came to the Dortmund-Ems Canal. Running parallel to the Ems River, the waterway was built to transport coal and other goods between the port of Emden and the industrial Ruhr Valley. It was yet another barrier the escapees would have to overcome before they reached Holland. Campbell-Martin had already shown himself to be a poor swimmer on their first night out when they were crossing the Weser, but neither of them wanted to chance using one of the canal's many bridges, particularly since the authorities were clearly on close watch for any of the Holzminden fugitives. A bridge that appeared unguarded at first glance could be hiding soldiers on the opposite side, just waiting to challenge anyone who crossed.

They would not have known that Bousfield, Morrogh, and Smith were planning to take exactly this risk that very same night, crossing a canal bridge to the south. Only Bousfield, the Cambridge champion runner, eluded capture, and he nearly took a bullet in the back as he sprinted away.

In the dark, Bennett and Campbell-Martin could not gauge how far they would have to swim to cross the canal, but they suspected it would be at least fifty yards. They had made a pair of water wings from the sleeves of Campbell-Martin's Burberry jacket to help him stay afloat. Bennett leaped in — to find that the canal was only three feet deep on its eastern shore. Campbell-Martin slipped down into the water with less of an abrupt splash. Both kept their clothes on, since they were already soaked through after their wade through the moor.

Water wings secure, Campbell-Martin held onto Bennett's shoulders. The canal soon grew deep, and Bennett lost his purchase on its bottom. They were almost halfway across when Bennett started to struggle against the current. Wanting to help, Campbell-Martin turned onto his back so he could kick with his legs. As he did, one of his water wings split open. Off balance, he flailed with his arm only to rupture the other water wing. Bennett grabbed him before he went under. Campbell-Martin held onto Bennett's back while he pushed his way to the west bank. To their surprise, the embankment was almost a sheer wall, ten feet high. There was no way to scale it, and Bennett was losing strength as he fought against the drag of the water on his clothes.

Something needed to be done, and quickly. As Campbell-Martin held onto the embankment to keep them steady, Bennett stripped off his clothes. He handed them to his friend, who balled them up and threw them onto the embankment to retrieve later. Now unburdened by the wet clothes, Bennett slipped downstream with Campbell-Martin beside him. Two hundred yards away, they found a place where they could climb out of the canal. Naked and exhausted, Bennett hiked back up the canal to find his clothes, but could not locate them among the reeds. The two got a good laugh out of his predicament. Bennett might well be the first to make his home run to Holland in nothing but his birthday suit. They hunted back and forth along the embankment until Bennett finally located the bundle of clothes underneath a bush.

They still had the Ems to cross the next night, followed by the border. They marched onward in their drenched clothes and sopping boots, their brief moment of mirth having given way to misery.

One foot after the other. In the late hours of Saturday, August 3, Gray was leading from the front, compass in hand. For their twelfth night out, he kept them mostly on the road. They never moved faster than a slow trudge, but it was a steady one, without detour for several miles. Near the hamlet of Wieste, the road took a sharp turn away from their northwest-ward course. They left its easy track for a tramp through a deep marsh, their boots sticking in the mud. The only sounds in the night were their grunts of exertion and the sucking sound of the mud taking hold of each step. Neither Gray nor Blain and Kennard had the energy to speak.

Over sixteen miles after they began, they collapsed in some woods before daybreak on Sunday. They slept soundly. Then, once dusk settled over the countryside, they set off on yet another trek. They passed through cultivated farmland from time to time, but their efforts to forage from the fields yielded nothing. The best nourishment they found was some rotten turnips that turned the stomach and raw potatoes that were better for cracking teeth than eating. Before morning, they intended to cross a point where the Ems River and canal met. That swim alone was enough to occupy their fears.

The same Sunday evening, southwest of Blenheim, perched high in the branches of a tree, Jim Bennett watched German soldiers go in and out of a camp just three hundred yards away. The camp housed the sentries who served the frontier a short distance from its gates. Early that morning, he and Campbell-Martin had taken cover in the tree's dense foliage. While there, they surveyed the best way to penetrate into Holland. It was one thing to see the border on the map, another to see its exact location and surroundings and to determine the best place to cross.

Armed sentries patrolled the 350-mile border, but there was no great high wall to separate Germany and the Netherlands, no single line of defense. In some places, there were manmade earthen embankments; in others, a canal or road to separate the two countries. There were woods and open fields divided by electrified fences or barbwire, and there were stretches where it was impossible to know whether you had passed the border or not unless you came across a guard or sentry post. In some senses, the border's irregularity, often dictated by terrain, was its own defense. The longer you looked for an undefended spot, the surer you were to be caught by roving patrols or by a farmer who would be rewarded handsomely if you were apprehended.

By observing the movements of the frontier sentries, Bennett had a good idea of where the border line was. He figured their best opportunity lay where it ran through some woods. Because of the nearby camp, he figured there might be an electrified fence serving as a barrier, but they were too far away to see. There were dogs, for sure.

Stuck in the tree until dark, the day passed slowly. There was nothing for them to do but watch the guard and try to forget how thirsty and hungry they were. They had eaten the last scraps of their food after swimming the Ems the night before. Connoisseurs of puddle water, they were desperate for something fresh to drink. Late in the day, a storm settled over them, turning the sky black. Rain beat down through the trees, and the thunder cracked and boomed in every direction. After a few hours, it was still fairly dark, and they might have set out early, but then the clouds broke, and the sun shone brightly. They waited in their perch until the sun set and night stole completely over the countryside.

The two men then dropped down to the ground, fixed their compass for southwest, and started off across the moor. Thoughts coursed through Bennett's head about what might prevent him reaching freedom — electrified fences, dogs, burly sentries — and how he would overcome each.

His general strategy would be to run as quickly and boldly as possible through any gap he could find. Only a bullet, and maybe not even that, would stop him setting foot in Holland before dawn the next day.

When they neared the woods, they dropped to their hands and knees and crawled into the trees. The earlier rain had done little to dampen the vegetation on the forest floor, which crackled beneath their weight. It seemed that the closer they were to where they thought the border was located, the more noise they unwittingly made in their advance. They both grabbed heavy sticks to use in the event they met with resistance. Finally, they straightened up and eased forward. Ahead, the darkness was lifting. Bennett figured they must be close to the edge of the woods. A few minutes later, he spotted the line of a barbwire fence. The border. It was a hundred yards away at the most. A lone sentry stood between them and freedom.

The two men crept through the trees. As of yet they had neither seen nor heard any dogs. But then a rustling sound came from the woods just a short distance away. Bennett stopped cold, and Campbell-Martin drew up alongside him. For a long moment, the two waited. There were no other sounds, yet Bennett sensed someone in the darkness ahead — someone on alert. He was sure of it. Still he advanced; there was no turning back now. He'd gone just a few steps when he heard the distinct cocking of a rifle.

"Halt!" a German sentry ordered.

Bennett and Campbell-Martin knew what they had to do. They barely gave each other a look before charging straight through the trees at the sentry, their sticks readied to swing. Their sudden movement came as a surprise to the guard, who stood motionless as Bennett swept past, running so quickly he did not have the time, nor the need, to use his stick. Campbell-Martin followed on his heels.

Finding a break in the barbwire fence, the two men raced through it. "Halt!" the sentry shouted again. The crack of a rifle echoed behind as the two officers charged headlong into Holland. The first shot, then the next, missed their mark. The men kept running and running until they both spilled into the Dinkel River, free of Germany at last.

Collapsing on the opposite bank, the two shook hands. "We've made it," they said at the same time.

On the morning of August 5, hidden in a stretch of woods outside Lathen, beyond the Ems River, Gray, Kennard, and Blain had their last meal — some Horlicks tablets (a mix of dried milk, barley, and wheat). Other than a couple of squares of chocolate each, they were completely out of food. To warm them, Blain served out the few ounces of cognac left in his flask. They had long since smoked their last cigarettes, but the spirits offered some relief before the rising chatter of birds in the trees signaled that it was time to sleep.

At twilight, Gray laid out the last remaining section of the map. This was reason enough to be encouraged. He sensed his partners' spirits needed bolstering — and maybe his own too. They were eight miles from the border now. Along their path, almost due west, there were no major roads to cross and but a few small hamlets to circumvent. Only the amorphous dark form representing the Walchumer Moor separated them from Holland. A single night's march and they would be past the map's border line by morning, hopefully eating a rich breakfast. Or, if things went the other way, dodging rifle fire.

The three airmen soon fell into the maw of the Walchumer. They trudged through its narrow channels, across islands of peat, and into hollows waist-deep in fetid water. Every step was unsure footing, their boots almost always either in a stream or buried in sticky mud. They slipped and stumbled, floundered backwards, sideways, every which way. Often it was impossible to move forward without one of them leaning on another — or asking for a hand or a yank on the rucksack straps to loosen them from the moor's sucking grasp. Night crawlers slithered underneath their clothes, and clouds of insects swarmed around them. If the three had known more about the Walchumer, they would have circumvented it for sure.

Hour after hour, they slogged their way through, never on a straight compass line. If there had been a trail left in their wake, it would have looked like a drunkard's tramp. Rain pelted down, mixing with the sweat in their eyes, and the sky was black. After fourteen nights of marching, the last two on little more than nibbles of chocolate, they had only their last reserves of mental endurance to drive them onward. They drew from the shame, unwarranted though it was, of being shot down and captured. The months, years, stolen from their lives. The separation from their squadrons and their families. The narrow escapes, only to be recaptured. The spells in solitary, sometimes at the brink of madness and death. The deprivations of Holzminden. The endless hours of tunneling, the terror of the dark, the fear of collapse, of being buried alive in the bowels of the earth. And Karl Niemeyer. The thought of Niemeyer, of the moment he would realize they had beaten him, was reason enough to continue.

It was approaching 4:00 a.m. on August 6 when Gray spotted a string of faint lights ahead. Unless they had trekked far off their line, these would be the arc lamps illuminating the border. There were no towns nearby to explain their presence. The first blush of dawn would come soon, and they needed to be across the frontier before then. They crept slowly through the moor, feeling the stir of danger and the enlivening thrill of their goal being at hand. The rain muffled their movements, but they made sure to proceed as quietly as possible. Soon they were close enough to see a high dike, and on top of it individual lamps hung on posts, each spaced roughly two hundred yards apart. German sentries paced back and forth between the posts, framed by the light.

The trio discovered that the dike was a sloped wall of mud and grass roughly twelve feet high. Backs flat against it, hidden from the eyes of the sentry patrolling above, they took a few minutes to calm themselves and ease their breathing. Then they started to watch the guard's routine: how

long it took him to walk from post to post across the gravel track on top
of the embankment; whether he made any pauses along the way. Unable
to see beyond the dike, they had to take on faith that it would be a contin-
uation of the moor. Once "over the top," Gray whispered, they would have
to run as fast as they could through the muck. Only the darkness would
protect them.

They needed to go. The guard paced away from their position, and
Kennard turned to climb the dike first. Digging the toes of his boots into
the wall, grasping some clusters of short grass in his hands, he made it a
few feet up before slipping down. Another attempt had the same result,
and for an instant they feared the embankment might be insurmount-
able. Gray had an idea. Bracing his body against the wall, he threaded his
fingers together, palms up, and told Kennard to use his hands as a foot-
hold. This Kennard did, and with a quick jerk, Gray launched him against
the embankment. Kennard gained some purchase on the wall, enough
to place his feet on Gray's shoulders to stop himself sliding back to the
moor. Suppressing a grunt as Kennard bore down on him, Gray cupped
his hands together again and heaved Blain up in the same way. Blain then
used Kennard as ballast to clamber to the top of the embankment.

At that moment, the sentry turned and headed back toward them.
Blain pressed himself against the edge of the dyke wall, fingers clawed
into the mud, trying to keep himself from tumbling backward. Kennard
supported him as well, with Gray holding up the human ladder at the
bottom under already exhausted legs.

The sentry passed close enough to kick gravel down on top of them,
but Blain remained unseen. After a short countdown, fearing Gray might
buckle at any second, Blain scrambled completely onto the track and hunkered down. As the sentry distanced himself, Blain yanked Kennard to his
side. Now they had to get Gray up before the German turned and headed
back in their direction.

Forming a chain to lean over the embankment, Blain at the top, grasping Kennard by the legs, they reached for Gray. Desperate as he was to join

them, his boots slipped on the mud as if it were ice. Every attempt Gray made to grasp Kennard by the hand ended in a tumble down to the dank moor. After several tries, Gray saw that the sentry was about to make an about-face. "Duck!" he warned.

Blain and Kennard slithered off the gravel track and clung to the embankment edge. With every second that passed, their fingers were losing the strength they needed to keep their hold. Both kicked their boots into the wall for further support only to create a tumble of mud that splashed into the puddles below. They were certain the sound would give them away, but the sentry continued on his beat.

Gray had one more idea, one more chance to join Blain and Kennard on the embankment. Otherwise, they would have to go on without him. He would have to find another way across the border.

He tied together the straps of the two rucksacks Blain and Kennard had left behind. Kennard looked down as Blain held tightly onto his legs. "Catch!" Gray half-shouted, half-whispered. He burst up the wall, at the same time throwing the bundle up, one hand grasping its end. Kennard grabbed the lead rucksack, and as he hauled Gray up the side of the wall Blain stepped backward on the embankment to bring them both up. Gray scrambled onto the top, and the three sat gasping together on the track.

Just as they realized their effort had been successful they heard the sentry barking and saw him striding toward them.

"Run!" Gray shouted. "Down the bank! Run!" They leaped over the side of the dike, tumbling and sliding down the embankment until they hit the moor at the bottom. Together they hurled themselves blindly through the uneven terrain. Several rifle shots rang out behind them, but the sentry was aiming at shadows in the dark and missed. Curses and shouts in German followed.

The three men rushed on until the sentry's threats faded away. They slowed their pace but kept moving until Gray was sure they were well out of range and far over the border. Then he drew to a halt. Blain and Kennard stopped beside him in the moor. "It's all over," Gray said, throwing an arm around each of their shoulders. "We've bloody well made it!" Together they yawped, leaped up and down, hollered, and splashed in the marshy moor like schoolchildren playing in puddles.

In his young life, Blain had never experienced such joy; it overwhelmed him. Kennard felt the same. He sat down on the grass and ate his last sliver of chocolate, the one he had saved to celebrate their successful home run. Then he wept.

"That, dear friends and fellow lunatics, is the Dutch village of Sellingen," Gray announced, rallying them to their feet. Looking northward to the halo of lights, he quickly resumed his role as the steadying hand. "Come on, then. Let's not waste time. There's a war on, you know." The three escape artists started toward the lights, their masterpiece complete.

Twenty-four

Outside Sellingen, Gray, Blain, and Kennard surrendered themselves to the first patrol they encountered. The Dutch soldiers received the three men as if they were honored guests and took them to the nearby town of Coevorden. Put up in top-class accommodations at the Hotel Van Wely, they ate, shed their filthy clothes, bathed and shaved, then collapsed into beds that must have felt like the most heavenly of clouds. The next day, they telegrammed their families. The notes were spare but victorious. Kennard's read: "Escaped and arrived safely in Holland. Expect me home shortly — Caspar."

The next day, Tullis, Purves, and Leggatt joined them at the hotel. They too had made their home runs. The six of them, wearing wooden clogs, had their photograph taken, together with the owner of the hotel. Although their faces were gaunt, they all wore the looks of conquering heroes. Soon after, the Dutch military escorted them by train to Enschede, where they idled for a week in quarantine, segregated from a large contingent of German deserters. Bennett, Campbell-Martin, and Bousfield met them at the camp soon after.

Including Rathborne, who had already gone ahead to England, ten of the twenty-nine who escaped Holzminden made it to Holland. It was the greatest escape of the war. Secret cables from the British Consulate in Rotterdam informed London, where Lord Newton and officials in the War Office, Military Intelligence, and the Air Ministry celebrated the triumph.

Even before the escaped officers left the quarantine camp, brief reports about the tunnel escape were already hitting newspapers across Europe and in the United States. The *New York Times* headlined, "British Prisoners Dig Out," but offered few details, since the sensational nature of the breakout had yet to be fully revealed. First, the men needed to be returned home and debriefed. On the evening of August 15, the Holzminden escapees boarded a small ship in Rotterdam. They had new clothes, temporary passports, and a pocketful of money for their journey to London. With them on the steamer was Henry Cartwright, the officer for whom Will Harvey had sacrificed his own escape from Aachen. As part of a large convoy escorted by destroyers, the ship pulled out of the Dutch harbor and traveled a circuitous route across the Channel.

The next morning, the officers were moved beyond words by the sight of the English shoreline. They docked soon after in Gravesend. From the window of their train to the capital, Gray watched the countryside pass. It all looked as it always had: the rise and fall of fields bordered by hedges, cows lazing in the sun, towns tucked into hollows. Although he and the others had received updates on the war's progress, including the renewed Allied offensive that began only a week before, they still feared that their homeland had been ground down into a hopeless state — as the "Confidential Liar" had promised for years now.

Arriving at the station, they found the platforms crowded with young men in uniform. Outside, buses and taxis crammed the streets, and pedestrians thronged the sidewalks. Shops were open and restaurants bustling. To their quiet relief, Britain was alive and eager still. Dispatched straight to the War Office, the men underwent a series of interviews, mostly run by the Intelligence Department, to learn about their experiences and what they had seen during their captivity in Germany. Gray delivered his well-worn report of prisoner abuses from earlier in the war. Then, as one escapee recounted, they were instructed to "take three months' leave and get fat."

Soon after their return, King George V invited them for a private audience at Windsor Castle, then sent a kind personal note to each. Blain's was similar to those of the others: "The Queen joins me in welcoming you on your release from the miseries and hardships which you have endured with so much patience and courage. During these many months of trial, the early rescue of our gallant officers and men from the cruelties of their captivity has been uppermost in our thoughts. We are thankful that this longed for day has arrived, and that back in the old Country you will be able to once more enjoy the happiness of a home and to see good days among those who anxiously look for your return."

As the tunnelers reunited with their families, reports of their breakout spread. They were feted in their hometowns and former schools, by their fellow soldiers and airmen. Now that the details could be revealed, their exploits captivated the nation and the world. "The Tunnel to Freedom: British Officers' Escape from German Black Hole" headlined the *Daily Sketch*. "Daring Escape" reported the *Evening Express*, in bold type. With so much sacrifice and horror on every front, the Holzminden escape was a bright banner of hope — not to mention proof of British derring-do — that portended an Allied victory over Germany.

The ten men were put up for Military Cross medals. Despite all the attention that the Holzminden breakout artists received, most of them simply wanted to get back into the fight. After their leaves were over, Gray and his fellow pilots Blain and Kennard returned to their duties, albeit in squadrons stationed in England. They still had a war to win.

On August 16, 1918, the day after the Holzminden tunnelers arrived in London, Will Harvey was being made to board a train to Stralsund. He spent the next two months in yet another camp, this one beside the Baltic Sea. The sunsets were remarkable, but Harvey could not see beyond the "green mold" that once again settled over him like a great weight. He rarely left his bed. He again grew out his beard. He wrote no letters home, and the only reading he could manage was *Chambers's Twentieth Century Dictionary*. Yet it was in words — in poetry — that he was saved. Written at that time, "The Treasury" speaks of the liberating power of the imagination.

I have such joy in my heart's coffer,
Little I care what Life may offer;
Little it matters if I lie
In dungeons, who possess the sky.
The sparkling morn, the starry night,
Are locked away for my delight.
But in my heart there hangs a key
To open them, called memory.
How should I ever lack a friend
Who so have lovers without end?
How can I ever lose my home
Who bear it with me where I come?
My home is in my heart, and there
In dreadful days I do repair;
And I have broken off the seal
Of that Dream-box, whose dreams are real
So rich am I, I do possess
Their overpowering loveliness;
And have such joy in my heart's coffer,
Little I care what Life may offer.

In late October, the Germans finally returned Harvey and dozens of other prisoners of war to Aachen. The camp commandant swore he would soon be free, but Harvey had lost faith in such promises. Several days later, however, he and a number of others were sent across the border at last. There, they were welcomed by a crowd of Dutch children with joyous shouts and blown kisses. Harvey was moved beyond measure by the sight. At a seaside resort outside The Hague, he was reunited with Colquhoun as well as Rogers, Mossy, and the other Pink Toes. Together they belted out

"The Old, Bold Mate," one of their favorite prison songs, set to a melody by Harvey's friend Ivor Gurney.

> *Oh, some are fond of red wine and some are fond of white,*
> *And some are all for dancing by the pale moonlight,*
> *But rum alone's the tipple and the heart's delight*
> *Of the old, bold mate of Henry Morgan.*

Months passed before Harvey finally made his way back to the Red-lands in Gloucestershire, the place he loved so well. On many nights after his return, he stayed in and read to his mother, listening to the crackle of flames in the hearth, gazing at the white moon through the window, and thinking, "This is the most wonderful thing that has ever happened to me!" He was once again home, in the countryside he celebrated in his poetry. There he would remain, a solicitor, and a writer, married to Anne, for the rest of his life.

In the period after receiving the telegram from Rathborne, Commandant Karl Niemeyer became unhinged, whether due to shame over the mass escape, too much drink, or the ravages of the Spanish flu then spreading among the prison population. Like never before he raged at his charges, accusing them of insurrection and firing his revolver into the air at the slightest provocation. William Leefe Robinson, the Zeppelin killer, endured the worst of the commandant's abuses and was scarcely hanging on to life in solitary.

Not content with abusing his charges, Niemeyer stabbed his cane at the laundry the prisoners hung from the wire fences, a sight that one officer likened to Don Quixote tilting his lance at windmills. The men's continued escape attempts, mostly by cutting through the perimeter wire, only enraged him further.

As promised, he court-martialed the nineteen prisoners who were recaptured after the tunnel breakout. On September 27, 1918, officials from

Berlin held the trial at Holzminden. The defendants were charged with mutiny and "conspiring to destroy Imperial Government Property." Finding the indictment a farce, some of the officers decided to give suitably farcical answers to questions about their name, rank, religion, and pre-war occupations. One declared himself a shepherd, others gave their professions as diamond trader, grammar-school pupil, and pensioner. The judges sentenced the lot to six months' solitary confinement in a prison fortress for "having made an escape by force with united forces." But with 250,000 American troops landing in France every month, Allied advances puncturing holes in the trench lines across the Western Front, mass desertions of German soldiers, and civil unrest in Berlin and elsewhere, the war promised to be over long before they could serve a fraction of that sentence. Negotiations for an armistice were already in the works.

Within days of the court-martial, Niemeyer effected a sudden change of heart toward the men, transforming himself into a pliant friend of the prisoners. He hired a photographer to come into Holzminden, and made awkward attempts to joke with the men and gather them into happy groups for shots. "They would all be home for Christmas" came the promise. No longer did he bluster around the yard, cock of the walk. He stayed mostly in the Kommandantur, inviting the senior British officer, Stokes-Roberts, to his office, making frequent approvals of any requests. Fewer roll calls, longer parole walks — whatever the men wanted. Throughout the camp, portraits of the kaiser disappeared.

Of course, Niemeyer was keen to the fact that the British knew all about his actions at Holzminden — Lord Newton having once demanded his removal. What he feared was a trial of his own, for war crimes. When some prisoners at the camp confirmed to him that justice would come calling, he claimed that he had "always done all he could for the officers and that if there had been any unpleasant orders, they came from above."

The prisoners were wise to his intentions. With their newfound freedoms came access to more than the *Continental Times*. On October 3 one wrote in his secret diary, "The war will soon be over. Austria has seceded to President Wilson's peace terms. Things look pretty cheery. Our boys at the Front are certainly working hard. They have sure pushed the Germans back a long piece." Most believed they would be home before Christmas. Apart from what the newspapers reported, the prisoners knew well that Germany could not hold out for long. Not if the stirrings of popular revolt in the town of Holzminden were any sign. There was a string of food riots, and many of the town's inhabitants were dying from starvation and the Spanish flu.

Finally, on November 11, the Armistice was announced, along with the news that Kaiser Wilhelm II had fled to the Netherlands, his rule over Germany at an end. At Holzminden, the prisoners tossed their caps in the air. They cheered and danced in the Spielplatz. They removed the German flag that flew atop Block A. They freed those still in the solitary cells in Block B. They drank and feasted in celebration into the wee hours of the night. Neither the guards nor Niemeyer tried to stop them. In fact, their commandant immediately shed his uniform for a plain suit and declared to the camp, "You see, I am no longer a Prussian officer, but a Hanoverian gentleman."

He had good reason to be worried. Socialist revolutionaries had already assassinated his superior, General Hänisch. The following day, while the officers and orderlies at Holzminden wondered how and when they would return home, Niemeyer disappeared, no doubt with the riches he had extorted from them. Most of the guards fled as well. A company of German soldiers was sent to watch over the camp, but they largely allowed the men to do as they liked. Dick Cash was one among many who used the new freedom to take walks into town. Its residents were in a desperate state, and a riot nearly broke out when he presented packages of rice and tins of cocoa for trade.

Weeks passed without word of their fate, and the prisoners' supply of food soon dwindled down to potatoes and cabbages. Instead of scheduling a departure date, the Germans handed out pamphlets sent from Berlin, entitled *A Parting Word*. They began, "The war is over! A little while

—you will see your native land again." The propaganda promised a new Germany and concluded, "The valiant dead who once fought against each other have long been sleeping as comrades side by side in the same earth. May the living who once fought against each other labour as comrades side by side upon this self-same earth. That is the message with which we bid you farewell."

Yet this farewell remained at a considerable remove: no help came from Berlin to evacuate the Holzminden camp. Finally, Stokes-Roberts commandeered a train to take the Holzminden men west. On the moonless night of their departure from the camp, December 10, there was one last hurrah. The men piled tables, boxes, chairs, trunks, old clothes, and anything else combustible they could find into the Spielplatz and lit a huge bonfire. The German soldiers tried to extinguish the flames, but the men stabbed holes in their hoses. Framed by the glow of the blaze, they assembled into four columns and marched out of the gates.

In town, the Germans lined the streets to watch them pass, a look of "awe, envy, and hate" on their faces, as one officer wrote. The officers and orderlies boarded their train, making no separation for rank as they packed the carriages. With a jolt, the train started forward down the rails, the bonfire at Holzminden growing fainter in the distance with each minute that passed, until they could see it no more.

Epilogue

On the evening of July 23, 1938, Lieutenant Colonel David Gray, commanding officer of the 48th Pioneers, headed down London's Fleet Street. He ducked through the door of Ye Olde Cheshire Cheese, the pub that had served Sir Arthur Conan Doyle and Charles Dickens under its famous dark vaulted ceilings. This night, it was hosting the twentieth anniversary of the Holzminden tunnel escape. Air Commodore Charles Rathborne chaired the dinner, and Jim Bennett was its organizer.

After two decades, Gray reunited for the first time with his former roommates Jack Tullis and Stanley Purves, their lead sapper, Walter Butler, and a number of other officers and orderlies involved in the breakout. His two closest friends from those dramatic days would sadly not be coming. In early 1919 Cecil Blain had crashed and died while test-piloting a Sopwith Dolphin for the RAF. He was in the middle of writing a memoir about the Holzminden escape. Gray was stationed in Russia at the time, battling the Bolsheviks in the Russian Civil War there, and could not return for the funeral. King George V sent his condolences in a letter to the Blain family, recalling the "gallant and able Officer" he had met only months before.

So too did Gray miss the burial of Caspar Kennard. After the war, Kennard had gone home to Argentina. He married and became the manager of a large ranch. In 1935 he was killed in a freak shooting accident. "Kennard was a stout fellow, a good pal," his obituary concluded. "His untimely death will leave a feeling of great regret in the hearts of his fellow officers."

There were many others missing at the dinner, albeit because of distance rather than tragic circumstance. Dick Cash had returned to Australia to reunite with his family. Likewise, the Holzminden prisoners had spread out far and wide after the Armistice — from South Africa to New Zealand, to Singapore, India, Hong Kong, Barbados, Vancouver, and New York City. Those absent were recognized, but most of the evening was spent in laughter and conversation over "weisse wine," recalling the moments both comic and horrifying they shared while tunneling to their freedom.

The breakout artists still wondered about the fate of Karl and Heinrich Niemeyer. At the Versailles Peace Conference, it had been agreed that certain "enemy officers" should be brought to justice for their crimes. The Niemeyer brothers made the list, particularly after the death of William Leefe Robinson was ascribed to the privations he suffered at Holzminden. The twins, however, were never found. One report had Karl committing suicide in Hanover; others said that he had escaped to South America.

Whatever the truth, perhaps the best laugh of the anniversary night came when a mocked-up telegram from one of their fellow tunnelers was delivered to the pub from Milwaukee, Wisconsin. "I know damn all about you and your dinner [Stop] Niemeyer [Stop]." The roars from Gray and others were heard into the night.

Over the next few decades, the tunnelers and other Holzminden prisoners — friends for life — would meet again for anniversaries. Over time, they would join with fellow escape artists from other camps — and other wars. Gray, however, would not attend another of these dinners. After Hitler invaded Poland in September 1939, Gray left the 48th Pioneers to join the RAF as a squadron commander. Although fifty-five years old and graying at the temples, he was still rigid of spine and eager to the fray.

When he had to leave the RAF in 1942, for reasons of age, he signed up for the Home Guard, a voluntary defense organization. That November, he died in a lorry accident — an inglorious end to an otherwise glorious and bravely led life. David "Munshi" Gray, the "Father of the Tunnel," was buried with honors in Wonston, Hampshire. Most treasured among the items he left his family, his wife, Violet, and their nineteen-year-old son, were the escape kit, old maps, fake identification, and compass he had used in his home run.

In total, 573 British and Empire prisoners (54 officers, 519 other ranks), escaped during World War I. Remarkably, by one historian's estimate, there were over ten thousand attempts. Those who succeeded were a small, select group out of the 192,848 POWs held in Germany.

Throughout World War II, Jim Bennett continued to travel for MI9, brown leather suitcase in hand, to base after base, for week after week. He usually began his talks by saying that becoming a POW was "improbable but possible." His message to the young men was always the same: in the event that they were taken prisoner, their war effort was not finished. Each and every one of them had a duty to escape.

Then he recounted his own experiences, his lack of preparation, the missed opportunities, the false starts, all before his final dash across the border. In his mistakes, and in those of his friends, there was much to learn. "Forewarned is forearmed," he liked to conclude.

As a speaker, Bennett played only a small part in the vast organization that coordinated escape and evasion across Europe and the Mediterranean, but he and his fellow breakout artists — Gray, Blain, Kennard, Leggatt, Medlicott, and so many others — were very much the inspiration for MI9 and its American counterpart, MIS-X. Their bravery and daring paved the way for the establishment of these organizations.

Before the collapse of Nazi Germany in 1945, 33,578 British, Commonwealth, and American members of the armed forces managed to return to Allied lines after finding themselves on the run or captured behind enemy lines. Further, some of the most remarkable escapes, including ones from Colditz and Stalag Luft III, bear too many echoes of Holzminden and other World War I breakouts to be a coincidence.

Outside his MI9 lectures, Bennett rarely spoke about his captivity or escape. His family had no idea about his subsequent service in World War II until they found a dusty folder with papers that included his speech notes and travel receipts after his death in 1983 at the age of ninety-one. Instead, he focused his life on building a business, being a good friend, investing in a happy marriage, and raising a son and daughter. He was there to ensure that his children, Graham and Laurie, followed his version of the Golden Rule — "Do as you would be done by" — and to teach them how to ride a bicycle and drive a car. The opportunity to do so in freedom, in his own country, was reward enough for his contribution to the greatest escape of the Great War.

The Holzminden Escape List —
July 23 to 24, 1918

SUCCEEDED IN HOME RUN

Jim Bennett

Cecil Blain

John Bousfield

Peter Campbell-Martin

David Gray

Caspar Kennard

Edward Leggatt

Stanley Purves

Charles Rathborne

John Tullis

RECAPTURED

Douglas Birch

Thomas Burrill

Walter Butler

Andrew Clouston

Frederick Illingworth

William Langran

Colin Laurence

Bernard Luscombe

Peter Lyon

Neil McLeod

Frederick Mardock

Arthur Morris

Jack Morrogh

Robert Paddison

Clifford Robertson

Frank Sharpe

Alan Shipwright

Philip Smith

David Wainwright

Acknowledgments

Years ago, in a more adventuresome lifetime, I took some flying lessons with a fellow author (and experienced pilot), Tom Casey. I still vividly remember the exhilaration — and heart-dropping fear — of swooping over the coastline of Long Island, then around the tip of Manhattan, and up the Hudson River corridor. The experience sparked an interest in aviation, pursued more safely within the confines of histories of the same. My most avid reading focused on the early days of the Royal Flying Corps and daring Oxbridge sorts who made up its ranks of pilots flying their wood, cloth, and wire contraptions. Among those volumes that inspired further reading were H. A. Jones's magisterial *The War in the Air*, Cecil Lewis's *Sagittarius Rising*, and Denis Winter's *The First of the Few*.

Besides a hasty path to death, these pilots also faced a good chance of being shot down behind enemy lines, particularly as their activities ramped up in advance of the Battle of the Somme in 1916. Those who survived a crash landing were inevitably captured and imprisoned by the Germans. Rascals of the highest sort, many of these men attempted elaborate escapes that might well have been pulled straight from the pages of *Boy's Own* adventures. Only the incurious could then resist picking up one of what became a genre of World War I breakout memoirs. They are too many to name, but among my early favorites were Gerald Knight's *Brother Bosch*, J. A. L. Caunter's *13 Days*, A. J. Evans's *The Escaping Club*, and J. L. Hardy's *I Escape!*. Time and again, these memoirs drew a line to what might best be described as the Alcatraz of Germany at the time: Holzminden.

I quickly fell under the spell of the classic *The Tunnelers of Holzminden* by H. G. Durnford, who played a bit part in the extraordinary events that led to the greatest breakout of the Great War. Upon consuming his memoir, I was sure I had my next book project in hand. That said, Durnford recounted the events — and characters of those involved — with the kind of emotionless British reserve that left me unsure of who these men were and what drove them. Then I came across the delightfully introspective, quirky, and beautifully written *Comrades in Captivity* by the poet and Holzminden survivor F. W. Harvey. He put flesh and bone on what it was to be a prisoner in the archipelago of German camps in World War I, and the desperation that pushed some to risk everything to be free.

All these books were inspiration — and great source material — but they were only the beginning of my journey to chronicle this narrative. One should always start with the low-hanging fruit, and I benefited from three previous works on the Holzminden escape: *Beyond the Tumult* by Barry Winchester, *Escape from Germany* by Neil Hanson, and Jacqueline Cook's *The Real Great Escape*. Each in their own way provided excellent guidance, same as the holistic study of British POWs in Germany by John Lewis-Stempel in *The War Behind the War*.

Given these events occurred almost exactly a century before I started my research, I knew firsthand interviews were out, and I would need to depend on a rich and diverse range of primary documents. Fortunately, I struck gold early and often over the course of the project thanks to the wonderful archivists at the Imperial War Museums, RAF Museum, the British National Archives at Kew (a treasure almost unparalleled), the Bundesarchiv, and the Liddle Collection at the University of Leeds. They provided unpublished memoirs, oral history interviews, repatriated POW reports, letters, maps, and even artifacts from the escape by many of the key participants in these extraordinary events. Of particular note was a handwritten memoir by Cecil Blain at the Imperial War Museums. My frontline researcher for many of these finds was Claire Barrett. At the time, she was studying for her master's in the history of war from King's College, London. She proved tenacious and a quick study, and I owe a great debt to her for following up my leads — and generating quite a few on her own. In a word, she is top-notch. Thanks also to early research by Norma Bulman and Almut Schoenfeld.

I would also like to make a special call out to the F. W. Harvey Collection at the Gloucestershire Archives, an extraordinary repository of letters, scrapbooks, personal documents, notebooks, and other papers from the soldier-poet. In writing this book, I am perhaps most proud to have played a part in resurrecting the memoir of this incredible individual. I was ably assisted in accessing this collection by James Grant Repshire and Steve Cooper of the F. W. Harvey Society. Thank you also to Mrs. Elaine Jackson of the Harvey family, who gave me permission to quote from the collection. It is truly a window into the soul of these heroes.

Where archives came up short, I depended on the kindness and generosity of the families of many of the principal individuals in this escape. After so many years, some were a challenge to track down across the world (online family trees and Facebook are a researcher's new best friend!), but perseverance paid off. Much of the incredible story of Royal Navy Air Service observer Leonard James Bennett had been lost to history, but thanks to his daughter, Laurie Vaughan, I had access to his unpublished memoirs, lecture notes, and page after page of letters he sent from Holzminden during his captivity. More important in some ways, Bennett verified the link between the breakout artists of World War I and the founding of MI9, the British escape and evasion service that saved so many lives during World War II. I would also like to thank Laurie's granddaughter, Lily Peschardt, who collected many of these writings in her graduate school project Home This Afternoon.

Many other families assisted with letters, unpublished memoirs, photos, and other bits of information. This book could not have been written without them. Thanks especially to Hugh Lowe, Brian Tullis, Keil Tullis,

Brenda Merriman, Pete Clouston, Jane Gray, Diana Gillyatt, Kit Kennard, Margaret Pretorius, Mal Lyon, Tony Wheatley, and Julyan Peard. Although I could not tell each prisoner's story in full, I hope the families know how instrumental their efforts were. Thank you also to Jacqueline Mallahan for her generosity in sharing her late husband Patrick's archival collection and research into the RFC and POWs in World War I.

Despite such a vast number of sources, there remained some mysteries, particularly as to the arrival and departure times of some of the prisoners to Holzminden — and their specific activities in the early foundation of the tunnel. The tremendous archive/tracking service of World War I POWs collected by the International Committee of the Red Cross was invaluable in accounting for some, but not all, of the prisoners' movements in and out of camps. Still, there remained a few gaps. I have endeavored to draw as accurate a timeline as possible. Any errors or misinterpretations are mine alone.

Much-deserved thanks go to my publishing team. First to my former Scholastic editor Cheryl Klein, who gave me that little extra nudge at a critical time to pursue this story. Second to my agent and friend Eric Lupfer, who is always there with steady guidance and cheerful encouragement; this book could not have happened without him. Thanks too to my film agent on the project, Ashley Fox, as well as the great folks at WME, Simon Trewin and Raffaella De Angelis. I also benefited from an early read by World War I aviation expert James Streckfuss. As always, my appreciation to the support of all at Houghton Mifflin Harcourt, including Jenny Xu, Lori Glazer, Bruce Nichols, Megan Wilson, and Michael Dudding. Thanks also to Melissa Dobson, for your skilled copyedit. To the late Carla Gray, I'll be absent your sharp wit and ever-at-the-ready cheer as we go to publication. You're missed.

This book is dedicated to my two longtime editors, Liz Hudson and Susan Canavan. We've been together now going on a decade and a half, and to be honest, I simply do not know how I'd do what I do without you at my side every step of the way. Thank you for your patience, insight, and crack-of-the-whip-but-with-kindness. Sometimes I may not show it, but I know how lucky I am.

Finally, to Diane and our girls (and Moses thrown in for good measure). Words couldn't do justice in describing your impact on every part of my life!

Notes

ABBREVIATIONS

AC — Family Papers of Andrew Clouston
AWM — Australian War Memorial, Campbell, Australia
BA — Archives, British Library, UK
BARCH — Bundesarchiv, Germany
CHALK — Chalk Collection, Tasmanian State Archives, Australia
CK — Family Papers of Caspar Kennard
CWB — Family Papers of Cecil W. Blain
DGB — Family Papers of David B. Gray
GA — F. W. Harvey Collection, Gloucestershire Archives, UK
HFD — Family Papers of Hector F. Dougall
HPA — Colquohoun Family, Archives and Special Collections, Hamilton Public Library, Canada
ICRC — Prisoners of the First World War, ICRC Historical Archives, Switzerland
IWM — Imperial War Museums, UK
IWM-B — Papers of C. Blain, Imperial War Museums, UK
JDM — Family Papers of John D. Morrogh
JKT — Family Papers of John K. Tullis
LIDD — Liddle Collection, University of Leeds Special Collections, UK
LJB — Family Papers of Leonard. J. Bennett
PM — Family Papers of Patrick Mallahan
RAF — Archival Collection, Royal Air Force Museums, Hendon, UK
SCHA — Private Papers of William Hugh Chance, Sandwell Community History and Archives, UK
TNA — National Archives, Kew, UK

PROLOGUE

page

xxi   *For all his wife:* Author interview with Laurie Vaughan.
      Its headlines read: Daily Express, July 14, 1941; *Daily Herald,* July 14, 1941; *Times* (London), July 14, 1941; *Daily Mirror,* July 14, 1941.
xxii *Three months before:* Bryan, p. 36.
      Bennett boarded: Application for P/W Lectures, July 14, 1941, LJB.
      Earlier that morning: Author interview with Laurie Vaughan.
      While running: Foot, pp. 22–26; Historical Record of I.S.9, TNA: WO 208/3242; History of Intelligence School No. 9, TNA: WO 208/3246.
xxiii *Crockatt did not:* Foot, pp. 2–3.
      "duty to escape": Notes, Bennett MI9 lecture, LJB.

CHAPTER ONE

3   *The sky lightened:* Blain, unpublished memoir, IWM-B; Papers of W. Chance, IWM; Tullis Flight Log, 8/7/16, JKT.
     "Contact!": Winter, pp. 91–92.
4   *Over a woolen:* Ibid., p. 87.
     After his squadron: Winchester, pp. 1–2; Bott, p. 239.
     For a limited: C. Lewis, pp. 47–48.
5   *"It looks from":* Grider, p. 270.
     "Open for us": Lee, pp. 5–6.
     On July 1: Keegan, pp. 292–94.
     For the No. 70: Bott, p. 161; Liddle, p. 28; Money, p. 21.
6   *On the port:* Winchester, p. 1.
     "plunging into a": Winter, p. 99.
     One aggressive move: Winchester, pp. 2–3.
7   *The ancient city:* Afferbach and Strachan, p. 294.
     The Sopwiths broke: Blain, unpublished memoir, IWM-B; Statement Regarding Circumstances of Capture, David Griffiths, TNA: AIR 1/1207/204/5/2619; Winchester, pp. 4–5; 70th Squadron Report, TNA: AIR 1/2395/258/1.
8   *"the introduction into":* Pamphlet: "The Diamond Jubilee," SCHA, FP-CH 15/7/10.
     "naval requirement": R. Barker, p. 9.
     "I hope none": Winter, p. 11.
9   *"skill, energy and perseverance":* Pamphlet: "The Diamond Jubilee," SCHA: FP-CH 15/7/10.
     "Do you ride?": R. Barker, p. 21.
     "High spirits and resilience": Ibid., pp. 213–14.
10   *Born in 1896:* Baptism Papers, CWB; Author interview with Hugh Lowe.
     The outbreak of: Blain Service Records, TNA: AIR 76/41.
     To start his: Blain Service Records, TNA: AIR 76/41; Unpublished memoir, Papers of G. Gilbert, RAF; Lecture notes, SCHA: FP-CH 15/6/4.
     "The whole contraption": C. Lewis, p. 12.
11   *For his maiden:* Unpublished memoir, Papers of C. Roberts, LIDD: AIR-264; Unpublished memoir, Papers of C. Illingworth, LIDD: AIR-170; Unpublished memoir, Papers of P. Playfair, RAF; Unpublished memoir, Papers of G. Gilbert, RAF; Liddle, pp. 70–72;

R. Barker, pp. 210–13; Winter, pp. 27–33; Money, pp. 11–15; Lee, pp. 14–22. In his own memoir, Blain gave scarce details of his RFC training. Nonetheless, the sources listed here provide a consistent view of what pilot cadets faced, and offer a great window into this period of the pilot's life.

At Northolt: Exact figures on training deaths within the RFC remain difficult to determine. In Denis Winter's book, *The First of the Few,* he accounted that half of the "14,166 dead pilots" were killed in training (p. 36). Other analyses, including some fine work by World War I air enthusiasts (www.theaerodrome.com), state that this number is far exaggerated. Drawing on statistics from Chris Hobson's *Airman Died in the Great War 1914–1918: The Roll of Honour of the British and Commonwealth Air Services* (DVD-ROM), they settle on fewer overall deaths — and fewer still from accidents (one-sixth from training). The author has erred on the side of the more limited number, though this is surely worthy of a more precise scholarly investigation.

On a typical: Michael Skeet, "RFC Pilot Training," Aerodrome, Forum, December 1998, www.theaerodrome.com.

When Blain took: Unpublished memoir, Papers of L. Nixon, IWM.

"Rudder—Elevator—Ailerons": C. Lewis, p. 14.

12 *Blain survived his:* Blain Service Record, CWB.

"maternity jacket": Unpublished memoir, Papers of W. Chance, IWM.

In June: Ibid.; Blain Service Records, TNA: AIR 76/41.

He left for: Letter from Winchester to Miss Blain, March 3, 1969, CWB.

Eight weeks later: Bott, p. 215.

"No use! Got": Winchester, p. 5; Statement Regarding Circumstances of Capture, David Griffiths, TNA: AIR 1/1207/204/5/2619.

As Griffiths tossed: Blain, unpublished memoir, IWM-B; Winchester, pp. 4–6; 70th Squadron Report, TNA: AIR 1/2395/258/1; Bott, p. 254.

14 *On the road:* Knight, pp. 25–29; Unpublished memoir, Anonymous War Diary, IWM: 73/181/1.

Blain and Griffiths: Blain, unpublished memoir, IWM-B; Winchester, pp. 17–22.

CHAPTER TWO

16 *Early on August:* Percy Douglas, "Life in the Ypres Salient," Papers of P. Douglas, LIDD: AIR-107; Ellis, pp. 9–15.

Those on sentry: Barnes, pp. 42–43.

"I never saw": Harvey, pp. 64–65.

17 *Only the day:* 2/5 Gloucestershire Regiment Diary, TNA: WO 95/3006/1/1; Barnes, p. 37; Fussell, p. 11.

Harvey tried: Harvey, p. 3; Report on the Capture of F. W. Harvey, TNA: WO 374/316910.

Later that morning: Thornton, p. 97.

18 *"intolerable grief":* Bridges, p. 7.

In the early afternoon: Harvey, pp. 1–7; Ellis, pp. 72–74; News Clipping, no date, Papers of F. W. Harvey, GA; Report on the Capture of F. W. Harvey, TNA: WO 374/31691.

19 *"Be damned if":* Harvey, p. 6.

Reaching the next: Report on the Capture of F. W. Harvey, TNA: WO 374/31691.

20 *"When earth was":* "Round Pool," GA.

Constructed by: Boden, pp. 3–29.

21 *"real me":* Boden, p. 30.

The same rumbling: Hattersley, pp. 1–3, 126, 175, 243, 266, 291, 362–367.

22 *Despite these reverberations:* Repshire, pp. 9-11.

Although the death: Keegan, pp. 16–87.

"world power or downfall": Tuchman, p. 14.

"forced into our": Keegan, p. 73.

Mustering in the: Ibid.

"honor" and "glory": Tuchman, p. 113.

23 "To turn, as swimmers": Brooke, "1914," as excerpted in Tuchman, p. 341.

Many believed the: Horrocks, p. 15.

Swept into this: Boden, pp. 43–46.

Under the Schlieffen: Keegan, pp. 28–29.

24 *On March 29:* Wyrall, pp. 128–29; Boden, pp. 64–76.

"I must say": Shephard, p. 33.

"wastage": Fussell, p. 44.

Affectionately nicknamed: Repshire, p. 11.

On August 3, 1915: News clipping, undated, Papers of F. W. Harvey, GA.

25 "This route march": Harvey, "This Route March," GA.

"Joy diadems thy": Harvey, "To Rupert Brooke," GA.

"I'm homesick for": Harvey, "In Flanders," GA.

26 *The first of its:* Boden, p. 59.

"His desire for": Thornton, p. 97.

"Local Poet Missing": Boden, p. 122.

"How did you": Harvey, p. 9. In his memoirs, Harvey recounted this brief interrogation in the first person. For sake of clarity, the author made slight amendments to account for who was addressing the questions to whom.

"Oh, we have": Ibid., p. 11.

27 *"By God":* Ibid., p. 12.

"No mortal comes": Harvey, "Solitary Confinement," GA.

"Shakespeare for the": Harvey, p. 15.

"Nein! Engländer!": Lewis-Stempel, p. 59; Harvey, p. 12.

28 *"Krieg. Nix gut":* Harvey, p. 17.

From the station: Unpublished memoir, Papers of J. Dykes, IWM; Phillimore, pp. 9–10.

"Bad sportsmen": Harvey, p. 18.

"Front-line troops": Horrocks, p. 19.

CHAPTER THREE

29 *"There is to":* Unpublished memoir, SCHA: FP-CH 15/7/8; Bott, pp. 32–33. The speech presented here is an amalgamation of these two versions, though primarily leaning on Bott's.

"Attack everything!": Hart, p. 74.

At Le Hameau: History of No. 11 Squadron, TNA: AIR 1/688/21/20/11.

30 *"solid grey wool":* Hart, p. 169.

Aided by tanks: Ibid., p. 172.

"The next moment": Unpublished memoir, Private papers of Colonel F. O. Cave, IWM.

Since the war: R. Barker, pp. 142–48.

At the start of: Whitehouse, p. 112.

"absolute master": Unpublished memoir, Papers of V. Coombs, LIDD: POW-016.

Air crews were: R. Barker, p. 171.

The RFC now: Winter, p. 156.

31 *"bloody murder":* R. Barker, p. 171.

What the British: Werner, pp. 1–7, 148–52, 199–201, 230–34.

Back at their aerodromes: Unpublished memoirs, Papers of F. Morris, RAF; Hart, pp. 152–53.

Even so, at: History of 11th Squadron, TNA: AIR 1/688/21/20/11; Unpublished memoir, Papers of C. Roberts, LIDD: AIR-264; Keegan, p. 360.

32 *Gray reviewed his:* Report from Captain Gray, August 21, 1918, TNA: AIR 1/501/15/333/1.

David Gray spent: Family Records, DBG; Weatherstone, pp. 60–83; Antrobus, pp. 145–53; Sharma, pp. 1–43.

In addition to: Family Records, DBG; Antrobus, pp. 145–53.

33 *He settled early:* Family Records, DBG; Guggisberg, pp. 103–81.

Upon graduation: Service Record of D. B. Gray, British Indian Army Records, BA.

"A capable and efficient": Ibid.

Despite his quick: Interview with Jane Gray. For reference, *munshi* is a Persian word for secretary or writer, but in India it was used to identify language teachers who taught the British.

34 *Soon after the outbreak:* Service Record of D. B. Gray, British Indian Army Records, BA; TNA: WO 95/5118/2; A. J. Barker, pp. 11–40.

In spring 1915: Lambert, pp. 45–60.

"There were no": Whitehouse, p. 97.

35 *Later that year:* Author interview with Jane Gray; Kieran, pp. 60–91.

After earning his: Family Records, DBG; Service Record of D. B. Gray, British Indian Army Records, BA; TNA: AIR 76/192.

After a dismal: Unpublished memoir, SCHA: FP-CH 15/7/8; Money, pp. 100–104; Winchester, pp. 6–11.

36 *Before crossing the: Destonian,* June 1918.

Suddenly the sky: Letter from David Gray to Mrs. Morris, November 25, 1916, Papers of F. Morris, RAF; Report from Captain Gray, August 21, 1918, TNA: AIR 1/501/15/333/1; Werner, pp. 240–242; Von Richthofen, pp. 74–78; Report on Capture of Leonard Helder, TNA: WO 339/11209.

38 *"You are my":* Winchester, p. 11.

Once reassured: Letter from David Gray to Mrs. Morris, November 25, 1916, Papers of F. Morris, RAF.

Gray remained: Winchester, p. 28.

"Fix bayonets and die": Lewis-Stempel, pp. xv, 3.

39 *"The war is over":* Unpublished memoir, SCHA: FP-CH 15/7/8; Money, p. 106.

The next day: Money, pp. 105–10; Tullis, unpublished memoir, JKT; Letter from David Gray to Mrs. Morris, November 25, 1916, Papers of F. Morris, RAF.

"Why do so many": Money, p. 111; Herwig, p. 226.

40 *on September 29:* Blain, unpublished memoir, IWM-B.

The train clanked: Winchester, pp. 34–35; Knight, pp. 41–43.

Several hours later: Unpublished memoir, SCHA: FP-CH 15/7/8; Tullis, unpublished memoir, JKT; Money, p. 113; Account of Edward Leggatt, TNA: WO 161/96.

41 *On September 3:* Money, p. 113; Bills, pp. 50–65. The story of Germany's plans to retaliate for the Zeppelin downing is difficult to corroborate, as some at Osnabrück attributed the proposed retaliation to British use of tracer fire.

CHAPTER FOUR

42   *October 9, 1916:* Letter from Caspar Kennard to Chris Kennard, October 13, 1916, CK; Letter from C. Kennard to his Parents, October 12, 1916, Papers of C. Kennard, IWM; "Shot Down Behind Enemy Lines," News Clipping, undated, Papers of C. Kennard, IWM.

43   *flying solo:* Pilot Logbook, Papers of C. Kennard, IWM.
     Seven months before: Author interview with Diana Gillyatt; Kennard Family Papers, CK.
     After earning his: Kennard Service Records, TNA: AIR 76/271.

44   *"Somewhere behind the":* Letter from C. Kennard to his Parents, October 12, 1916, Papers of C. Kennard, IWM.
     Days later, their: Winchester, p. 36.
     "Those vanquished in": Krammer, p. 3.

45   *During the Middle:* Garrett, pp. 17–25.
     "sticked with daggers": Ibid., p. 25; Krammer, p. 5.
     "None shall kill": Krammer, pp. 17–18.

46   *"merely men, whose":* Speed, p. 3.
     With the rise: Ibid., p. 2.
     "like your own": Garrett, p. 28.
     "sinkholes of filth": Krammer, p. 19.
     "humanely treated": Report on Certain Violations of the Hague and Geneva Conventions, TNA: HO 45/10763/270829.

47   *"a spoilt darling":* Speed, p. 5.
     In the first six: Doegen, pp. 21–29; Jackson, p. 54.
     In the act: Lewis-Stempel, p. xix.
     The moans of: Gilliland, p. 9.
     Those who reached: Lewis-Stempel, pp. 1–20. For a full account of the vagaries suffered by British POWs in World War I, John Lewis-Stempel's *The War Behind the Wire* is a finely detailed study.
     Wood-slatted huts: Report of the Conditions of the Camp for Prisoners of War at Friedrichsfeld, TNA: HO 45/10763/270829. The British archives contain numerous inspection accounts verifying the same.

48   *"The patients were":* Report on the Typhus Epidemic at Wittenberg, TNA: HO 45/10763/270829.
     Roughly 80 percent: Lewis-Stempel, pp. 68–111; Spoerer, pp. 121–36.
     According to one: Heather Jones, p. 21.

49   *"take no prisoners":* Herwig, p. 79.
     "screw up the most": Ibid., p. 256.
     "in case of overwhelming": Morgan, p. 97.
     Other nations: Panayi, *Prisoners of Britain*, p. 90; Speed, pp. 102–5.

50   *In mid-October:* Winchester, pp. 35–36; Unpublished memoir, SCHA: FP-CH 15/7/8; Tullis, unpublished memoir, JKT; Account of Edward Leggatt, TNA: WO 161/96.
     When Kennard emerged: Report by Gerald Knight, TNA: FO 383/272; Money, pp. 114–15; Winchester, p. 36.
     A guard brought: Blain, unpublished memoir, IWM-B; Report on Prisoners Camp at Osnabrück, TNA: FO 383/267.

51   *The British Red:* Hanson, pp. 106, 113–18.

Throughout his first: Blain, unpublished memoir, IWM-B.

His fellow prisoners: Ibid.; Winchester, pp. 37–38.

53   *"My deaarest Mother":* Blain, unpublished memoir, IWM-B.

"Will they twig": Ibid.

While they waited: Letters from Hugh Chance to his Family, October–November 1916, SCHA: FP-CH 15/7/3; Money, pp. 116–19; Diary, October 5–November 30, 1916, SCHA: FP-CH 15/7/8.

54   *"stout heart and steady":* Letter from David Gray to Mrs. Morris, November 25, 1916, Papers of F. Morris, RAF.

Every day: Winchester, pp. 38–41.

"Dear old Mum": Ibid.

55   *In early December:* Tullis, unpublished memoir, JKT.

Then, on December: David Gray, ICRC.

CHAPTER FIVE

56   *Gütersloh was a:* Harvey, pp. 91–95; Gilliland, p. 55.

"pine-shadowed cage": Harvey, p. 19.

Crushed by this: Phillimore, pp. 24–26.

"bad German wine": Harvey, p. 70.

A few days later: Report by Captain C. V. Fox, TNA: FO 383/271; *Continental Times,* December 18, 1916; David, p. 279; Keegan, pp. 306–9.

57   *When Harvey first:* Harvey, pp. 19–25; Lewis-Stempel, p. xxi.

"Walking round our cages": Harvey, "Gütersloh," GA.

58   *"less important":* Harvey, p. 39.

"the Poet": Ibid., p. 26.

It was not the: Phillimore, pp. 26–29.

Harvey missed: Boden, p. 140.

"He cannot help": Harvey, pp. 27–28.

His bunkmates: Ibid., pp. 30–35; Boden, pp. 154–57.

59   *A former coal-mine:* Phillimore, pp. 37–44.

a camp in Crefeld: Reflects pre-1929 spelling; it is spelled "Krefeld" today.

"foolish": Ibid., p. 29.

Cecil Blain and: Blain, unpublished memoir, IWM-B; Tullis, unpublished memoir, JKT; Chance, unpublished memoir, SCHA: FP-CH 15/7/8.

60   *"evil swine":* Blain, unpublished memoir, IWM-B.

61   *"Ready?":* Winchester, p. 44.

"covered with blood!": Blain, unpublished memoir, IWM-B; Knight, p. 49.

admitted they had: Blain, unpublished memoir, IWM-B.

Blankenstein decided to: Knight, pp. 50–54.

62   *"Raus!":* Ibid., p. 51; Letters from Hugh Chance to his Family, March–April, 1917, SCHA: FP-CH 15/7/5.

After a couple: Lewis-Stempel, p. 122; Letters from Hugh Chance to his Family, March–April, 1917, SCHA: FP-CH 15/7/5; Tullis, unpublished memoir, JKT.

Surrounding the retreat: Evans, pp. 19–21.

Blain, Kennard, and: Blain, unpublished memoir, IWM-B; Knight, pp. 70–77.

63   *"cunning attack":* "Begalubigte Abschrift," April 7, 1917, Papers of C. Kennard, RAF.

They spent it: Blain, unpublished memoir, IWM-B; Tullis, unpublished memoir, JKT.

Captain David Gray: Winchester, p. 103. In his book, *Beyond the Tumult,* Winchester references the escape described in this passage to have taken place during June 1917. At that time, Gray would have been at Schwarmstadt camp, having been moved from Crefeld. That said, it is clear this escape was attempted from Crefeld, and given the weather and window of opportunity, spring was the most likely time.

With its warm: Report on Crefeld, Bundesarchiv 901/84359; Letter from Burlow to his mother, April 14, 1917, Papers of R. Burrows, LIDD: POW-010.

He shared the: December 12, 1916, Diary, Papers of D. Grant, IWM. Lyall Grant kept a wonderful diary through his years of captivity, a Monty Python–esque daily accounting of his life.

"I wish I had": June 2, 1916, Diary, Papers of D. Grant, IWM.

some eight hundred: Report by Lieutenant Russell, TNA: FO 383/275; Phillimore, pp. 44–49; Unpublished memoir, Papers of L. McNaught-Davis, Leeds: POW-043.

64   *Gray remained desperate:* Crefeld Secret Inquiry, Winchester, Appendix II.

      With Crefeld only: Winchester, pp. 104–5.

      "evading your fate": Caunter, p. 7.

65   *In the months:* Unpublished memoir, Papers of J. Dykes, IWM; January–May 1917, Diary, Papers of D. Grant, IWM; Caunter, pp. 27, 38; Unpublished memoir, Papers of L. McNaught-Davis, Leeds: POW-043.

      Of late, Gray: Phillimore, pp. 45–49; Harvey, pp. 124–28.

      After a long: Winchester, pp. 105–16.

67   *Something was afoot:* May 1917, Diary, Papers of D. Grant, IWM.

      sorry to lose them: Ibid., May 20, 1917.

68   *Early the next:* Ibid.; Report by Captain Hudson, TNA: WO 161/96; Report by Walter Haight, TNA: WO 161/97; *Flesherton Advance,* February 6, 1919; Caunter, pp. 45–64.

69   *"mouldy atmosphere":* Harvey, p. 117.

      "Cannon fodder": Caunter, pp. 53–57.

70   *"thanked his god":* May 26, 1917, Diary, Papers of D. Grant, IWM; Unpublished memoir, Papers of G. Gilbert, RAF; Phillimore, pp. 51–54.

      Finally they came: Report by J. A. L. Caunter, TNA: FO 383/271.

CHAPTER SIX

71   *Jim Bennett scanned:* Bennett and Tullis Interview, LJB.

      Three months before: Keegan, pp. 329–53.

72   *Leonard James Bennett:* Author Interview with Laurie Vaughan.

      After his twenty-first: Record of Service, LJB.

      A little over: Jerrold, pp. 1–40.

      By spring the: Author interview with Laurie Vaughan; Record of Service, LJB.

73   *"There it is!":* Bennett and Tullis Interview, LJB.

      Laurence pushed his: Ibid.; Bennett, "A Little Introduction Speech," LJB.

74   *"As you see":* Letter from Bennett to his Mother, May 30, 1917, LJB.

      From Bruges: Ibid.

75   *He shared the:* Schwarmstedt Report, BARCH: R 901/8443; Letter to Mrs. Harvey, August 27, 1917, Papers of F. W. Harvey, GA.

"I'm sorry": Report by C. V. Fox, TNA: FO 383/271; Phillimore, pp. 53–54; Harvey, pp. 134–35.

76   That Friday morning: June 8, 1917, Papers of D. Grant, IWM.
      The prisoners knew: Report by Alan Wilken, TNA: WO 161/96; Clausthal Camp, Diary and Comments, SCHA: FP-CH 15/7/5.
      After a short speech: News clipping, undated, Papers of H. Needham, IWM.
      "There is only": June 8, 1917, Papers of D. Grant, IWM.

77   Schwarmstedt had a: Unpublished memoir, Papers of L. McNaught-Davis, Leeds: POW-043; Unpublished memoir, Papers of J. Dykes, IWM.
      For the run: Phillimore, p. 42. This method recounted by Phillimore was one of several ways the prisoners engineered compasses on their own. Another way was to cut a razor blade and repeatedly run a magnet along the edges.

78   Seventy-five miles: Evans, p. 41; Clausthal Report, BARCH: R 901/84348.
      Commandant Wolfe: Clausthal Report, BARCH: R 901/84348; Statement by Lieutenant Anderson, Papers of F. Mann, IWM; Knight, p. 71. Some accounts give the Clausthal commandant as Wolfe; others give Puttenson. There are similar discrepancies between reports and prisoner memoirs at many of the camps.
      "Cut up their": Clausthal Camp, Diary and Comments, Papers of W. Chance, LIDD: AIR-72.
      The prisoners made: Unpublished memoir, Papers of A. Martin-Thomson, IWM.

79   Compared to their: Blain, unpublished memoir, IWM-B; Money, p. 128.
      It began with: Blain, unpublished memoir, IWM-B; Report on Visit to Detention Camp at Clausthal, TNA: FO 383/270.
      One of the: Series of undated newspaper clippings, HPA.

80   "Are all Canadians": Spectator, December 5, 1966; Series of undated newspaper clippings, HPA.
      One day, in: Knight, pp. 78–81.
      A squadron mate: Tullis, Unpublished memoir, JKT.

81   Blain and Kennard: Blain, unpublished memoir, IWM-B.
      The punishment wielded: Garrett, p. 85.
      "subject to the": Lewis-Stempel, p. 239.

82   "restriction of privileges": Morgan, p. 95.
      commandant was aided: Report on Visit to Detention Camp at Clausthal, TNA: FO 383/270.
      Shooting Sam: Clausthal Camp Diary and Comments, Papers of W. Chance, LIDD: AIR-72.
      "court-martialed": Lewis-Stempel, p. 188.
      failed "to rejoin": Ibid., p. 189.

83   Undaunted, Blain: News clipping, undated, Papers of E. Leggatt, RAF; Blain, unpublished memoir, IWM-B.

CHAPTER SEVEN

87   Swamp Camp was: Note Verbale, TNA: FO 383/273; Unpublished memoir, Papers of G. Gilbert, RAF; Unpublished memoir, Papers of J. Dykes, IWM; Report from Captain Harrison, TNA: FO 383/272; June 27–29, 1917, Diary, Papers of D. Grant, IWM.
      "one of the bravest": Harvey, p. 144.

88 *Life at Schwarmstedt:* Report by Captain C. V. Fox, TNA: FO 383/271; Report by J. A. L. Caunter, TNA: FO 383/271; June–July 1917, Diary, Papers of D. Grant, IWM.

On July 9, Dr. Rudolf: Schwarmstedt Report, BARCH: R 901/8443; July 1917, Diary, Papers of D. Grant, IWM.

"there has never": Schwarmstedt Report, BARCH: R 901/8443; Report on Visit to Officer Prisoner's Camp at Schwarmstedt, July 11, 1917, TNA: FO 383/270.

After Römer left: "Draft of an Agreement Between British and German Governments," July 1917, TNA: CAB 24/19/39.

89 *The inmates:* Report by Captain C. V. Fox, TNA: FO 383/271.

Although physically: Harvey, pp. 170–71.

"The wearisome sameness": Lewis-Stempel, pp. 117–18.

"Laugh, O laugh": Harvey, "Prisoners," GA.

He copied a: Harvey, pp. 146–47, 159.

90 *Looking for:* Thornton, pp. 183–84.

"cad": Report on Conditions of Officers' Camps in Xth Army Corps, TNA: FO 383/399; Notes on Holzminden, Papers of M. Pannett, IWM.

The root of: Report on Conditions of Officers' Camps in Xth Army Corps, TNA: FO 383/399; *Auckland Star,* March 22, 1919; "Torture of Our Officers," news clipping, undated, Papers of R. Milward, Leeds: POW-046.

91 *"had been enough":* Hanson, p. 74.

On his first day: A series of "Memorandum for Communication to the Netherland Minister," Strohen Report, BARCH: R 901/84455.

"Los! Los!": Report by Gerald Knight, TNA: FO 383/272; Report by Captain Harrison, TNA: FO 383/272.

92 *"I had nothing":* Report by Lieutenant Insall, TNA: FO 383/272.

"making the best": Letter from Bennett to his Mother, July 25, 1917, LJB.

Since arriving at: Bennett, "A Little Introduction Speech," LJB.

93 *Niemeyer knew well:* Grinnell-Milne, p. 217.

Knight had been: Knight, pp. 112–15.

Bennett and his fellow: Report by Roy Fitzgerald, TNA: WO 161/96.

94 *on the front lines:* Bennett, "A Little Introduction Speech," LJB.

"What is it like?": Report by J. A. L. Caunter, TNA: FO 383/271.

Then he returned: Ibid.; Report by Captain C. V. Fox, TNA: FO 383/271.

The guards permitted: Phillimore, pp. 109–12. Solitary confinement within the 10th Division was fairly standardized. This account, drawn from fellow prisoner Phillimore, illuminates the deprivation Gray would have suffered.

95 *Guards led him:* David Gray, ICRC.

CHAPTER EIGHT

96 *Charles Rathborne:* Report by Charles Rathborne, TNA: FO 383/399; Report by Samuel Ellis, TNA: WO 161/96. The exact arrival date of the Karlsruhe contingent, the first at Holzminden, was left unreported in most accounts. Ellis provided the most accurate timeline, as he arrived two days afterward from Schwarmstadt.

Founded in 1245: Mitzkat, pp. 1–80.

97 *"prisoner's Mecca":* Durnford, p. 15.

They had no way: Letter from Barlow to his parents, September 26, 1917, Papers of A. Barlow, LIDD: POW-002.

on April 14: Wise, pp. 274–75.

After the bombers: Rathborne Account, TNA: AIR 1/7/726/129/1.

"the face of": Cook, p. 176.

Private-school-educated: "The First Great Escape?," *Cross & Cockade International* (Spring 2016), https://www.crossandcockade.com/uploads/Great_Escape.pdf.

"keen": Rathborne Service Record, TNA: ADM 273/2/18.

As a POW: Rathborne Account, TNA: AIR 1/7/726/129/1; Report by Rathborne, TNA: WO 161/96.

98   *It was after:* Durnford, pp. 18–21; Hargreaves, p. 193.

      The former infantry: Report on Conditions of Officers' Camps in Xth Army Corps, TNA: FO 383/399; Unpublished memoir, Papers of R. Gough, LIDD: POW-029.

      "glad to see": Durnford, p. 19.

99   *"bedroom candles and":* Ibid.

      They were divided: Letter, June 16, 1918, Papers of L. Nixon, IWM.

      In the morning: Rathborne Account, TNA: AIR 1/7/726/129/1.

      The prison was: Spectator, May 19, 1928; Unpublished memoir, Papers of R. Gough, LIDD: POW-029; Ackerley, p. 78; October 14, 1917, Diary, Papers of D. Grant, IWM; Notes, Papers of M. Pannett, IWM; Hanson, pp. 43–45.

100   *At morning roll call:* Durnford, pp. 19–21; Report on Conditions of Officers' Camps in Xth Army Corps, TNA: FO 383/399.

      "you wouldn't get": Warburton, p. 96.

      "You damn well": Recollections of L. J. Bennett, Oral History, LIDD.

      On September 20: September 14–20, 1917, Diary, Papers of D. Grant, IWM; Warburton, pp. 92–93.

101   *As the guards:* Harvey, pp. 210–11.

      The following day: October 14, 1917, Diary, Papers of D. Grant, IWM.

      He had his route: Phillimore, pp. 104–5.

102   *"rob you of vitality":* Harvey, pp. 152–56.

104   *The other Schwarmstedt:* Warburton, pp. 94–95.

      "Bury your notes!": Durnford, p. 17.

105   *"meaningless now":* October 14, 1917, Diary, Papers of D. Grant, IWM; Unpublished memoir, Papers of L. McNaught-Davis, LIDD: POW-043; Unpublished memoir, Papers of A. Barlow, LIDD: POW-002.

      Harvey arrived: Harvey, pp. 219–21.

CHAPTER NINE

106   *"mad keen":* Letter from Blain to Hugh Reynolds, August 28, 1918, CWB.

      "Confidential Liar": MacDonald, p. 136.

      "Utterly Hopeless": Continental Times, July–September, 1917.

107   *Blain's time in:* Blain, unpublished memoir, IWM-B.

      Dressed in civilian clothes: Ibid.

      The rain had: Ibid.; Winchester, pp. 62–65; Letter from Leggatt to Family, November 30, 1917, Papers of E. Leggatt, RAF.

109   *"Wohin gehen si?":* Blain, unpublished memoir, IWM-B.

      The policeman examined: Letter from Blain to Hugh Reynolds, August 28, 1918, CWB.

      Over the course: Durnford, pp. 18–25.

110   *Prisoners practiced:* Thorn, p. 65. In his memoir, Thorn offers a compelling portrait of

the early escape at Holzminden described here, not to mention of life in the camps. Well worth a read.

Both of the: Unpublished memoir, Papers of R. Gough, LIDD: POW-029; Durnford, pp. 52–60; September 28, 1917, Diary, Papers of D. Grant, IWM.

111 *Thorn and Wilkins:* Thorn, pp. 66–68; Unpublished memoir, Papers of L. Mc-Naught-Davis, LIDD: POW-043; Rathborne Account, TNA: AIR 1/7/726/129/1; Garland.

112 *Back at the:* Rathborne Account, TNA: AIR 1/7/726/129/1.

"had left the": Thorn, p. 87.

A great cheer: Ibid., pp. 87–88; Hanson, pp. 15–52.

113 *The commandant who:* Tullis, unpublished memoir, JKT.

114 *Knight, who had:* Report by Gerald Knight, TNA: FO 383/272.

Another gang tried: Harding, p. 113.

Another scheme, led by: Grinnell-Milne, pp. 212–18.

115 *Although his previous:* Tullis, unpublished memoir, JKT.

After almost three: Bennett, "A Little Introduction Speech," LJB.

CHAPTER TEN

116 *October 1, 1917:* Durnford, pp. 24–25; Report by A. E. Haig, January 20, 1918, Papers of A. Haig, IWM.

"barbarians": Report by Captain F. B. Binney, TNA: WO 161/96; Report by Samuel Ellis, TNA: WO 161/96.

117 *"the penalty for":* Precis of part of interview between Major Wyndham and General Hänisch, TNA: FO 383/399; Letter in Code Despatched from Holdminden, October 9, 1917, TNA: FO 383/275.

118 "Baralong!": Durnford, pp. 29–30.

In his office: Report by Samuel Ellis, TNA: WO 161/96; Report on Conditions of Officers' Camps in Xth Army Corps, TNA: FO 383/399.

In some of: October 1917, Diary, Papers of J. Chapman, RAF; Letter in Code Despatched from Holdminden, October 9, 1917, TNA: FO 383/275; Horrocks, p. 21.

"Three more out": Harvey, p. 221.

Harvey was glad: Boden, p. 199.

For almost two: November 5, 1917, Diary, Papers of D. Grant, IWM.

119 *There were others:* Papers of J. Whale, IWM.

"It is not": Harvey, p. 222.

120 *In Cell 5 at:* Blain, unpublished memoir, IWM-B.

An ace of: "Lieutenant H. W. Medlicott (1895–1918)," Medlicott Family History, http://www.fam.medlicott.uk.com/HEM_files/7_HWMedlicott.html; Tullis, unpublished memoir, JKT; Hare, p. xx.

One time: Cook, p. 151.

121 *"For this":* Winchester, p. 68.

Medlicott was sent: Blain, unpublished memoir, IWM-B; Letter from Blain to Hugh Reynolds, August 28, 1918, CWB; Tullis, unpublished memoir, JKT. Blain left two similar versions of this remarkable escape narrative in his unfinished memoir. All quotes and details come from these two sources, but are also corroborated in Tullis, unpublished memoir, JKT.

125 *Throughout October:* Letter from Bennett to his mother, October 17, 1917, LJB; Report

on Holzminden, November 22, 1917, TNA: FO 383/275; Report by A. E. Haig, January 20, 1918, Papers of A. Haig, IWM.

126   *"Look at these"*: Horrocks, p. 26; *Auckland Star*, March 22, 1919; Durnford, pp. 16–23; Unpublished memoir, Papers of A. Barlow, LIDD: POW-002; Warburton, pp. 91–97; *Sydney Mail*, August 6, 1919. The behavior depicted here was typical of Niemeyer as recorded in a number of memoirs relating to prisoners' arrival at Holzminden.
Once they had: October 1917, Diary, Papers of D. Grant, IWM; Letter in Code Despatched from Holdminden, October 9, 1917, TNA: FO 383/275; Unpublished memoir, Papers of L. McNaught-Davis, Leeds: POW-043.

CHAPTER ELEVEN

127   *"Get up!"*: Unpublished memoir, Papers of R. Gough, Leeds: POW-029.
Since arriving: Unpublished memoir, Papers of L. McNaught-Davis, Leeds: POW-043; Report on Conditions of Officers' Camps in Xth Army Corps, TNA: FO 383/399.

128   *"Cost price"*: Durnford, p. 37.
Gray found that: Harvey, p. 228. As with his depiction of most elements of prison life, Harvey writes eloquently of the torturous amount of time the men spent merely waiting.

129   *The small tyrannies:* Unpublished memoir, Papers of L. McNaught-Davis, Leeds: POW-043; Report by Lieutenant Purves, TNA: FO 383/399.
when a more: Harvey, p. 227.
Theft was pervasive: Notes on Holzminden, Papers of M. Pannett, IWM; Letter from Nixon, Papers of L. Nixon, IWM.

130   *Across Germany:* Herwig, pp. 232–39, 255, 285–89.
"I guess, you": Report on Conditions of Officers' Camps in Xth Army Corps, TNA: FO 383/399.
For no reason: Letter to Nixon family, Papers of L. Nixon, IWM.

131   *"Time drags slowly"*: Coombes, p. xx.
In late October: Report on Holzminden, November 1917, BARCH: R 85/4337; Unpublished memoir, Papers of L. McNaught-Davis, Leeds: POW-043; Garland, "My Dashes for Freedom."
The barricades in: Hanson, pp. 167–68.

132   *The Holzminden inmates:* Newsclip, "Bucks Officer's Adventures in Germany," undated, Papers of J. Shaw, IWM.
"You see, gentleman": Durnford, p. 50.

CHAPTER TWELVE

135   *Shorty Colquhoun:* Ackerley, p. 78.
Scouting the camp: Recollections of L. J. Bennett, Oral History, LIDD; Durnford, pp. 71–75; Hanson, pp. 183–85; "The Holzminden Tunnellers Want to Meet Again," *Answers,* June 11, 1938.

136   *Colquhoun recruited:* Letter from Bennett to Lyon, May 13, 1938, LJB.

137   *"Will you join"*: Beyond Colquhoun and Ellis, the founding members of the tunneling team that November are rarely mentioned in sources. In his memoir, Harvey states that Rogers, Mossy, and the Pink Toes were there from the start, and given their ex-

perience, they were ideally suited for the engineering of the trapdoor. Note Harvey, pp. 239–40. The timing of David Gray's participation is slightly more elusive. Durnford, the best firsthand chronicler of the tunnel, states unequivocally that Gray was the "Father of the Tunnel, and in every way one of the most important personages concerned." Note Durnford, p. 119. Further, according to the *Otago Daily Times,* November 23, 1918, written with the aid of Lieutenant John Bousfield, only one of the originators of the tunnel eventually made the successful escape through it. Given that, by their own admissions, the others had all come to the tunnel later, this leaves Gray.
First they would: Recollections of L. J. Bennett, Oral History, LIDD; Tullis, unpublished memoir, JKT.

138   *The next day:* Ackerley, pp. 78–79; Recollections of L. J. Bennett, Oral History, LIDD; Tullis, unpublished memoir, JKT. Although this critical scouting mission was clearly recorded, the individuals responsible remained unmentioned in all accounts. Given the intricate engineering of the the the slide panel, and the demonstrated capacity of the Pink Toes, namely Mossy and Rogers, to create such a contraption, the author surmised these two were responsible.

139   *Willing accomplices:* Holzminden Tunnelers 20th Anniversary Dinner, Attendee List, LJB. The names of the orderlies who aided the tunnel effort were never mentioned in Durnford's memoir, nor in almost any other chronicle. Only in Bennett's papers did I find mention of them; Bennett wrote them letters thanking them for their assistance and also invited them to the anniversary dinners.

140   *"It's a case":* Winchester, p. 147.
One of the: New Zealand Herald, August 27, 1938.
A bribe of: Hanson, pp. 194–95.
Like the other: Unpublished memoir, Papers of D. Morrish, LIDD: ADD-001; Unpublished memoir, Papers of J. Dykes, IWM.
The British born: Schmitt, IWM.

141   *"I have no":* Ibid.
He lived with: Hanson, pp. 49–53.

142   *At 7:00 a.m.:* Unpublished memoir, Papers of J. Dykes, IWM. Private Dykes provided a lengthy, detailed account of his time as an orderly at several camps during World War I, well worth the read for anyone interested in the "Upstairs/Downstairs" character of their lives.
"Taking the officers": Ibid.
"There was a": Fussell, p. 89.

143   *Cash, with his:* Schmitt, IWM.
On November 5: November 5, 1917, Diary, Papers of D. Grant, IWM.
That morning: Rathborne Account, TNA: AIR 1/7/726/129/1; November 5, 1917, Diary, Papers of J. Chapman, RAF.
"eye-wash": Harding, p. 92.
Some of the: Letter from Robert Vansittart, December 21, 1917.

144   *The men tried:* Report on Holzminden, November 1917. BARCH: R 85/4337.
"not yet able": Letter from Bennett to his mother, October 17, 1917, LJB.
Every day, he: Bennett, "A Little Introduction Speech," LJB.

145   *"A considered plan":* Ibid.
Bennett began: Ibid.
"By the way": Letter from Bennett to his Mother, November 25, 1917, LJB.

146   *In late November:* Letter from Leggatt to Family, November 30, 1917, Papers of E. Leggatt, RAF.

"Good luck!": Blain, unpublished memoir, IWM-B.
"rabbit warren": Ibid.

CHAPTER THIRTEEN

147   *the head of:* Panayi, pp. 80–86.
"could be obviated": Report on Holzminden, BARCH: R 85/4337.

148   *"professionally incapable"*: Letter from British Vice Consulate, May 16, 1917, TNA: FO 383/270.
"The first officer": Letter in Code, November 12, 1917, TNA: FO 383/275.
"Holzminden was an": Letter from W. R. C. Green, Papers of R. Burrows, LIDD: POW-010.
In the past: Summary of Reprisals Taken by British and German Governments, TNA: CAB 24/6/375; Meeting Minute, October 26, 1917, TNA: FO 383/273.
When it came: Letter from Adelaide Livingstone, December 19, 1917, TNA: FO 383/275.

149   *at 11:00 a.m.:* Durnford, pp. 71–88.
One orderly: Tullis, unpublished memoir, JKT.
"All clear": Durnford, p. 79.

150   *Gray and his:* Australian, March 3, 1922.
Thin lines: Durnford, pp. 71–88.

151   *Using spoons: Sunday Express,* May 8, 1938; Morrogh, unpublished memoir, JDM; Recollections of L. J. Bennett, Oral History, LIDD.
Initially, they: Australian, March 3, 1922.
Since being released: Harvey, pp. 230–31.
There was never: Cook, pp. 20–21.

152   *Niemeyer continued:* Report by A. E. Haig, January 20, 1918, Papers of A. Haig, IWM.
"The latrine, sir": Letter from Christie-Miller, March 13, 1918, Papers of G. Christie-Miller, IWM.
"The Scots are": Harvey, p. 228.
The greatest resistance: Ibid., p. 230.
Another madcap: December 1917, Diary, Papers of D. Grant, IWM; Unpublished memoir, Papers of R. Gough, Leeds: POW-029.

153   *"What the devil"*: Harvey, p. 231.

154   *"From troubles"*: Harvey, "Ducks," GA.
At Christmas: Durnford, p. 75.
The men sang: December 1917, Diary, Papers of D. Grant, IWM; Hanson, p. 200.

155   *at one point:* Hanson, p. 199; Hargreaves, pp. 281–82.
The following morning: Unpublished memoir, Papers of L. McNaught-Davis, Leeds: POW-043.
into this cascade: Notes, Papers of M. Pannett, IWM; Durnford, p. 75; J. W. Shaw, "The Holzminden Escape Tunnel," News clipping, Papers of J. Shaw, IWM.

CHAPTER FOURTEEN

157   *Caspar Kennard wriggled:* Winchester, p. 112. According to Winchester, Kennard joined the tunnel project in January 1918. Kennard left no record of the exact date, but according to his archival files, he was clearly working with Gray at this point in bribing

a Holzminden dentist for supplies. Gerichtsschreiber des Landgerichts Brief, January 18, 1918, Papers of C. Kennard, RAF. Given Kennard's arrest and imprisonment after escape, this timeline figures well.

On reaching the: Harding, pp. 135–39; J. W. Shaw, "The Holzminden Escape Tunnel," news clipping, Papers of J. Shaw, IWM; Unpublished memoir, Papers of W. English, RAF.

159 *January 26, 1918:* January 26, 1918, Diary, Papers of D. Grant, IWM; Unpublished memoir, Papers of L. McNaught-Davis, LIDD: POW-043.

Searches were common: Horrocks, p. 28.

Bennett was worried: Bennett, "A Little Introduction Speech," LJB.

A mad scramble: Unpublished memoir, Papers of L. McNaught-Davis, LIDD: POW-043.

160 *"You know my":* Hanson, p. 245.

Inspired by the: Bennett, "A Little Introduction Speech," LJB.

Since the recent: Bennett Family Album, LJB.

"'First Day — Got up'": Hargreaves, p. 317.

161 *"A motley crew":* Unpublished memoir, Papers of G. Gilbert, RAF.

They filled their: Hanson, pp. 136–41.

"There was a": V. Coombs, Oral History Interview, IWM.

162 *"Nothing has the":* Harvey, pp. 83–85.

The night after: January 27, 1918, Diary, Papers of D. Grant, IWM.

Other productions: Hanson, pp. 136–39.

James Whale, who: Curtis, pp. 15–26.

"Pots of paint": James Whale, "Our Life at Holzminden," *Wide World Magazine*, undated, Papers of J. Whale, IWM.

"They insisted on": Harvey, p. 238.

163 *"the comradeship of":* Ibid., pp. 168–73.

The arrival in December: Letter from M. R. Chidson, May 15, 1936, Medlicott Family History, http://www.fam.medlicott.uk.com/HEM_files/7_HWMedlicott.html.

A legend even to: Evans, p. 56.

Dick Cash provided: Unpublished memoir, Papers of J. Cash, IWM; February 1918, Diary, Papers of D. Grant, IWM.

At 3:30 p.m.: Ibid.; Durnford, pp. 60–63; Letter from M. R. Chidson, May 15, 1936, Medlicott Family History, http://www.fam.medlicott.uk.com/HEM_files/7_HWMedlicott.html.

165 *"All my boys:* Unpublished memoir, Papers of N. Birks, IWM.

When the officers: Report on Conditions of Officers' Camps in Xth Army Corps, TNA: FO 383/399.

"unblemished record": Durnford, p. 63.

"it was impossible": Letter from M. R. Chidson, May 15, 1936, Medlicott Family Papers, http://www.fam.medlicott.uk.com/HEM_files/7_HWMedlicott.html.

CHAPTER FIFTEEN

166 *In late February:* Durnford, p. 95.

Since the Boxing: December 1917–February 1918, Diary, Papers of D. Grant, IWM.

Rather than welcoming: Lewis-Stempel, pp. 246–247.

"I felt like": Vance, p. 68.

167   *At the end*: Harvey, pp. 239–40.
      They left: *King Country Chronicle*, September 27, 1919; TNA: ADM 273/23/137; Morrogh, unpublished memoir, JDM.
      Quietly, usually: P. Mallahan. "The Big Breakout," unpublished article, PM.
168   *Since being captured*: Cook, pp. 147–48.
      In early 1918: Report by Clifford Campbell-Martin, TNA: WO 161/96.
169   *"The turn had"*: *King Country Chronicle*, September 27, 1919. Garland states that this diversion came in December 1917, but this was unlikely, since it was clear that Gray — and Mardock — were at the time in charge, which did not occur until late February 1918.
      Just before dawn: Herwig, p. 381.
      "We will punch": Ibid., p. 389.
170   *"If an English delegation"*: Ibid., p. 394.
      "England ist kaput": Diary, March 24, 1918, Papers of D. Grant, IWM.
      "Well, gentleman, for": Unpublished memoir, SCHA: FP-CH 15/7/8.
      "German Offensive": *Continental Times*, March 25, 1918.
171   *Another inspector came*: Letter from Netherland Legation, April 4, 1918, TNA: FO 383/398; Note Verbale to Germany, April 5, 1918, TNA: FO 383/398; *Times*, March 13, 1918; Memorandum for War Cabinet, TNA: FO 383/440.
172   *in Schweidnitz*: Rathborne Account, TNA: AIR 1/7/726/129/1.
      "commercial traveler": Ibid.
      Cecil Blain was: Blain, unpublished memoir, IWM-B; Recollections of L. J. Bennett, Oral History, LIDD.
173   *At Neunkirchen*: Ibid., Grinnell-Milne, pp. 252–72.
      Finally, Blain arrived: Blain, unpublished memoir, IWM-B.
174   *Back by the*: Recollections of L. J. Bennett, Oral History, LIDD; Tullis, unpublished memoir, JKT.
      Kennard stood just: Durnford, pp. 96–99.

CHAPTER SIXTEEN

176   *Whether they were*: Harvey, pp. 142–43.
177   *There was a*: Speech Notes, AC; Tullis, unpublished memoir, JKT.
178   *"black gusts of"*: Hanson, pp. 79–80.
      "Letter Boy," the: David, p. 442; Durnford, pp. 81–85; P. Mallahan, "The Big Breakout," unpublished article, PM.
      "I do not": Durnford, pp. 84–85.
      With his photography: Schmitt, IWM.
179   *With each additional*: Rathborne Account, TNA: AIR 1/7/726/129/1; Tullis, unpublished memoir, JKT.
180   *"We must be"*: Harvey, p. 135.
      In early May: Letter from Mardock to Bennett, July 4, 1958, LJB.
      Every additional foot: Morrogh, unpublished memoir, JDM.
      Already exhausted, and: Recollections of L. J. Bennett, Oral History, LIDD.
181   *Despite all*: Peschardt, p. 84.
      Bennett's kit: Letter to Bennett's Mother, sender unknown, February 9, 1918, LJB; Secret letter from Bennett, addressee unknown, LJB.
      Finally, Niemeyer: Hargreaves, p. 330.

Although Holzminden was: April 1918, Papers of D. Grant, IWM; Report by F. J. Ortweiler, TNA: WO 161/96.

"I am in very": Letter to Bennett's Mother, June 6, 1918, LJB.

182 *"accidentally":* Tullis, unpublished memoir, JKT.

In mid-May: Notes, Papers of M. Pannett, IWM; Summary of Reprisals Taken by British and German Governments, TNA: CAB 24/6/375.

The tunnelers tried: Durnford, pp. 108–10; Morrogh, unpublished memoir, JDM.

183 *"worst man in":* Harvey, p. 248.

"What, when all": Ibid., p. 278.

184 *"They would never":* Letter from M. R. Chidson, May 15, 1936, Medlicott Family History, http://www.fam.medlicott.uk.com/HEM_files/7_HWMedlicott.html.

Beetz ordered: Durnford, pp. 283–90.

"Herr Commandant": Ibid., pp. 284–85.

"Yes, they are": Ibid., p. 289.

"sudden dash": Letter from M. R. Chidson, May 15, 1936, Medlicott Family History, http://www.fam.medlicott.uk.com/HEM_files/7_HWMedlicott.html.

185 *While the guards:* Grinnell-Milne, pp. 303–4.

"one of the": Flight, June 20, 1918.

CHAPTER SEVENTEEN

186 *At the eastern:* Durnford, pp. 108–9; Morrogh, unpublished memoir, JDM.

187 *At the start:* Hargreaves, p. 392.

188 *They would no longer:* Ibid., pp. 109–13; Papers of M. Pannett, IWM; Rathborne Account, TNA: AIR 1/7/726/129/1.

A lunatic who: Winchester, pp. 142–44.

189 *Gray would be:* Forged Document, Papers of C. Kennard, RAF.

190 *"I hope you":* Letter from Bennett to his mother, June 6, 1918, LJB.

"true German style": Rathborne Account, TNA: AIR 1/7/726/129/1.

To help with: Schmitt, IWM.

191 *On June 6:* Diary, June 6, 1918, HFD.

nickname was Fluffy: Harvey, pp. 237–38; Durnford, pp. 120–24.

192 *"To prevent the":* Sydney Mail, August 6, 1919.

Niemeyer had: Document from Holland, Harsh Treatment of Captain Robinson, TNA: FO 383/399; Report by Ortweiler, TNA: WO 161/96.

"simple disobedience": Court Martial of David B. Gray, June 12, 1918, TNA: FO 383/401; Durnford, p. 119.

193 *One night:* Notes on Holzminden, Papers of M. Pannett, IWM.

"last lap": Durnford, p. 118.

A few days later: Rathborne Account, TNA: AIR 1/7/726/129/1; Tullis, unpublished memoir, JKT; Bennett, "A Little Introduction Speech," LJB.

194 *"nosed its way."* Recollections of L. J. Bennett, Oral History, LIDD.

CHAPTER EIGHTEEN

195 *The tunnelers had:* Morrogh, unpublished memoir, JDM; Notes, Papers of M. Pannett, IWM.

196   *When not on:* Bousfield, "An Exciting Escape."
       "Bone dry": Tullis, unpublished memoir, JKT; Notes. AC.
       No one had: Forged Identity Card, CWB.
       "We hereby certify": Günther Note, Papers of C. Kennard, RAF.

197   *"In our parole":* Durnford, pp. 128–29.
       Home John: Angus McPhail, His Book Holzminden, LJB.
       "Are you in": Ackerley, p. 75.

198   *"Expect something big":* Diary, July 1918, HFD.
       Livewire reluctantly: Durnford, p. 129.
       Far from Holzminden: Harvey, pp. 291–30.

199   *"oysters and stout":* Letter from Frank Moysey, March 6, 1918, Papers of F. W. Harvey,
       GA.

200   *Gray led the:* Durnford, pp. 124–27; *King County Chronicle,* September 27, 1919. Gar-
       land lends support to Gray being in charge of the men's actions during the night of the
       breakout.
       The first party: Bousfield, "An Exciting Escape."
       Once they were: Papers of M. Pannett, IWM; Blain, unpublished memoir, IWM-B.

201   *one to oversee:* Recollections of L. J. Bennett, Oral History, LIDD.
       Commandant Niemeyer: Report by Lieutenant Purves, TNA: FO 383/399.

202   *"impossible peace ideas":* *Continental Times,* July 19, 1918.
       "the situation is": Herwig, pp. 404–5.
       Meanwhile, the Spanish: Ibid.
       "Well, gentlemen": Edgar Garland, "My Dash to Freedom," *Wide World Magazine,* June
       1919.
       The next night: Durnford, pp. 129–30.

CHAPTER NINETEEN

207   *"Tonight!":* Freeman, James, "The Holzminden Tunnelers Want to Meet Again," *An-
       swers,* June 11, 1938; July 21–24, Diary, HFD.

208   *"A decorated officer":* Unpublished memoir, Papers of G. Gilbert, RAF.
       "If B house": Durnford, pp. 131–32.
       "Holzminden — Escaped": Winchester, p. 152.
       "Oh, shut up": Ibid., p. 154.
       Throughout Block B: Morrogh, unpublished memoir, JDM.
       Bennett remained sober: Recollections of L. J. Bennett, Oral History, LIDD.

209   *"wonderfully Teutonic":* Durnford, pp. 132–33.
       the team assembled: Ackerley, pp. 84–86.

210   *"finale of a gigantic":* Max Gore, "The Long Dim Tunnel," CHALK.
       A religious man: *News Chronicle,* July 24, 1948; Butler Account, as quoted in Durnford,
       pp. 159–60.

211   *Minutes before, Private:* Hanson, pp. 263–64.
       They were depending: Letter from Ernest Collinson to Bennett, May 25, 1938, LJB; Er-
       nest Collinson Record, ICRC.

212   *"Mr. Blain":* Winchester, pp. 157–58.
       Dick Cash was: Extract of letter from June 29, 1918, John R. Cash file, AWM: 2875.
       "Chocks away": Winchester, pp. 158–59.

During one stretch: Blain, unpublished memoir, IWM-B.

213 *"What's up?":* Winchester, pp. 160–61.

The guard paced: Tullis, unpublished memoir, JKT.

214 *Taking care:* Blain, unpublished memoir, IWM-B.

As he reached: Morrogh, unpublished memoir, JDM.

In the distance: Foot, p. 18.

215 *"Bet Niemeyer":* Winchester, pp. 161–63; Blain, unpublished memoir, IWM-B.

CHAPTER TWENTY

216 *Charles Rathborne thrust:* Rathborne Account, TNA: AIR 1/7/726/129/1.

"all-clear": Bennett, "A Little Introduction Speech," LJB; Bousfield, "An Exciting Escape."

217 *After over an:* Rathborne Account, TNA: AIR 1/7/726/129/1.

"Your turn, Major": Morrogh, unpublished memoir, JDM; Letter from Tony Wheatley to author, July 12, 2016; Senan Molony, "Titanic: The Last Photograph," April 23, 2004, https://www.encyclopedia-titanica.org/titanic-the-last-photograph.html.

218 *"All clear":* Morrogh, unpublished memoir, JDM.

219 *David Gray scanned:* Ibid.; Winchester, pp. 163–68. Barry Winchester provides the best account of the run to Holland by Gray, Kennard, and Blain. His description is backed up by the maps.

221 *When Bennett and:* Recollections of L. J. Bennett, Oral History, LIDD; Bousfield, "An Exciting Escape"; Peschardt, p. 93.

Six miles south: Rathborne Account, TNA: AIR 1/7/726/129/1.

There was trouble: Notes, Papers of L. Nixon, IWM.

222 *"What's the idea?":* Garland, "My Dashes to Freedom."

Back at the: Ibid.

223 *Soon after, Hartigan:* Unpublished memoir, Papers of R. Gough, Leeds: POW-029; Notes on Holzminden, Papers of M. Pannett, IWM.

224 *"So, a tunnel!":* Durnford, p. 139.

"The tunnel has gone": "The Moles of Holzminden," *Popular Flying,* December 1938.

"Neun und zwanzig": News clipping, undated, Papers of F. W. Harvey, GA.

225 *"Niemeyer's jaw":* Durnford, p. 139.

Then Niemeyer went: Unpublished memoir, Papers of R. Gough, Leeds: POW-029; Report by Lt. Ortweiler, TNA: WO 161/96; July 25, 1918, Diary, HFD.

CHAPTER TWENTY-ONE

226 *Hunkered in:* Bennett, "A Little Introduction Speech," LJB; Bousfield, "An Exciting Escape."

The hunt was: Tullis, unpublished memoir, JKT.

227 *"full view of":* Morrogh, unpublished memoir, JDM.

228 *slipped his rucksack:* Winchester, pp. 175–77.

Gray drew out: Günther Note, Papers of C. Kennard, RAF.

230 *1. No officer of:* Statement by Captain Batty-Smith, TNA: FO 383/399.

231 *"Go away!":* Ibid., Hanson, p. 274.

He grew even: Statement by Lieutenant Ortweiler, TNA: WO 161/96; Harvey, pp. 241–42; V. C. Coombs, "Sixty Years On," *Royal Air Forces Quarterly* (Summer 1976); July 26, 1918, Diary, HFD.

232   *"We urgently and":* *Täglicher Anzeiger* (Holzminden), August 2, 1918.
      The reward offered: Bennett, "A Little Introduction Speech," LJB.
      On Thursday afternoon: Rathborne Account, TNA: AIR 1/7/726/129/1.

234   *Jim Bennett and:* Recollections of L. J. Bennett, Oral History, LIDD; Bennett, "A Little Introduction Speech," LJB.

CHAPTER TWENTY-TWO

236   *After their antics:* Winchester, pp. 178–80.
237   *Twenty-four hours:* Rathborne Account, TNA: AIR 1/7/726/129/1.
      On his arrival: Speech Notes, Officer POW Dining Club, Leeds: POW-072.
238   *Although the skyline:* Rathborne Account, TNA: AIR 1/7/726/129/1; Herwig, p. 288.
239   *On their own:* Durnford, pp. 143–47; July 24–August 3, 1918, Diary, HFD.
240   *Never one to:* Durnford, p. 145.
241   *"Having a lovely time":* "The Men Who Dug a Tunnel," *Evening Standard,* July 24, 1958.
      Always careful, but: Bennett and Tullis Interview, LJB; Bennett, "A Little Introduction Speech," LJB; Recollections of L. J. Bennett, Oral History, LIDD.
242   *"cheerio":* Bousfield, "An Exciting Escape."
      Tullis and Purves: Tullis, unpublished memoir, JKT.
      After Bennett and Campbell-Martin: Bousfield, "An Exciting Escape."
243   *The dogs were:* Winchester, pp. 182–83.
244   *They had rations:* Letter from Cita Kennard, August 1918, CK.

CHAPTER TWENTY-THREE

245   *As the sky:* Bennett and Tullis Interview, LJB.
246   *Later that day:* Morrogh, unpublished memoir, JDM.
247   *In the dark:* Recollections of L. J. Bennett, Oral History, LIDD; Bennett, "A Little Introduction Speech," LJB.
248   *One foot after:* Winchester, pp. 183–84.
      The same Sunday: Bennett and Tullis Interview, LJB.
249   *Armed sentries:* Caunter, pp. 209–13; Gilliland, p. 230.
      By observing the: Bennett, "A Little Introduction Speech," LJB.
250   *"Halt!":* Recollections of L. J. Bennett, Oral History, LIDD.
251   *On the morning:* Escape Route Map, Papers of C. Kennard, RAF; Winchester, pp. 184-85
      At twilight, Gray: Letter from Cita Kennard, August 1918, CK.
      The three airmen: Winchester, pp. 185–88.
252   *mental endurance to:* Blain, unpublished memoir, IWM-B.
      It was approaching: Cypher telegram from Rotterdam, August 8, 1918, TNA: FO 383/381.
      They crept slowly: Winchester, pp. 185–88.
254   *"Duck!" he warned:* Ibid., p. 187.
255   *Together they yawped:* Letter from Blain to Uncle Hugh, August 28, 1918; Letter from Cita Kennard, August 1918, CK.

CHAPTER TWENTY-FOUR

256 *"Escaped and arrived":* Telegram from Kennard, August 1918, Papers of C. Kennard, RAF.
    Secret cables: Return to U.K. of British Prisoners-of-War Escaped from Germany, August 7, 1918, TNA: FO 383/381.

257 *"British Prisoners":* New York Times, August 7, 1918.
    On the evening: Cypher Telegram, August 7, 1918, TNA: FO 383/381; Harrison, p. 183.
    The next morning: Tullis, unpublished memoir, JKT.
    From the window: Gilliland, pp. 256–59.
    "take three months'": Harrison, p. 183.

258 *"The Queen joins":* Letter to Blain, 1918, CWB.
    "The Tunnel to": Daily Sketch, December 18, 1918.
    "Daring Escape": Evening Express, August 26, 1918.
    Despite all the: Service Record of D. B. Gray, British Indian Army Records, BA; Money, p. 151; Service Record of C. Blain, CWB.
    On August 16, 1918: Harvey, pp. 301–5.

259 "I have such": Harvey, "Treasury," GA.

260 *"This is the":* Harvey, p. 316.
    In the period: Cypher Telegram from Netherlands, August 24, 1918, TNA: FO 383/399; Durnford, pp. 146–54; Statement by M. S. Fryer, TNA: FO 383/400.
    continued escape: August–September 1918, Diary, HFD.

261 *"conspiring to destroy":* Hanson, pp. 300–304.
    Finding the indictment: Beglsubigte Abschrift, Papers of R. M. Paddison, LIDD: POW-049.
    "having made an": Schmitt, IWM.
    But with 250,000: Herwig, p. 403.
    "They would all": September 29–October 2, 1918, Diary, HFD.
    Of course, Niemeyer: Durnford, p. 159.
    "always done all": New York Times, December 15, 1918.
    "The war will": October 2–5, 1918, Diary, HFD.

262 *"You see, I":* New York Times, December 15, 1918.
    "The war is over!": "A Parting Word," Pamphlets for Repatriates, IWM.

263 *Yet this farewell:* Unpublished memoir, Papers of R. Gough, LIDD: POW-029; December 9–10, 1918, Diary, HFD.
    "awe, envy": James Whale, "Our Life at Holzminden," Wide World Magazine, undated, Papers of J. Whale, IWM.

EPILOGUE

264 *On the evening:* Holzminden Tunnel, 20th Anniversary Dinner pamphlet, JKT.
    "gallant and able": Letter from Keeper of the Privy Purse, February 5, 1919, CWB.

265 *"His untimely death":* "Prisoners in Germany," unsourced newsclip, March 9, 1935, Papers of C. Kennard, IWM.
    "enemy officers": Hanson, p. 329.
    "I know damn": Ibid., p. 337.
    Although fifty-five: Author Interview with Jane Gray.

266   *In total, 573:* Lewis-Stempel, pp. 190–91.
       "improbable but possible": Notes, Bennett MI9 lecture, LJB.
       Before the collapse: Foot, p. 5, Appendix I. As Foot and Langley admit, these numbers
       are but a best-guess approximation.
267   *"Do as you":* Author interview with Laurie Vaughan.

Bibliography

ARCHIVES

Australian War Memorial, Australia
British Library, UK
Bundesarchiv, Germany
Tasmanian State Archives, Australia
F. W. Harvey Collection, Gloucestershire Archives, UK
Archives and Special Collections, Hamilton Public Library, Canada
Prisoners of the First World War, ICRC Historical Archives, Switzerland
Imperial War Museums, UK
Liddle Collection, University of Leeds Special Collections, UK
Royal Air Force Museum, Hendon, UK
Sandwell Community History and Archives, UK
National Archives, Kew, UK

PERSONAL PAPERS

Bennett, Leonard J. (Courtesy of Laurie Vaughan)
Blain, Cecil (Courtesy of Hugh Lowe)
Clouston, Andrew (Courtesy of Pete Clouston)
Dougall, Hector (Courtesy of Brenda Merriman)
Gray, David (Courtesy of Jane Gray)
Harvey, F. W. (Courtesy of Gloucestershire Archives and the Harvey Family)
Kennard, Caspar (Courtesy of C. A. Kennard and Diana Gillyatt)
Leggatt, E. W. (Courtesy of Margaret Pretorius)
Lyon, Peter (Courtesy of Louise Lyon)
Mallahan, Patrick (Courtesy of Jacqueline Mallahan)
Morrogh, John (Courtesy of Julyan Peard and Tony Wheatley)
Tullis, John K. (Courtesy of Keil Tullis and Brian Tullis)

INTERVIEWS

Jane Gray

Laurie Vaughan

Diana Gillyatt

Hugh Lowe

BOOKS AND ARTICLES

Ackerley, J. R. *Escapers All: Being the Personal Narrative of Fifteen Escapers from War-Time Prison Camps, 1914–18*. London: The Bodley Head, 1932.

Adam-Smith, Patsy. *Prisoners of War: From Gallipoli to Korea*. New York: Viking, 1997.

Afferbach, Holger, and Hew Strachan. *How Fighting Ends: A History of Surrender*. New York: Oxford University Press, 2012.

Antrobus, H. A. *A History of the Jorehaut Tea Company Ltd.: 1859–1946*. London: Tea and Rubber Mail, 1948.

Barker, A. J. *The Bastard War: The Mesopotamian Campaign of 1914–18*. New York: Dial Press, 1967.

Barker, Ralph. *A Brief History of the Royal Flying Corps in World War I*. London: Constable & Robinson, 1995.

Barnes, A. F. *The Story of the 2/5th Battalion Gloucestershire Regiment 1914–18*. Gloucester, UK: Crypt House Press, 1930.

Bean, C. E. W. *Official History of Australia in the War of 1914–1918*. Sydney: Angus & Robertson, 1941.

Bills, Leslie. *A Medal for Life: Biography of Captain Wm. Leefe Robinson*. Kent, UK: Spellmount Limited, 1990.

Boden, Anthony. *F. W. Harvey: Soldier, Poet*. Gloucestershire, UK: Sutton, 1988.

Bott, Alan. *An Airman's Outings*. London: Blackwood and Sons, 1917.

Bousfield, J. K. "An Exciting Escape from a German Prisoners' of War Camp." *Caian: The Magazine of Gonville and Caius College* (undated).

Bradbeer, Thomas. "Battle for Air Supremacy over the Somme." PhD diss., U.S. Army Command and General Staff College, Fort Leavenworth, KS, 2004.

Bridges, Robert. *The Spirit of Man: An Anthology*. London: Longman, 1927.

Bryan, Tim. *The Great Western at War, 1939–1945*. Sparkford, UK: Patrick Stephens, 1995.

Caunter, J. A. L. *13 Days: The Chronicle of an Escape from a German Prison*. London: G. Bell and Sons, 1918.

Connes, George. *The Other Ordeal*. Oxford: Berg, 2004.

Cook, Jacqueline. *The Real Great Escape: The Story of the First World War's Most Daring Mass Breakout*. Sydney: Vintage Books Australia, 2013.

Coombes, David. *Crossing the Wire: The Untold Stories of Australian POWs in Battle and Captivity During WWI*. Wavell Heights, Queensland: Big Sky, 2016.

Curtis, James. *James Whale: A New World of Gods and Monsters*. Minneapolis: University of Minnesota Press, 1998.

David, Saul. *100 Days to Victory: How the Great War Was Fought and Won 1914–1918*. London: Hodder & Stoughton, 2013.

Doegen, Wilhelm. *Kriegsgefangene Völker, Der Kriegsgefangenen Haltung und Schicksal in Deutschland*. Berlin: Tafel, 1921.

Douglas, Sholto. *Years of Combat*. London: Collins, 1963.

Durnford, H. G. *The Tunnellers of Holzminden*. Cambridge: Cambridge University Press, 1920.

Ellis, John. *Eye-Deep in Hell: Trench Warfare in World War I*. New York: Pantheon, 1976.

Evans, A. J. *The Escaping Club*. London: Lane, 1921.

Foot, M. R. D. and James Langley. *MI9: Escape and Evasion*. London: Bodley Head, 1979.

Fussell, Paul. *The Great War and Modern Memory*. New York: Oxford University Press, 2013.

Garland, Edgar. "My Dashes for Freedom." *Wide World Magazine*. June 1919.

Garrett, Richard. *POW: The Uncivil Face of War*. New York: David & Charles, 1981.

Gerard, James W. *My Four Years in Germany*. New York: Doran and Company, 1917.

Gilliland, Horace. *My German Prisons*. Boston: Houghton Mifflin, 1919.

Grider, John MacGavock. *War Birds: Diary of an Unknown Aviator*. College Station: Texas A&M University Press, 1988.

Grinnell-Milne, Duncan. *An Escaper's Log*. London: Bodley Head, 1926.

Guggisberg, F. G. *The Shop: The Story of the Royal Military Academy*. London: Cassell & Company, 1900.

Hanson, Neil. *Escape from Germany: The Greatest POW Break-Out of the First World War*. London: Corgi, 2011.

Harding, Geoffrey. *Escape Fever*. London: John Hamilton, 1935.

Hardy, J. L. *I Escape!*. London: Pen & Sword Military, 2014.

Hare, Paul R. *Fokker Fodder: The Royal Aircraft Factory BE2c*. Stroud, UK: Fonthill, 2014.

Hargreaves, Aura Kate, ed. *My Dearest: A War Story, a Love Story, a True Story of WWI by Those Who Lived It*. UK: Property People, 2014.

Harrison, M. C. C., and H. A. Cartwright. *Within Four Walls: A Classic of Escape*. London: Penguin Books, 1930.

Hart, Peter. *Somme Success: The Royal Flying Corps and the Battle of the Somme 1916*. London: Pen & Sword, 2001.

Harvey, F. W. *Comrades in Captivity: A Record of Life in Seven German Prison Camps*. London: Sidgwick & Jackson, 1920.

Hattersley, Roy. *The Edwardians*. London: Little, Brown, 2004.

Hennebois, Charles. *In German Hands: The Diary of a Severely Wounded Prisoner*. London: William Heinemann, 1916.

Hervey, H. E. *Cage-Birds*. London: Penguin, 1940.

Herwig, Holger. *The First World War: Germany and Austria-Hungary 1914–1918*. London: Bloomsbury, 2014.

Hoffman, Conrad. *In the Prison Camps of Germany: A Narrative of "Y" Service Among Prisoners of War*. New York: Association Press, 1920.

Horrocks, Brian. *Escape to Action*. New York: St. Martin's, 1960.

Hynes, Samuel. *The Edwardian Turn of Mind*. Princeton, NJ: Princeton University Press, 1968.

Jackson, Robert. *The Prisoners: 1914–18*. London: Routledge, 1989.

Jerrold, Douglas. *The Royal Naval Division*. London: Hutchinson & Company, 1923.

Jones, H. A. *The War in the Air: Being the Story of the Part Played in the Great War by the Royal Air Force*. Vol. 2. Oxford: Clarendon, 1928.

Jones, Heather. *Violence Against Prisoners of War in the First World War: Britain, France, and Germany, 1914–1920*. Cambridge: Cambridge University Press, 2011.

Keegan, John. *The First World War*. New York: Vintage Books, 2000.

Kieran, R. H. *Captain Albert Ball*. London: Aviation Book Club, 1939.

Knight, Gerald. *Brother Bosch: An Airman's Escape from Germany*. London: William Heinemann, 1919.

Krammer, Arnold. *Prisoners of War: A Reference Handbook*. London: Praeger, 2008.

Lambert, Peter. "The Forgotten Airwar: Airpower in the Mesopotamian Campaign." Master's thesis, U.S. Army Command and General Staff College, Fort Leavenworth, KS, 2012.

Lee, Arthur Gould. *Open Cockpit: A Pilot of the Royal Flying Corps.* London: Jarrolds, 1969.

Lewis, Cecil. *Sagittarius Rising.* New York: Harcourt, Brace and Company, 1936.

Lewis, G. H. *Wings over the Somme, 1916–18.* Wrexham, UK: Bridge Books, 1994.

Lewis-Stempel, John. *The War Behind the Wire: The Life, Death and Glory of British Prisoners of War, 1914–18.* London: Weidenfeld & Nicolson, 2014.

Liddle, Peter. *The Airman's War: 1914–18.* London: Blanford, 1987.

Ludendorff, Erich. *My War Memories, 1914–1918.* Vol. 1. London: Hutchinson, 1920.

MacDonald, Frank. *The Kaiser's Guest.* Garden City, NY: Country Life Press, 1918.

McCarthy, Daniel. *The Prisoner of War in Germany.* New York: Moffat, Yard, and Company, 1918.

Mitzkat, J. *Stadt Holzminden und Umgebung Mitten im Weserbergland.* Holzminden: Jorg Mitzkat, 2016.

Money, R. R. *Flying and Soldiering.* London: Ivor Nicholson & Watson, 1936.

Morgan, J. H., trans. *The War Book of the German General Staff.* New York: McBride, Nast, 1915.

Morton, Desmond. *Silent Battle: Canadian Prisoners of War in Germany: 1914–1919.* Toronto: Lester, 1992.

Moynihan, Michael, ed. *Black Bread and Barbed Wire.* London: Leo Cooper, 1978.

Neave, Airey. *Saturday at MI9: History of Underground Escape Lines in Northwest Europe in 1940–45 by a Leading Organizer of MI9.* London: Leo Cooper, 1969.

Panayi, Panikos. *The Enemy in Our Midst: Germans in Britain during the First World War.* New York: Bloomsbury, 1991.

——. *Prisoners of Britain: German Civilian and Combatant Internees During the First World War.* New York: Manchester University Press, 2012.

Repshire, J. Grant. "'The Well-Loved Fields of Old': F. W. Harvey and Ivor Gurney's Friendship and Creative Partnership During the First World War as Seen Through Study of the F. W. Harvey Collection." *Ivor Gurney Society Journal* 20 (2014): 7–30.

Phillimore, Godfrey. *Recollections of a Prisoner of War.* London: Edward Arnold, 1930.

Sharma, Jayeeta. *Empire's Garden: Assam and the Making of India.* Durham, NC: Duke University Press, 2011.

Shephard, Ben. *A War of Nerves: Soldiers and Psychiatrists in the Twentieth Century.* Cambridge, MA: Harvard University Press, 2001.

Speed, Richard. *Prisoners, Diplomats, and the Great War: A Study in the Diplomacy of Captivity.* Westport, CT: Greenwood Press, 1990.

Spoerer, Mark. "The Mortality of Allied Prisoners of War and Belgian Civilian Deportees in German Custody During the First World War." *Population Studies* 60 (2006): 121–36.

Thorn, J. C. *Three Years a Prisoner in Germany.* Vancouver: Cowan and Brookhouse, 1919.

Thornton, R. K. R., ed. *Ivor Gurney War Letters.* Manchester, UK: Carcanet New Press, 1983.

Tuchman, Barbara. *The Guns of August: The Outbreak of World War I.* New York: Random House, 2014.

Vance, Jonathan. *Objects of Concern: Canadian Prisoners of War Through the Twentieth Century.* Seattle: University of Washington Press, 1994.

Vischer, A. L. *Barbed Wire Disease: A Psychological Study of the Prisoner of War.* London: John Bale and Sons, 1919.

Von Richthofen, Manfred. *The Red Air Fighter.* London: Aeroplane & General Publishing, 1917.

Warburton, Ernest. *Behind Boche Bars.* London: John Lane, 1920.

Waugh, Alec. *The Prisoners of Mainz.* New York: George Doran, 1918.

Weatherstone, John. *The Pioneers, 1825–1900: The Early British Tea and Coffee Planters and Their Way of Life.* Shropshire, UK: Quiller, 1986.

Werner, Johannes. *Knight of Germany: Oswald Boelcke German Ace.* London: Casemate, 1991.

Whitehouse, Arch. *The Years of the Sky Kings.* New York: Curtis Books, 1959.

Winchester, Barry. *Beyond the Tumult.* New York: Charles Scribner's Sons, 1971.

Winter, Denis. *The First of the Few: Fighter Pilots of the First World War.* Athens: University of Georgia Press, 1982.

Wise, S. F. *Canadian Airmen and the First World War: The Official History of the Royal Canadian Air Force.* Vol. 1. Toronto: University of Toronto Press, 1980.

Wyrall, Everard. *The Gloucestershire Regiment in the War.* London: Methuen, 1931.

Yarnall, John. *Barbed Wire Disease: British and German Prisoners of War, 1914–19.* Gloucestershire, UK: History Press, 2011.

Index

Page numbers in *italics* indicate maps.